TUDORESQUE

02/01/15/9 Post Sc (25)

TUDORESQUE

In Pursuit of the Ideal Home

Andrew Ballantyne
& Andrew Law

REAKTION BOOKS

Published by
Reaktion Books Ltd
33 Great Sutton Street
London EC1V 0DX, UK

www.reaktionbooks.co.uk

First published 2011

Copyright © Andrew Ballantyne and Andrew Law 2011

This book has been supported by the
Arts & Humanities Research Council.

All rights reserved
No part of this publication may be reproduced, stored in a retrieval system,
or transmitted, in any form or by any means, electronic, mechanical,
photocopying, recording or otherwise, without the prior permission
of the publishers.

Printed and bound in Great Britain by
CPI/Antony Rowe, Chippenham, Wiltshire

British Library Cataloguing in Publication Data

Ballantyne, Andrew
Tudoresque: histories of a poular architecture.
1. Architecture, Tudor. 2. Architecture, Domestic.
3. Architecture, Modern – British influences.
4. Decoration and ornament – Tudor style.
I. Title II. Law, Andrew
728-DC22

ISBN 978 1 86189 811 1

Contents

Preface *by* Andrew Ballantyne 7

One
An Indigenous Architecture 15

Two
Reviving a Tradition 43

Three
Tudoresque Paternalism 75

Four
Tudoresque Self-Reliance 105

Five
Backstage Tudoresque 131

Six
Britannia 'Outre-mer' 171

Seven
A Global Brand: Beyond the Tropics and Back Again 203

References 241
Bibliography 261
Acknowledgements 275
Index 276

Preface

I wish I could find again, to see how it would look to me now, a book that I read when I was thirteen or fourteen. My memory of it is quite clear, but memories can play tricks. There was a description of a house that had been sensibly organized for life as it was lived then, in the 1960s. The kitchen, which in those days was securely the wife's domain, was at the front of the house. That was good because the housewife would be in the kitchen most of the time, and she would be able to see visitors as they approached. The main living room was at the back of the house, which was good because that made for a link with the garden, where children would be playing. This exemplary dwelling looked to me like houses built by the local authority near the primary school, to house people who did not have the wherewithal to buy their own home. In the book it was contrasted with an idiotic house, which looked a bit aloof. It had its kitchen round the back, in the way that used to make sense when kitchens were staffed by servants. There was an imposing front door and a prominent black-and-white gable, which the book told me was meaningless. It gave unnecessary prominence to one of the upstairs windows, probably belonging to one of the smaller bedrooms. What was the sense in that?

It looked to me like a much smarter house, with its sweep of driveway and a passing resemblance to the big houses up by the church;

but the text told me that this house was all wrong. I remember it clearly because I think that this was the first time I had read a book that was authoritatively telling me something I knew to be wrong. I didn't understand why it would be doing that, and the effect was unsettling. It was my first encounter with the professional architecture world and its values.

In retrospect, having spent my adult life in the architecture world, it seems less surprising that the book said what it did, than that I had such a problem with it. I would have expected my opinions at that age to be very malleable, but actually there were opinions already in place. I have been educated away from them in some ways, but they still seem to be the general views of the public, even of highly educated people who have not been inducted into the world of architecture and design. Of course, the substantial Tudoresque house on the hill is in various ways preferable to the small architect-designed house for the local authority's tenants, and most of those ways have nothing whatsoever to do with architectural style, but a great deal to do with social status.

Many commentaries on architecture exclude any mention of issues other than form and style, as if such matters as money and status are not properly architectural issues at all. These commentaries tend to end up presenting the best architecture as a succession of temples, cathedrals and palaces, and they are appealing in their way. But they do not directly connect back to the world that most of us inhabit. If you reflect on the choices that had a bearing on where you live: didn't the cost come into it? And was the quality of the neighbourhood an issue? For most people there is a compromise to be made that involves the constraints of affordability while realizing some aspiration – whatever is most pressing at that stage in one's life – having some space to call one's own, trading up for a higher-status property, moving to somewhere smaller and easier to manage.

Few of us see our more outlandish dreams come true, but we learn to aspire to the things we can achieve, or to accept that a gesture indicating our aspirations will have to be enough to be going on with. Whether it works or not depends not just on the gesture, but also one's circle of friends. In some exalted stratosphere it would make a difference whether I decided to buy an Old Master painting to hang on my wall or an Abstract Expressionist. Each alternative would show that I had some discernment, but each would suggest a very different aspiration. I know that I am never going to be able to afford a Rothko or a Rembrandt, but if I pin up a poster of one or the other on my wall then some of my friends will understand that in my dreams I would have one, and if they share that dream then we feel closer as friends. I would be indicating the aspiration, and would hope to be given some credit for it. If all my friends have real Rothkos on their walls, though, they will also feel pity for my relative poverty. Now, in a modest Tudoresque house, the statistical likelihood is that the picture on the wall will be a small traditional landscape painting, maybe a reproduction of a Constable, and almost certainly in a gilt frame. For someone with a design education, this is difficult territory, likely to produce a reaction of panic.

This is exactly the reaction that the Tudoresque has been producing since the 1950s. From the 1930s to the 1960s it used to be condemned by people who had a concern with the future of architecture, but then the architecture world stopped noticing it. There have been appreciative studies from time to time, but they could be dismissed as sentimental or nostalgic. These authors seemed to be talking about architecture that was no longer current, and to be addressing the 'general public' rather than architects.[1]

Tudoresque buildings are found all over the world, especially in England, where they seem to have been the 'default' preference for twentieth-century builders. They now look old-fashioned, but they were never supposed to look modern, and they are still being built – still looking old-fashioned, even when they house the most up-to-date facilities. How did that state of affairs arise?

The greatest quantity of Tudoresque buildings was constructed during the 1920s and '30s, especially in the suburbs, but they were not created out of the void. They are twentieth-century Britain's most characteristic buildings, and there are deep-seated reasons for this, but they are not often acknowledged as such, because the design-educated elite became embarrassed by them.

Anthony Bertram had been a soldier in the First World War, then wrote novels and gave talks about design that were broadcast on the radio and reached a wide public. In 1938, when every self-effacing building was Tudoresque, he said: 'These are insecure and frightening times and I believe that economic depression and the fear of war are the chief promoters of the Tudoresque.'[2] It is a difficult hypothesis to test, but it proposes in effect that the Tudoresque is a national illness, which would be shaken off once the British had the confidence and prosperity to face the future without being cowed. It is indeed still to be hoped that at some point the nation might be relieved of economic depression and the fear of war. A corollary, if Bertram's analysis were accepted, would be that we could demonstrate our confidence in the future by building modern designs in 'the genuine and legitimate style of our century', as Nikolaus Pevsner had put it.[3] The new architecture, Pevsner said, had been 'fully achieved' back in 1914, but somehow, to his and Bertram's dismay, instead of embracing genuine and legitimate architecture the British built more than ever in the Tudoresque style.

There is a problem here. If we look at the archaeological remains of the buildings of vanished cultures, then we have no doubt that what we see is evidence of the society that built them. We have no doubt that ancient Roman buildings tell us something about ancient Rome, even though their concrete structures were covered up with stone veneers and often decorated with pretend columns, made to patterns learnt from the Greeks. If the bulk of the evidence shows that British twentieth-century building was Tudoresque, why not accept it as a genuine and legitimate style of twentieth-century Britain? It does tell us about the decisions that were actually made by British people about how they wanted to live. They might have been prepared to listen to Bertram and Pevsner, and to buy their books, but when it came to buying a house, deeper instincts prevailed. If indeed it tells us that the British lived in fear during that time, then we should be noticing the fact, not just insisting that it should have been otherwise.

In fact, around the world the Tudoresque is seen precisely as the British national style: the black-and-white gabled twentieth-century house is readily recognized, understood and used as an image of English domesticity from Miami to Shanghai. British architects and designers are uncomfortable with that, but heigh-ho, there it is. Somehow, the Tudoresque has taken root at a popular level, and people – not only British people – keep choosing it. Architects on the whole hope that one day people will want to live in houses that look as modern as the places where they go to work, but actually people show no sign of doing that. There is in fact a popular version of the modernism that Pevsner thought was the only genuine and legitimate style of the twentieth century. It goes by the name 'Retro', and treats mid-twentieth-century modernist designs as antiques.[4] Modernism has found a place among the range of stylistic alternatives for life and is comfortably accepted now that it has become a new way of being old-fashioned.

Different groups of people have chosen the Tudoresque, and when they did so, they saw different things in it that addressed their needs. 'Tudoresque' is the answer to many different questions. For an English aristocrat at the end of the eighteenth century, after the French Revolution, it answered the question: 'What is the best style to adopt to remind my tenants that they are English and not French?' A person of modest fortune in the twentieth century might ask: 'What style of architecture best shows that I have a sound, dependable character and am not a fashion victim?' and find the answer readily enough; while a Malaysian doctor might ask himself: 'What style of house can I build to show that I have a sophisticated cosmopolitan education?' and reach the same conclusion.

Nothing connects these questions, except that the answer keeps being the same. The same questions would have different answers if different people asked them. The Tudoresque style does not have a coherent narrative, from inception to exhaustion. It keeps changing character. It also keeps changing its name, and 'Tudoresque' is used here because of the way it suggests an affinity with the Picturesque, which was important in the style's development. The twentieth-century versions of the style in the UK have come to be called 'Mock Tudor', which sounds derisive, with echoes of 'mockery' and the suggestion that this style is less real than others. When Georgian style is resurrected it is called 'Neo-Georgian', which means 'New Georgian', and makes it sound as if the genuine Georgian style has been re-born. 'Neo-Tudor', however, sounds conflicted as a name for a style that so often aims to look anything but new. In the USA the usual term is 'Tudor Revival', and that seems appropriate in the more careful uses of Tudor precedent in grand houses and college building, but not for the more casual appropriations, which far outnumber them. So I have used 'Tudoresque' as the most general term, meaning anything that seems Tudorish, for whatever reason.

Each chapter tells its own story, and there are gaps, but also overlaps and strong resonances from one chapter to another. The questions keep changing, but the answer is always the same. No one could hope to catalogue every example of the Tudoresque, which has at times been a mass phenomenon, and the specific buildings that are mentioned here are not always particularly good buildings, while, sad to say, some finer buildings have not been included. The aim is to show the wide range of questions that the Tudoresque has been made to answer, not as part of a campaign to have more Tudoresque buildings in the future, but to understand why it is that we already have so many of them.

Most Tudoresque buildings were designed by people who did not have carefully articulated reasons for their stylistic decision, but who just did what felt right. One of the surprises is to realize just how wide a range of people has felt that the Tudoresque was right, from eighteenth-century squires and nineteenth-century nabobs to property developers in twentieth-century Manhattan and twenty-first-century China. There is so much of the Tudoresque that it can take on that primary quality of ordinariness: invisibility. The first step, the most important one, is to notice that Tudoresque architecture exists. Then, with attention a little more sustained, one can begin to realize what an extraordinary and versatile phenomenon it has already proved itself to be.

Andrew Ballantyne

Chapter One

An Indigenous Architecture

The memorable Tudors

Our relations with the past are always complex. People believed different things then, and acted for reasons that we cannot always understand. They did not always take the trouble to explain themselves, even to other people who were alive at the time, perhaps because their intentions were clear to all and did not need explaining, perhaps because they felt it better to act secretly, perhaps because the explanation was said aloud and never recorded in a more durable way, or perhaps because the person acting did not feel accountable. If we can write a history at all, and would call it 'history' rather than 'fantasy', then we need to draw upon evidence, and buildings are among the biggest pieces of evidence we have. But they are also ambiguous. They can be damaged and destroyed so that nothing survives, as have many more-fragile documents, though some important ancient texts that circulated in multiple copies are with us still. The vast numbers of Tudoresque buildings around the world must mean something – but what? And first of all, what is a 'Tudor'?

We are dealing with multiple viewpoints, and various classes of information, much of it debatable in one way or another. A statement that looked like a self-evident truth to its aristocratic author in the sixteenth century might have looked like a self-serving calumny to a twentieth-century Marxist. Things that look like common sense in one era sound like weird superstitions in another. Aristocrats used to think that unrefined peasant bread would mortify them, but we now think that the roughage in it will help us to live longer. The king used to be able to cure the sick, by touching them. It is usually impossible to be sure what a sixteenth-century peasant would have thought, because the thought went unrecorded. Without direct testimony we have to rely on empathy – a flawed method since it assumes that people in the past felt the same as we do now. For more recent times, however, there is more surviving evidence of popular culture, which is important for this study, which considers popular architecture.

We will be looking not at what actually happened to architecture under the Tudor monarchs, but rather how ideas of Tudor architecture influenced buildings in later times. There is some connection between the events that happened and the various accounts of those events, but there are confusions, errors, omissions and above all a tendency to see in the events of the past the details that address the interests of the present. So there are multiple versions of the Tudors in the historiography, ranging from the scholarly and exacting to the unsupported but often popular stories that circulate in song, on stage or on film. *The Private Lives of Elizabeth and Essex* (starring Bette Davis and Errol Flynn) and *1066 and All That* are important documents for understanding the role of the Tudors in the popular imagination, but unreliable about actual events at the Tudor court.[1]

So, what is a Tudor? 'Tudor' is now taken to be the family name of the dynasty that ruled England and Wales (but not Scotland) from the accession of Henry VII to the death of Elizabeth I, that is to say, 1485–1603 – the whole of the sixteenth century. In the popular imagination the important figures are Henry VII's son Henry VIII (who had six wives and an argument with the pope) and Henry VIII's daughter Elizabeth (who defeated the Spanish Armada and never married). Henry VII seized power after defeating the previous king, Richard III, at the Battle of Bosworth. There were great upheavals across the whole of Europe as the military forces of feudal barons found themselves outmanoeuvred or allied with the great commercial fortunes made by bankers, adventurers and merchants.² At the beginning of Henry VII's reign the culture was medieval, by the end of Elizabeth's it was early modern, a transition that took several generations, but in British history Henry VII's accession is often seen as the point of rupture, where the Middle Ages came to an end.

There were other significant cultural events at about this time, which are sometimes (in retrospect) seen as break points. In art history the Italian Renaissance of the fifteenth century is the thing. Compared with the Fall of Constantinople (1453) or the development of Protestantism and the excommunication of Martin Luther (1521), the Battle of Bosworth (1485) was a local affair. It looks like a break because it arguably brought to an end the line of succession that stretched back to the invasion from Normandy in 1066, and whose monarchs, as we shall see, continued to be portrayed as foreigners, whereas the Tudors were portrayed as British – Welsh, in fact, and not until later known by the name 'Tudor', but indigenous nonetheless.

The thing that makes the Tudors compelling as historical figures is that they were colourful, in two senses of the word. We have their portraits, commissioned from the best artists of the day, and can imagine what they looked like; and rather publicly they fell in and out of love, ordered executions, behaved heroically or wilfully.³ It is those episodes that are remembered. Martin Luther's theology is abstract and unfathomable to a modern schoolchild, but the practical issues at stake in the Tudors' family politics make the royal family a concrete microcosm of that abstract world and give them a hold on the imagination that is comparable with the Greek tragedies. Ordinary adulteries are tawdry, but in the royal houses of Thebes and Tudor they are as deadly as at some level of the unconscious one feels they should be, and therefore they become mythic. The executions of Anne Boleyn, Katherine Howard, Lady Jane Grey, Mary, Queen of Scots, Sir Walter Raleigh, the Earl of Essex – the list goes on – were enacted for political reasons (each was found guilty of a treasonable crime), but what makes them compelling in the history books or on the stage is the harrowing emotion involved. The schisms that caused bloodshed across Europe are played out for us in the early modern era on a domestic scale by characters as well defined as Oedipus and Jocasta.

Building style did not change as dramatically as the monarchs. Henry VII's chapel at Westminster Abbey, and the chapel at King's College, Cambridge (which was finished under Henry VIII), are both fine Gothic buildings, recognizably belonging to the tradition of ecclesiastical architecture that had been developing for centuries under the Plantagenet kings. There is a distinct 'Tudor arch' – still a pointed arch, as we would expect in the Gothic tradition – but it is integrated into the established style, and does not mark a break with the tradition. It was not called a 'Tudor' arch at the time, and nor was the church architecture then called 'Gothic' – these categories were invented much later. At the death of Elizabeth I, the throne passed to James I, whose family name was Stuart. He was already king of Scotland, where he was James VI. There was a change of dynasty, and a redefinition of the kingdom, but stylistically architecture continued as if nothing had happened, and although the adjective pertaining to James's reign is 'Jacobean' ('Jacobus' being the Latin form of 'James'), the architectural style tends to be called 'Jacobethan' in order to signal that Jacobean architecture is indistinguishable from Elizabethan. We should not be mesmerized into thinking that the change of a head of state always has an immediate influence on the taste of its subjects.

When times are changing rapidly enough for the change to be noticeable, the 'old' starts to have a value in providing a link with the past. It acquires authority and gives a comforting feeling of stability. In fact, British people have tended to show a marked preference for the old-fashioned when it comes to buildings, most often for the pragmatic reason that old buildings survive and they are expensive to replace. Up until the end of the eighteenth century the most numerous new buildings were the cottages of the rural poor. Most people lived off the land, and the rural labourers' cottages were most likely to need renewing – especially those built of cob, which was basically mud and straw – much like adobe, or the biblical sun-baked bricks.[4] These cottages changed little over centuries. The end of medieval

An Indigenous Architecture

1 Robert Smythson, Hardwick Hall, Derbyshire, 1590–97. An Elizabethan 'prodigy house': high courtly style.

serfdom brought social change, but the cottages continued to be built as simply as possible with local materials, and there was no scope for fashion to take a hold.

At the other end of the scale, the extremely wealthy might have inherited medieval castles from their ancestors, but the need to build defensively faded away, which opened up new freedoms in architecture. For example, buildings by the Elizabethan architect Robert Smythson, such as Hardwick Hall, represent the novel high-style architecture of the era (illus. 1), but they are not typical of everyday building. They were for the super-rich who desired new settings for their activity, and they were designed to be far from ordinary, as sites for displays of magnificence. We tend to see them as the defining monuments of the time, but they were unfamiliar to the sixteenth-century public. The people who had new houses by Smythson were outnumbered by others of equally high rank and equally rich, who spent their money in other ways and continued to live in their ancestral homes, making some adjustments (a new hall, a new wing). And they in turn were vastly outnumbered by people who lived in more modest circumstances, such as the squires who lived in manor houses and belonged to a more local elite. They used older buildings to support their way of life, or built new houses that tended to continue the patterns set by the past. If they gave the matter thought, then they were upholding tradition rather than trying to set a fashion, but probably they were more interested in the accommodation's facilities than its style, and left that to the builders.[5]

If a building is well constructed and well maintained, then it can last for centuries. People in the past lived in new buildings no more than they do now, and buildings that were new in the sixteenth century were not demolished as soon as they became old-fashioned. Henry Fielding published *Tom Jones* in the middle of the eighteenth century, and if there is one character in the novel who is beyond all reproach it is the supremely benevolent Squire Allworthy. His good character is established by the novelist equipping him with an old-fashioned house. By that time the term 'Gothic' was in use, but it was a much less specific term than it is now, and could include buildings of any not particularly classical style, especially if they were old. The contrast that is implied here is between Allworthy's old-fashioned house and a modern house – in a style that would now be called 'Georgian' – the detail of which we now call classical, but which Fielding calls 'Grecian':

> The Gothic stile of building could produce nothing nobler than Mr Allworthy's house. There was an air of grandeur in it that struck you with awe, and rivalled the beauties of the best Grecian architecture; and it was as commodious within as venerable without.
>
> It stood on the south-east side of a hill, but nearer the bottom than the top of it, so as to be sheltered from the

north-east by a grove of old oaks which rose above it in a gradual ascent of near half a mile, and yet high enough to enjoy a most charming prospect of the valley beneath.[6]

The fact that the house is 'commodious within' suggests that it belongs to the sixteenth century rather than an earlier, more feudal time, but of course this is a fictional house, so one cannot verify archaeologically what the author had in mind. Fielding gives further detail about its imaginary landscape, which is presented as ideally Arcadian, with old elements surviving in it: not only the old oaks, but also villages that have not been swept away for the sake of the view, and a pre-Bosworth abbey, thrown into dilapidation by Henry VIII, which has been allowed to remain as a romantic ruin. The lands confiscated from the monasteries were sometimes the sites for sixteenth-century manors, and Allworthy's house might be one such, were it not fictional.

In the midst of the grove was a fine lawn, sloping down towards the house, near the summit of which rose a plentiful spring, gushing out of a rock covered with firs, and forming a constant cascade of about thirty feet, not carried down a regular flight of steps, but tumbling in a natural fall over the broken and mossy stones till it came to the bottom of the rock, then running off in a pebbly channel, that with many lesser falls winded along, till it fell into a lake at the foot of the hill, about a quarter of a mile below the house on the south side, and which was seen from every room in the front. Out of this lake, which filled the centre of a beautiful plain, embellished with groups of beeches and elms, and fed with sheep, issued a river, that for several miles was seen to meander through an amazing variety of meadows and woods till it emptied itself into the sea, with a large arm of which, and an island beyond it, the prospect was closed.

On the right of this valley opened another of less extent, adorned with several villages, and terminated by one of the towers of an old ruined abbey, grown over with ivy, and part of the front, which remained still entire.

The left-hand scene presented the view of a very fine park, composed of very unequal ground, and agreeably varied with all the diversity that hills, lawns, wood, and water, laid out with admirable taste, but owing less to art than to nature, could give. Beyond this, the country gradually rose into a ridge of wild mountains, the tops of which were above the clouds.[7]

All Fielding's trustworthy characters are immune to the lure of fashion, and the most fashionable are the most wrong-headed. He equates good sense with nature, seeing truth and goodness most clearly in the places where fashion does not reach. So for Fielding the past acts as a guide for the present, and whatever is novel and fashionable in the present is not to be trusted. If there is to be progress, then it should be progress guided by nature, which will give us a good grounding. The stance is plainly anti-modern. What we have here is a presentation of an ideal: Allworthy, the embodiment of practical wisdom, is presented as absolutely at one with his estate, which is beautiful mainly because it is natural, and his house is long established and as indigenous as he is himself. There is nothing Grecian or Italianate about it, nothing 'classical' or foreign. It is indigenous, old-fashioned and presented as an image of perfection.

There had been political and cultural upheavals between Elizabeth's time and Fielding's — the Civil War and the execution of Charles I in 1649, the Commonwealth, the Restoration of Charles II and the 'Glorious Revolution' of 1688, which removed Charles's brother, James II, from the throne to install William and Mary; and then the accession of George I (from Hanover) in 1714, a distant cousin of his predecessor, Queen Anne, but her closest Protestant relative. When looking back from the eighteenth century one saw recent trouble, preceded by an age of domestic harmony and prosperity under Elizabeth, when the enemies were overseas and the state seemed to be at peace with itself.

British antiquity

There are old histories, such as Bede's history of the English Church and Geoffrey of Monmouth's semi-mythological history of British kings, but the first British work to take a systematic interest in old things *because* they were old was William Camden's *Britannia* (1586). Camden used the island's Roman name as his book's title, wrote in Latin, and took a particular interest in relics of the Romans' presence; but he also took note of medieval remains.[8] It is not a history, but rather a gazetteer of ancient and medieval sites, organized by county. Camden was one of the founders of a College of Antiquaries, which met regularly between 1587 and 1614, when it was suppressed by James I because of suspicions about the tenor of political discussion at the meetings.[9] The publication of *Britannia* and the formation of the society are clear signals that there was antiquarian activity. The society being disbanded did not mean that the interest stopped, only that it no longer had a central point of focus. It continued quietly as a more local kind of interest.[10] In the eighteenth century it became more visible again with the formation of the Society of Antiquaries in 1707 and the more aristocratic Society of Dilettanti in 1732.

The Society of Dilettanti was founded as a club for people who had been on the Grand Tour, and according to Horace Walpole (who had been on the Grand Tour, but who was not a member), its main condition of membership in its early days was 'being drunk'.[11] Sir Francis Dashwood was one of the leading lights in those days, but his Hellfire Club gained him more notoriety. The meetings were chaired by the president, wearing a Roman toga, and might have been too robust for Walpole to be at his ease. He had himself painted in Van Dyck costume, with a lace collar and cuffs, and was more at home with the Society of Antiquaries' sedate manners. The Dilettanti, despite their carousing, supported important pioneering archaeological expeditions to Greece, and lavishly published James Stuart and Nicholas Revett's folios of *The Antiquities of Athens*, as well as a notorious *Discourse on the Worship of Priapus*.[12] The Society of Antiquaries had less sensational interests, closer to home, including medieval Britain.

The antiquary's image contrasts with the historian's. The stereotypal antiquary falls in love with old things because they are old, and can be lost in the accumulation of detail, held in thrall by curiosities, neglecting to try to connect them into a broader narrative, while the stereotypical historian's narrative preoccupations will lead him or her to try to make sense of things in a more general way, at the expense of inconvenient detail.[13] The Grand Tour was an educational rite of passage for the young gentleman – an extended journey that sent him away from familiar surroundings to learn about civilized accomplishments and to have romantic adventures in far-away places where he could escape from any lasting consequences of recklessness, except perhaps disease. He would come back a man of the world, and with a taste for Italy and the antique, about which he would feel intuitively nostalgic when it was evoked in English buildings, landscapes or statuary. It might have been a feeling of nostalgia for the dreams and dalliances of his youth, rather than a passion for antiquity as such, but the two were fused together. So graduates of the Grand Tour who took up antiquarian enthusiasms, as many did, tended to focus on the antiquity of Greece and Rome, and gentlemen's magazines catered to this interest in their prints and articles.[14] By the middle of the eighteenth century an interest in antiquity was a normal gentlemanly accomplishment, extending also to people who had not been to Italy, who were more likely to fix on British subject matter.[15] The British Museum opened its doors in 1759, and institutionalized the activity. Charles Townley's bequest of his collection of statuary, and then the acquisition of the Parthenon sculptures from Lord Elgin, confirmed the absolute prestige of Greek and Roman antiquity, which also supplied the style for the museum's new building, designed by Sir Robert Smirke in 1823.[16]

Another element of polite culture from the mid-eighteenth century was an enthusiasm for the Picturesque, which could lead landowners to remodel their estates so as to make them resemble Arcadian countryside, and which took them, as well as people without estates, on journeys to appreciate natural scenery. A certain level of education and polite accomplishment was necessary to participate convincingly in the enterprise, but these things were not beyond the reach of the middle classes, and the Reverend William Gilpin, for example, made a significant contribution to it with his accounts of picturesque travels, beginning with his *Observations on the River Wye* of 1782. His published thoughts made possible a new appreciation of natural scenery and picturesque ruins, and helped to establish the Wye Valley as a middle-class tourist destination. He had aristocratic readers, including Horace Walpole and George III, but they were heavily outnumbered. George Lipscombe, writing in the same genre, said that his own work was aimed at 'men of business and persons of very moderate incomes',[17] and the same could be said of Gilpin's – it is not necessary to own the land in order to appreciate its picturesque beauties. The attitudes of Picturesque tourists were not necessarily in complete alignment with the preservationist instincts one would expect of an antiquary. Gilpin could say that 'a ruin is a sacred thing', and could look at it as if it were a work of nature rather than art; and he could imagine that Tintern Abbey might be made more picturesque if only it were a little more ruined; but, consistently, he did nothing to encourage anyone actually to dismantle it.[18] He was clearly promoting an aesthetic appreciation of old things, along with natural things, that became established and still remains firmly a part of British culture, now supported and facilitated by the National Trust and English Heritage. The popular antiquarian impulse is nurtured and developed in antique shops, which are to be found everywhere (even on Ocean Beach in San Diego, where the main activity seems to be surfing, but a fine folio page from the Society of Dilettanti's *Specimens of Antient Sculpture* turned up there). One of the BBC's most enduringly popular broadcasts, the *Antiques Roadshow*, attracts crowds of thousands, who bring along family 'treasures' for expert appraisal, mostly to be told that their heirlooms have no commercial value, despite the strong sentiment that the family has invested in them. These activities – taking an interest in antiques, visiting historic houses and their grounds – are ingrained as part of the polite discourse of the middle classes, and that process began in the eighteenth century, broadening out from the enthusiasms of isolated hoarders of curiosities, such as John Tradescant and Hans Sloane, whose collections formed the basis of the Ashmolean and British Museum respectively. Collections in private hands were not necessarily inaccessible to visitors, and guidebooks to London gave the details of houses with collections that a tourist would want to visit. By the end of the eighteenth century it was clear that it was not only the treasure-owning aristocrats who had access to the means of developing a fine sensibility, but also those with some leisure that had been used to cultivate knowledge and receptivity to encounters with nature and relics of the past.

The engagement with the natural and antiquarian phenomena of a place became the mark of a sense of national identity, and middle-class authors criticized cosmopolitan aristocratic culture for lacking it.[19] When eighteenth-century aristocrats said they 'loved their country', they were thinking of it as a place owned and managed by themselves and their friends.[20] The peasantry was part of the scene, to be managed in the same way as crops and livestock. Agricultural labourers were not expected to behave as moral agents, and were not allowed to vote; but the inherited land was idealized and invested with a sacred character. If landed aristocrats noticed populist nationalism they saw in it an expression of 'intensely vulgar sentiments' and 'an invasion of the sphere of public life by plebeians'.[21] In the twenty-first century we expect 'the people' to include the poor as well as the rich, the successful as well as the high-born. The eighteenth-century aristocrat was quite capable of thinking that 'real people' were those who lived off the income from inherited land. They were the fully-realized humans, firmly in charge of managing their estates and the country, while the rest were dependent relatives, servants or livestock on the estate. They could be great company, but their circumstances meant that they would not be suited to public life. Nowadays eighteenth-century aristocratic culture looks anti-democratic, and the eighteenth-century nobility would without hesitation have agreed – for it the words 'democracy' and 'anarchy' were interchangeable. There was a dominant culture of deference, but where popular sentiment found expression it is possible to piece together non-aristocratic perspectives, ranging from the peasants to the educated and prosperous middle class, where this aristocratic view was seen as patronising, standing against the culture of the indigenous population and therefore against the real interests of the nation.[22]

It was taken for granted, not only by the aristocracy, that French and Italian luxuries and arts were finer than domestic products, while the sturdy British yeoman thrived on boiled beef and saw luxury as synonymous with corruption and decadence. 'Those who have conversed with persons of different ranks, that have been in France,' said an anonymous contributor to the *Gentleman's Magazine* in 1766, 'will find the account favourable, in proportion as their rank is high. The man of fashion is always captivated with his journey to France; the man who moves in a lower circle there always disgusted.'[23]

The eighteenth-century use of the word 'disgusted' always sounds over-emphatic. Eighteenth-century 'disgust' translates to something more like modern 'distaste'. 'The man who moves in a lower circle would not find it to his taste' would be a more accurate understanding of the sense than the expression of moral outrage or horror that the original 'disgust' might bring to mind – though that might be the only possible English reaction to a peasant dish of *andouillettes* or *tête de veau*.

While the pleasures of Paris and the antiquities of Athens and Rome continued to enjoy unrivalled prestige among the elite, the increasing confidence of middle-class voices, which had not been formed by foreign travel, made it seem important to recognize and value Britain's indigenous culture. Such efforts are evident in the work of Henry Fielding, Samuel Johnson and the painter William Hogarth. The enthusiasm for British antiquity is characterized as 'middle-class' rather than 'aristocratic', but there was not a sharp division between the two cultures. Horace Walpole, Lord Orford, was one of the most enthusiastic medievalists of his generation, and Henry Fielding's background was aristocratic, but he was short of money and relied on patronage.[24] The enthusiasm for British antiquity is also evident in northern Europe's willingness to fall for Ossian, who might have been an ancient Scottish or Irish bard and a local equivalent for Homer; but in fact he was a forgery perpetrated by one James Macpherson.[25] Goethe translated him into German, and there is a heroic painting of him on prominent display in the Louvre – a ghostly, white-robed figure, long-established in heaven, welcoming in a legion of newly arrived French soldiers.[26]

Ossian's poetry, as Samuel Johnson pointed out at the time, is not good. That might not have been evidence against its being real, but the only reason for the forgery's sensational success was that there was a widespread desire for such a cultural figurehead. 'Some seem to admire indiscriminately whatever has been long preserved', said Johnson, not himself believing that Ossian's works had in fact been long preserved, and finding problems in accepting a mediocrity as the nation's literary foundation.[27] Johnson was helped to meet that need for an indigenous literary giant by promoting the cause of Shakespeare – a much more recent poet, but by the eighteenth century firmly a historical figure. The sense of a British identity was constructed by looking to history, and finding continuity with the past, including the old England of Elizabeth, and more remote epochs: medieval, Saxon, Roman and even quite fictionally mythic.

British antiquaries

When British antiquarian activity began in earnest, it was preoccupied with Romano-British artefacts, transferring the enthusiasms of the Grand Tourists to the local scene.[28] Inigo Jones, who had travelled in Italy and was thoroughly imbued with aristocratic values, looked at Stonehenge and saw it as a Roman temple.[29] The idea was markedly more scientific than the previous hypothesis: according to Geoffrey of Monmouth's history, the monument had been brought over from Ireland by Merlin.[30] In the eighteenth century it was reassigned by the Reverend William Stukeley to the Druids, whom he more or less invented in the 1740s.[31] They are mentioned, glancingly, in Roman texts, and from scant clues Stukeley fleshed out an idea of their religion and customs, bolstered by recondite knowledge and a fertile imagination. The Druids were in Britain before the arrival of the Romans, but we do not really know what they were like. Significantly, more is known about the population that was there when the Normans came. The eighteenth-century historian John Whitaker saw the Anglo-Saxon period as the 'greatest seed plot of national history', when English Common Law was established under Alfred the Great, so there was some appreciation of the developmental importance of the era, but little was known about the buildings.[32]

If we look for a style of building that is profoundly rooted in the island's ancient past, we will encounter problems. Stonehenge certainly exists and is certainly old, but it has little to offer as an example for modern domestic arrangements. Most Anglo-Saxon buildings were timber and have perished, while the few churches that were built in stone were mostly rebuilt in later centuries. In the eighteenth century knowledge of Anglo-Saxon buildings seemed irretrievable, and we still do not know much.[33] Some churches survive, but the domestic buildings have had to be reconstructed from conjectures based on limited evidence, such as post holes, where timbers have rotted in the earth and have altered the chemical composition of the soil. Their analysis has depended on twentieth-century laboratory techniques, but the settlements are often detected because their patterns show up when seen from the air, in raking light when there has been uneven growth, or with melting snow. But even the most meticulous excavation and soil analysis is not going to tell us much about these buildings' architectural style.

Much more survives from the era between 1066 and 1485: street patterns, great cathedrals, city walls, castles and parish churches.

But because they were not codified or understood, they were seen to belong together as a great unprincipled mass, unguided by any defined taste. It came to be known as 'Gothic', after the Goths who had laid waste to the Roman Empire. This state of affairs was gradually remedied, but it took the care and insight of more than one generation to achieve it. As the youngest son of Robert Walpole, Lord Orford, Horace Walpole did not expect to inherit his father's title or the family's seat, Houghton Hall in Norfolk (though eventually he did inherit them, from his nephew). He had a house in central London, and his villa at Strawberry Hill in Twickenham was his personal space where he could follow his own whims. The Gothickery there began frivolously enough, with *papier mâché* pinnacles that had to be replaced when it rained. But over the years it became a serious scholarly enterprise, and experts were enlisted to help make accurate reconstructions of medieval work. Walpole also invented the 'Gothic novel', with *The Castle of Otranto*, which spawned the 'Gothic horror' genre.[34]

The serious scholarly researches remained as the preserve of antiquarian enthusiasts until the publication of a book by Thomas Rickman in 1817: *An Attempt to Discriminate the Styles of English Architecture from the Conquest to the Reformation*. It was Rickman who gave the names 'Early English', 'Decorated' and 'Perpendicular' to the styles of English medieval architecture, and made sense of their chronology. His book was concerned with church rather than domestic buildings, and his end-point, the Reformation, is the break with Rome (1531). The example from Fielding given above indicates that the way the boundaries of styles were drawn in the eighteenth century meant that an old-fashioned house could be called 'Gothic' and might have seemed to be medieval. No one would have called such a house 'Tudor' when Fielding was writing, because the term was not yet in use, not even when referring to sixteenth-century royalty.

In order to stress the legitimacy of their claim to the throne, the relatives of Henry VII drew attention to the already-royal branch of their family. The name 'Tudor' was introduced when Henry V's widow, Catherine of France, married Owain ap Maredudd ap Tudur. One of her sons from this second marriage, Edmund, Earl of Richmond, fathered the future Henry VII, but died before his son was born, so at birth Henry inherited his father's title, and was always known as 'Richmond' rather than by a personal surname. The name 'Tudor' was not associated with the dynasty until 1757, when David Hume used it in his *History of England under the House of Tudor*.[35] It is really a mistake, since 'ap Tudur' was a Welsh patronymic, not a surname. So if Henry had grown up in Wales he would have been 'ap Edmund', which could have been anglicized to Edmundson. The change of royal 'house' helps to establish the idea of a radical break in 1485, which in retrospect seems appropriate enough, but Henry VII was keen to show that he was related to earlier monarchs, not to look as if he were making a clean break. It was eighteenth-century historians who established the idea that the period before 1485 was medieval (of recreational antiquarian interest), and that history after that was a preamble to the present state of affairs and was therefore worthy of serious study.[36]

A historian's aim, said Lord Bolingbroke, was to 'instruct posterity by the example of former ages', and he dismissed medieval chroniclers as 'monkish annalists' and 'antiquaries'.[37] Samuel Johnson criticized would-be historians for whom 'history was a series of actions, with no other than chronological succession, independent on each another, and without any tendency to introduce or regulate the conclusion'; they failed to rise to 'the majesty of history'.[38] The point of history on this view is its moral effect, rather than the accumulation of detailed facts. So Shakespeare's history plays are exemplary, even if their factual accuracy is not to be trusted. Thomas More had already portrayed Richard III as a disaster, but it was Shakespeare's portrayal of him as an incarnation of duplicitous evil that sealed the sense of rupture between the medieval past under the French kings and the glorious present, inaugurated by Henry VII and flowering under his granddaughter Elizabeth.[39] David Hume, for example, said that after 1485 'a general revolution was made in human affairs throughout this part of the world; and men gradually attained that situation, with regard to commerce, arts, sciences, government, police, and cultivation, in which they have ever since been preserved'.⁴⁰ On this view, under the Plantagenets there was confusion and disorder, and afterwards, under the Tudors, there was peace, prosperity and stability. The foundation of the modern age, the bringing of order, and the escape from medieval superstition into Protestantism, were associated with the Tudor dynasty in general, and with 'the Age of Elizabeth' in particular, embodied in the spectacular image of the queen as Gloriana – with a nimbus of delicate lace around her face, and the defeat of the Spanish Armada to her credit (illus. 2).

It was a powerful image, and it was not forgotten. The memory of Elizabeth was invoked by Queen Anne when she came to the throne in 1702, and then as a measure of good monarchy, to encourage the Hanoverian kings (the Georges who ruled through the eighteenth century) who succeeded her in 1714.⁴¹ Elizabeth's example was also being used in the 1730s to criticize Robert Walpole, when he was prime minister. He had thought it best to avoid war with Spain (because of its cost), despite Spanish depredations on British interests in the West Indies. Elizabeth's success was contrasted with Walpole's 'weakness'. The Tudor age became emblematic as a time of prosperity and success; also as a time when feudalism was dismantled, bringing an end to serfdom. Hume tells the following story about the dismantling of feudal relationships between a lord and the men in his service:

> There scarce passed any session during [Henry VII's] reign without some statute against engaging retainers, and giving them badges or liveries; a practice, by which they were, in a manner, inlisted under some great lord, and were kept in readiness to assist him in all wars, insurrections, riots, violences, and even in bearing evidence for him in courts of justice. This disorder which had arisen during turbulent times, when the law could give little protection to the subject, was then deeply rooted in England; and it required all the vigilance and rigour of Henry to extirpate it. There is a story of his severity against that abuse ... The Earl of

An Indigenous Architecture

2 Crispin van de Passe, *Elizabeth 1*, 1596. Elaborate costume and symbols of office turn the human into spectacle.

Oxford, his favourite general, to whom he always gave great deserved trust, having splendidly entertained him at his castle of Heningham, was desirous of making a show of his magnificence at the departure of his royal guest; and ordered all his retainers, with their liveries and badges to be drawn up in two lines, that their appearance might be more gallant and splendid. 'My Lord', said the King, 'I have heard much of your hospitality; but truth far exceeds the report. These handsome gentlemen and yeomen, whom I see on both sides of me, are surely your menial servants. The earl smiled and confided that his fortune was too narrow for such magnificence. 'They are most of them' subjoined he, 'my retainers, who are come to do me service at such a time, when they knew I was honoured with your majesty's presence'. The king started a little and said 'By my faith, my lord I thank you for my good cheer, but I must not allow my laws to be broken in my sight. My attorney must speak with you'. Oxford is said to have payed no less than fifteen thousand marks, as a composition for his offence.[42]

The importance of this anecdote lies in the way it establishes that the ordinary British people owe their independence and liberty to the Tudor monarchy. The feudal system was being dismantled across western Europe, not only in England, but Henry was leading the way.

There was also a growing importance in international commercial activity, which was recognized and encouraged by the monarchs, the most famous examples being Sir Walter Raleigh's expeditions to America and the setting up of the East India Company under Elizabeth. The nation's wealth and prosperity were increased beyond the aggregated productive capacities of English farmers, drawing in exotic goods and minerals from overseas. Then there was the work of Francis Bacon, under Elizabeth and then James, credited with inaugurating experimental science.[43] He became one of the great heroes of the eighteenth-century Enlightenment. The building blocks of a recognizably modern culture were, in the eighteenth century, depicted as being set in place under the guidance of the Tudor monarchs.

The confirmation of the greatness of the age came with the elevation of Shakespeare to his position of cultural supremacy. There is no doubting the quality of Shakespeare's poetry, and the power of the moments of sublimity that can be found in his greater works. The things that have taken his reputation beyond that of a fine poet and playwright, and made him something more like a patron saint, are his history plays. They present a national dramatic pageant, showing British history through the persons of its monarchs, and in a manner that helps to reinforce the legitimacy of the Tudors. There is also the fact that Shakespeare's birthday coincided with the feast of St George, England's official patron saint, so Shakespeare seems easily to take on the mantle of being the national genius, and in France the English language has become *la langue de Shakespeare*.[44]

This status was gained incrementally, from a period of neglect and near oblivion in the decades after his death in 1616 and a ban on theatrical productions during the Commonwealth under Oliver Cromwell. New editions of the plays started to appear in the early years of the eighteenth century, and they were championed on the stage especially by David Garrick. His efforts to promote Shakespeare reached a climax in the Shakespeare Jubilee in Stratford in 1769, which drew popular attention to not only the plays, but also to his birthplace.[45] In 1597 Shakespeare bought a large house, New Place, in Stratford, built in the fifteenth century, but it was demolished by its disobliging owner as late as 1759, leaving Shakespeare's more modest birthplace to take on the role of a shrine. Its image circulated widely (illus. 3), and a hundred years later a replica was made for exhibition at the Crystal Palace at Sydenham, where it was marketed to a popular audience.[46] It is a puzzling idea that a replica of a house might have cultural value, not on account of its artistic merit, but because someone noteworthy once lived in the original in a different place, but it indicates very clearly the kind of cultural icon Shakespeare had become, and his Tudoresque dwelling was the very model of Englishness.

Old-fashioned buildings

During the eighteenth century it became normal for buildings to have classical detail, whether following the example of Palladio, or later perhaps something more archaeologically specific from Greece. The Italianate mansion with a columned portico became the cliché of aristocratic decorum. Landscape settings, especially under the influence of 'Capability' Brown, brought the rolling Arcadian countryside right up to the front door. Sixteenth-century houses clearly belonged to another age, with their lively silhouettes and their box-hedge topiary. The will to modernize was sometimes resisted. We have seen Fielding's description of Squire Allworthy's old-fashioned house, and how that helped to position him as a man of sound character, unswayed by fashion, eschewing a taste for foreign things – here Italian architecture.

In the world of practical building William Kent can be found in 1729 making alterations to a late fifteenth-century tower at Esher Place. It dates from 1475–80, so it is actually pre-Bosworth, but Kent's alterations play up its antiquity in an eighteenth-century way. He added an ogee arch, which comes to a sharp point, but curves in a serpentine line to reach it. The ogee is less characteristic of genuine medieval work than it is of the eighteenth-century 'take' on Gothic. The nineteenth-century Gothic Revival, especially when influenced by Viollet-le-Duc, would stress the rational engineering that underpinned Gothic vaults and arches, but the ogee arch has no engineering logic behind it. It looked bizarre and exotic, and was therefore an appropriate sign to evoke the barbarism and superstition of the Middle Ages. Kent was certainly making the building look older rather than modernizing it, self-consciously adopting an outmoded style.[47]

The most widely circulated eighteenth-century image of a Tudor or Tudoresque building was drawn by Thomas Hearne and used as an illustration for Richard Payne Knight's poem *The Landscape*, published in 1794 and again in 1795 (illus. 4). It is one of a contrasting pair of images, one of which shows a conventional 'modern' house in a 'Capability' Brown-style landscape. The second shows how things ought to be, with the landscape overgrown and the house blended into the scene by planting close to it. The poem itself has a complex agenda, both promoting the Picturesque aesthetic that is exemplified in the image and expressing sympathy for the revolutionaries in France – an inflammatory position to take in a work for a genteel audience, given that the country was at war with France at the time, on account of the

An Indigenous Architecture

3 Shakespeare's birthplace in Henley Street, Stratford upon Avon, early 16th century. A prosperous 'middle-class' dwelling.

revolutionaries' activities.[48] Knight defended himself against the charge of sedition by explaining that he was arguing for the retention of old gardens, and the image certainly shows an old or old-fashioned house. Having said that, the poem's imagery has nature throwing off oppressive artificial constraints, and the symbolism is quite clear, but in Britain the free-born soul had no need to throw off any oppression since the government was already just, so there was no need for any uprising.

The choice of building is interesting because it was presented in the context of an exhortation to change design practices, and it was not a conventional choice. Indeed, it seems to be the first post-Tudor appearance of a Tudor-style building in anything other than a topographical picture or a depiction of a historic setting.[49] It is an old-fashioned building from the beginning of the current age, not a quaint exotic building from the Middle Ages, but a building of good character. It looks larger than Allworthy's house might have been, but might have taken its cue from him, since Knight wrote warmly about Fielding's work and lavished praise on him as much as his great hero Homer.[50] Knight's culture was cosmopolitan. He was supported by

4 Thomas Hearne, plate from Richard Payne Knight's *The Landscape, a Didactic Poem* (1794). The Tudor-style house commended for harmonizing with nature and defining the Picturesque.

one of the first great industrial fortunes, which gave him the means to travel in France and Italy, and to build a remarkable house. He tried to live like an ancient Greek and collected Greek and Roman antiquities. Nevertheless, he recommended the use of indigenous plants and trees in the landscape, and the avoidance of aping ancient temples in the design of modern houses. In the absence of convincing Druidic or Anglo-Saxon models for architecture, the Tudoresque building signals indigenous architecture, settled and old-fashioned, blended harmoniously into the scene.

'Olden Time'

In the imagination there is a historically non-specific 'mythic' time populated by figures whom history would keep apart, and the further distant the period, the greater the slippage and the greater the blurring into outright fiction. Horace Walpole's early playful Gothickery at Strawberry Hill was overtaken by his more serious British antiquarianism, but his party-costume portrait in Van Dyck satin and lace was not medieval. It suggests that Strawberry Hill started out as an architectural dressing-up box of general old-fashionedness, with no great fuss about stylistic purity. Walpole was a learned gentleman, and the heterogeneity did not bother him. He was more interested in amusing, mystifying and scandalizing his guests. At a popular level there was less learning and greater scope for slippage across the centuries. Actual historical knowledge is not the point here: we are dealing with popular myths about the national past and its general character. By the early nineteenth century this 'Olden Time' had settled on the age of the Tudors and the early Stuarts, and there it more or less remains.[51] 'Everybody' knows, for example, that the gallant Sir Walter Raleigh spread his cloak across a puddle, so that Elizabeth could avoid spoiling her shoes; and 'everybody' also knows that this mythical event did not happen. Nevertheless, it is endlessly alluded to – obliquely and glancingly, with a smile, floating free from the world of facts into something strangely enduring and resilient.[52] Similarly, in 1821 the coronation of George IV was an elaborate pageant designed to connect with ancient tradition. It was held in Westminster Abbey, which had been founded by Edward the Confessor, the last of the Anglo-Saxon kings, and George and his attendants wore Tudoresque ruffs round their necks – an odd spectacle, but one that must have looked plausibly old-fashioned at the time.[53]

In nineteenth-century England the exposure to old-fashioned things became an important part of culture, not only for the elite who could collect museum-quality artefacts, but also with 'popular antiquities' that seemed to embody an idea of Englishness with the 'middling sort of people'. An idea of an old-fashioned, pre-industrial 'Merry England' took shape at a popular level, and had a powerful appeal to the popular imagination.[54] Stylistically, it was not very specific, and it could be vague about the distinction between the Middle Ages and the Tudor era. The things that were on sale in the curiosity shop in Dickens's novel are united by the fact that they are old, and make an odd jumble: 'There were suits of mail standing like ghosts in armour, here and there; fantastic carvings brought from monkish cloisters;

rusty weapons of various kinds; distorted figures in china, and wood, and iron, and ivory; tapestry, and strange furniture that might have been designed in dreams.'[55] These are not useful things that are being recycled, but evocative random tokens of a vanished age. Whereas in the eighteenth century most educated people (with notable exceptions) thought of the medieval era as ignorant and superstitious, that changed as more became known about it, and Augustus Pugin, for example, recast it as an age of piety and virtue, and paved the way for the nineteenth century's Gothic Revival.[56]

The feudal castle could be seen as either romantic and nationalistic or as a symbol of political repression, particularly the Norman castles, which were the seats of power for an occupying force that held dominion over the native Britons.[57] Major new monuments were built in Gothic style, the most important being the New Palace of Westminster, the competition for which in 1835 stipulated that 'the style of the buildings be either Gothic or Elizabethan'.[58] The American and French had given classicism republican overtones, and William IV was keen to see that the new parliament had no such agenda, but demonstrated continuity with the British past.

The Gothic became a familiar style in the Victorian repertoire, especially for parish churches. Its drawback as a style for domestic buildings was that it was more readily evocative of piety than comfort, whereas a generic Old English style drew on the popular culture of Merry England, fed by such popular novels as *Kenilworth*, by Sir Walter Scott (published anonymously in 1821). Here the age of Elizabeth is presented as a golden age, with some knights in armour evocative of feudalism and chivalry, but also with a new sensibility of fair play and romance. Elizabeth is presented as principled and humane, commanding everyone's respect. There are historical inaccuracies, but Scott convinces the reader that the period saw an increase in artistic elegance and poise, with the presence of Shakespeare and a level of prosperity that contrasted favourably with the medieval world's harsh conditions. Scott's novel was widely read, and informed the historical sensibility of the masses, promoting the merits of Elizabethan culture.[59]

It is worth mentioning also at this stage the most popular of Tudoresque works: Edward German's operetta *Merrie England*, which dates from 1902 and became twentieth-century England's most-performed dramatic work, on account of a vast number of amateur performances between the wars.[60] It cannot be recommended as art – the music now sounds trite, and its wit is laboured – but it is good evidence of the persistence at popular level of the idea that there was an Elizabethan golden age, ruled by a wise and well-liked queen, who is one of the characters in the drama. Another folk hero, Robin Hood, also makes an appearance when Sir Walter Raleigh dresses up as him, and in addition to the few courtly characters there are woodcutters and honest tradesmen, representing 'the people'.

When Tudor architecture is referenced in buildings after the 1650s, it is often in order to prompt recognition of the warm feelings that are associated with the popular reputation of Elizabeth's reign. Those feelings seem to have been around since the eighteenth century, when the Tudor name was invented and the Battle of Bosworth adopted as the point of rupture that brought in not only a royal dynasty but also the modern world.

The associations of ideas are all indigenous, since the Tudors are always portrayed as Welsh, despite their claim to the throne being from their Plantagenet relatives by way of Catherine of France. They are always presented as the most British of monarchs, by contrast with the French kings before and the Dutch and then German kings afterwards. The era is remembered as a peaceable time, when the threats were from Spain and France, not from civil war – again in contrast with the Wars of the Roses before and the Roundheads and Cavaliers afterwards – finally resolved with the Glorious Revolution of 1688. This means turning a blind eye to the various martyrdoms under Henry VIII and his older daughter ('Bloody Mary'). Somehow, after his accession, Henry VII, Edward VI, Lady Jane Grey and even Mary rather fade from the picture, leaving Henry VIII, Anne Boleyn and their daughter Elizabeth as the dominant figures in the popular imagination. It is not coincidental that these were the crucial figures in establishing Protestantism in the kingdom, meaning that the country no longer felt answerable to Rome, but could be spiritually as well as politically independent. It seemed to mean at a national scale an equivalent of what the abolition of serfdom and the end of the feudal order meant at the personal one. Just as the ordinary working man was not in thrall to his overlord, and was free to make up his own mind about where and how he would live, so the nation's religion would not be answerable to Rome, but could settle things with its own conscience. That sense of the free-born, self-reliant subject is a continuing theme in Tudoresque buildings, and the Tudoresque style itself was seen not as something that had been learnt from classical Athens or Rome, but as indigenous – part of the island Britannia.

Chapter Two

Reviving a Tradition

What every schoolboy knows

In a Christmas pantomime, if someone strides on to the stage wearing green tights, with a bow and a quiver of arrows slung across his back, then the audience knows that the character is Robin Hood. It will not help the enjoyment of the show to wonder at that moment whether the real Robin Hood dressed like that, or whether there ever was a real Robin Hood. The thing that makes the character work for the audience is not the historical accuracy of the portrayal, but the fact that the conventional allusions are recognized.[1] In architecture, sometimes the allusions seem to be entirely hermetic – sealed in the architect's mind, or accessible only to those with arcane knowledge. There are ideas of proportion or sacred geometry that are built into structures, which can be decoded only by adepts. The stained glass and sculptural programmes of the medieval cathedrals were allusive in a more direct way, but would have needed a guide to explain their symbolism to the faithful.

Eighteenth-century Neoclassicism was given fresh impetus by archaeological discoveries, and the publication of Stuart and Revett's *Antiquities of Athens*, which made people want to incorporate evocations of specific Athenian temples and decorations in their new buildings and furnishings.[2] It was a type of elegance that was archaeologically informed, and prestige attached to the accuracy of the copy and the ingenuity with which it was used. Being able to notice such things was part of the polite discourse of the day.

The everyday Tudoresque is, and always has been, different from the styles of architecture that exhibit this kind of learned accomplishment. By contrast, it is an open book, more like the example of Robin Hood than the antiquities of Athens. The models, whether they were in masonry or timber-framed, could be adapted freely, and there are enough of them around to make the point that slavish imitation of one particular model would be beside the point. There are exceptions, but they are unusual.[3] In the twentieth century there were so many Tudoresque buildings around that the idea of allusion in them starts to seem less significant as a determinant of form than does the idea of habit, since the builders certainly contracted a habit of building in this manner, and the 'allusions' would be as much to the neighbours as to any more remote precedent.[4] It was more a matter of making the houses look the way they were expected to be, than of creatively incorporating elements of revered precedents.

'Everybody' knows that a wall (especially a small gable) with contrasting black-and-white work signifies 'Tudor', and that is the accepted signification. It comes as a surprise to learn that the black-and-white colouring is quite a new tradition, which goes back no further than the nineteenth century.[5] Older survivals suggest that the timbers were usually hidden under a coat of thick 'daub', so that the walls appeared more like stuccoed masonry. The timber frame was expressed, and decorative work was carved in it, but the timber was then unpainted. If it were oak, as structural timbers usually were, then it would have weathered to a silvery grey that darkens with age. The idea of blackening the timbers seems to derive from the tarring of the timber hulls of boats, and to have migrated from shipyards into wider use, but this is speculative and the idea did not begin at an identifiable time or port.[6] The less-vulnerable infill could then be painted in a contrasting colour to prevent the general effect becoming too sombre. The tradition of black-and-white building looks much older because surviving buildings from earlier centuries have often

5 William Lockwood, St Michael's Row and Arcade, 31–55 Bridge Street, Chester, Cheshire, 1911. In Chester there is a seamless blend of survivals, reproductions and reinterpretations of Tudor buildings.

been painted to bring them into line with the later idea of how they ought to look. For example, the brilliant black-and-white show of Chester's central area incorporates buildings from the seventeenth century and earlier, but they have been dressed in the manner that was seen as appropriate in the nineteenth century (illus. 5).[7] The result is spectacular, but it is a nineteenth-century aesthetic sensibility that is on display, persuading us that it belongs to a more ancient past. It has been suggested that the adoption of the colouring originates in the preservation of soot-blackened structures to be found in the industrial north-west of England, including Chester.[8] The origins are still open to speculation, but there is no doubt that it belongs in the late nineteenth century, maybe becoming the norm only in the twentieth, and definitely not in the sixteenth. Current scholarly thinking about how the old buildings should look is well represented by the exposed timbers and buff-coloured daub of Shakespeare's birthplace. It may look dull, but it is correct, and the mud-brown-and-buff colouring would be more plausible also for Robin Hood's clothes than the expensive 'Lincoln green' pigment by which everybody recognizes him.

The ways of building modest cottages seem to have continued unchanged across centuries, with regional variations to take advantage of the availability of local building materials, such as field-stones, slate and thatch. The principal alternatives for low-cost dwellings were to build either in rammed earth (*pisé*, or cob – basically mud, which had to be protected from rainwater) or a timber frame with a non-structural infill of wattle and daub. These methods were in use for centuries before they found their way into printed descriptions, but they are accessible in 'Kent's *Hints*' – Nathaniel Kent's book, *Hints to Gentlemen of Landed Property* – which gives specifications for decent dwellings for agricultural workers.[9] The presentation is utilitarian. The designs are plain and severe, and Kent makes no claims for their aesthetic merit. He does not present them as a continuation of a tradition, but that is what they are. It is a straightforward practical presentation that is completely unselfconscious about its place in a culture. The book is addressed to the landowners who would be in a position to build such houses for their workforce, and it is hinted that the expenditure would be worthwhile, but there is no mention of any stylistic considerations, which is perhaps what one would expect where such basic buildings are concerned.

The position changed, however, in the wake of the French Revolution of 1789, the ramifications of which spread from the political sphere to the culture in everyday life. On the political plane there was anxiety verging on panic in some quarters, and from 1793 – after the execution of Louis XVI – Britain declared war on France. Before the 'Industrial Revolution', France, a much larger country with more agricultural land and consequently able to support a larger population, seemed prosperous and stable, but then went into catastrophic spasm. It seemed to many that the same thing could happen in Britain. One of the ways in which the idea of a revolt of the labouring poor could be defused was by improving their lot. They did not at that time have a vote, and it was generally agreed that their dwellings were squalid and that they had little to lose.

A Board of Agriculture was established to advise landowners, and its reports were published. They include designs for modest cottages that could be built at minimal cost, and which would have the effect of improving the living conditions of the rural poor and thus dissipate the undercurrents that might build up to revolution.[10] These exhortations were supported by architects, who were short of work because taxes had been raised in order to pay for the war, leaving landowners feeling less prosperous and significantly less inclined to embark on major building and landscaping projects. Small-scale works that helped with political stability, however, seemed imperative, and during these years various architects published books that included designs for cottages.

It is striking, looking back, how few books on architecture were written in Britain before this time. The first was John Shute's *The First and Chief Groundes of Architecture used in all the Auncient and Famous Monymentes*, published in 1563, when Elizabeth was on the throne. It explains with illustrations how to use the classical orders. There was Sir Henry Wotton's free translation of Vitruvius, *The Elements of Architecture* of 1624, and then through the eighteenth century Colen Campbell's *Vitruvius Britannicus*, which presented plans, sections and elevations of British buildings, following the model of Palladio's *I quattro libri*, but promoting the merits of British designs – albeit designs in a classical style.

Vitruvius Britannicus was the first publication to promote a self-consciously 'British' view of architecture, rather than try to raise the standard of British architecture by inculcating admiration for Roman models. The designs steer the reader away from the excesses of the Continental Baroque, recommending a Palladian restraint.[11] It fits with the sense of national identity that had formed around the Glorious

Revolution, seeing Britain's architecture as independent of Rome's, and the book was dedicated to the new king, George I.

The major British treatise on architecture from the middle of the eighteenth century was William Chambers's *Treatise on Civil Architecture*, which has an absolutely cosmopolitan outlook.[12] Chambers had been born in Sweden, and published a book of Chinese-style designs, drawing on knowledge acquired on his travels in China in the service of the Swedish East India Company.[13] In contrast to this exotica, there were publications, such as John Wood's, that further developed Nathaniel Kent's architectural agenda, and others that started showing how the simple cottage could take a picturesque turn, and could enhance the scenery while at the same time making a decent and inexpensive dwelling.[14] The most significant for the developing sense of the Tudoresque was the first book since *Vitruvius Britannicus* to announce in its title that it was specifically concerned with the character of British architecture: James Malton's *British Cottage Architecture* of 1798.

Malton was Irish, which perhaps gave him a way to notice what was characteristic about the modest buildings he saw in England, and the book's subtitle explains that his aim was to 'perpetuate on principle the peculiar mode of building, which was originally the effect of chance'.[15] He proposed an 'old English' style, which was the very opposite of original. Some of his illustrations bring with them a jolt of recognition, because they look so strikingly like the products of twentieth-century speculative builders (illus. 6). Their applied 'half-timbering' effects are not black and white, but seem to show unpainted timbers. There are leaded lights in some of the windows, while others seem to have timber latticework to screen them, rather than expensive glass.

It would be a mistake, though, to see Malton's designs as the primary influence on subsequent developments. They were an attempt to consolidate and make principled a mode of building that was already well established. The great difference between his work and Nathaniel Kent's or John Wood's is that these designs are alive to the picturesque potential of modest buildings, and they are recommended

6 James Malton, Design 8, Plate 10, in *British Cottage Architecture* (1798). An Irishman defining the British sense of style.

for their charm as well as their utility. Also, they are presented as characteristically British. Malton had worked in the Dublin office of the architect James Gandon (who had earlier worked for William Chambers) and Malton's best-known works are views of Dublin, including watercolour perspectives of Gandon's monumental works. In his book about cottage architecture Malton endorsed and encouraged the taste for the Picturesque, along with an anti-exotic agenda.[16] He argued that public buildings, including royal palaces, should be splendid, but that the houses of private citizens should be modest, so there is denigration of private magnificence, and praise of simplicity:[17]

> With fixed depressed brow, is beheld the stately edifice on the eminence, confounding admiration with regarding it as the seat of cares and inquietude; but glancing at the view below, we smile with serene delight on the cottage in the valley, whose narrow confines seem adequate to all real needs and wants, and speaks the residence of 'Those calm desires that ask but little room'.[18]

The quotation here is from *The Deserted Village*, by another Irishman, Oliver Goldsmith, which is frequently cited when an idyll of the olden days is evoked. The poem portrays a vanished golden age of village life before the 'progress' of enclosures and landscaped parkland swept it aside. In fact, the particular stanza from which this line comes was an exact amplification of Malton's theme:

> But times are alter'd; Trade's unfeeling train
> Usurp the land, and dispossess the swain;
> Along the lawn, where scatter'd hamlets rose,
> Unwieldy wealth and cumbrous pomp repose;
> And every want to luxury allied,
> And every pang that folly pays to pride.
> Those gentle hours that plenty bade to bloom,
> Those calm desires that ask'd but little room,
> Those healthful sports that graced the peaceful scene,
> Lived in each look, and brighten'd all the green –
> These, far departing, seek a kinder shore,
> And rural mirth and manners are no more. [19]

The departure for 'a kinder shore' was more characteristic of Irish than English villagers, but both countries saw rural depopulation as common land was enclosed in private estates, and the towns began to present more opportunities for paid employment. Malton's designs avoid 'affectations', such as Gothic windows and coloured glass, which he saw as characteristic of the *cottage orné* – a 'second home' for someone who wanted to be able to retreat to the countryside for leisure and tranquillity. A *cottage orné* might look just the same as a 'real' cottage, but it would be used differently. It would be better decorated and furnished, and less crowded. Giving such a cottage a cosmopolitan French name signals the expectation of education and pretension. Malton was proposing decent family dwellings for people of relatively modest means, who would be at home in their cottages, and in the British landscape, not as visitors or *arrivistes*, but as an indigenous part of the social fabric.

Reviving a Tradition

Malton's book was a success, and went into a second edition in 1804. It does not mark a fresh departure in British architecture, but a consolidation of what everybody already knew British architecture to be. The grandiose domestic monuments had been itemized and represented in *Vitruvius Britannicus*, but the buildings that the people actually knew and lived in were represented generically and codified in *British Cottage Architecture*. Buildings that reflect these concerns can be found across the whole range of society, from dwellings for the poorest to the nobility, but since the books were clearly addressed to landowners it is through their commissions that the books' influence is to be found.

The undoubted high point of artistic accomplishment in the genre of cottage building was the hamlet that John Nash designed at Blaise, near Bristol, in 1810 (illus. 7). These small dwellings were built for people who had worked on the Blaise estate, and presented to

7 John Nash, Blaise Hamlet, Bristol, 1810. An idyll of pre-industrial village life.

perfection the vision of a rustic life in the olden days. Tudor elements can be isolated, but the aim is to evoke the vernacular tradition, which is less specifically tied to architectural fashions than is the architecture of the elite. The remarkable thing here is that the work is not vernacular at all, but by the architect who designed Regent Street and Buckingham Palace.

While Nash's cottages were designed to house the genuinely poor, who would have had these dwellings as their only home, the cottage could be adapted into something very much more commodious, such as Endsleigh, in Devon, by Sir Jeffry Wyatville (1809) for the Duke of Bedford. Wyatville, like Nash, had royal commissions, and here the client was scarcely less regal. He had been developing the West End of London and had very ample means, but against the background of grumbling civil unrest and the Napoleonic wars he was disinclined to make his new house a showy affair. After all, he already had Woburn Abbey.

8 Jeffry Wyatt (Sir Jeffry Wyatville). Endsleigh Cottage. A large house styled as a cottage. Devon, 1809.

Endsleigh was sited with Humphry Repton's advice in a superbly picturesque setting, and by anyone else's standards it was a substantial country seat. But the building used its irregular planning to diminish its apparent mass, and contrived to look like a large cottage (illus. 8).[20] It makes play with Tudoresque chimneys, oriels and square-headed windows with stone mullions and transoms, and hood-mouldings over some of the windows, so there is no doubt about the Tudoresque aspect of its comfortable old Englishness, but its aspirations are closer to Malton's British cottages than to Smythson's prodigy houses, which would have been within the duke's means. This building was considerately designed to feel at home in the landscape and to be comfortable to inhabit. It was not designed to impress, but the owner's rank made it aspirational.

Burke's 'Reflections'

The role that these buildings had in representing British character can be seen most clearly if we turn to another Irishman, Edmund Burke, whose celebrated analysis of that character in his *Reflections on the Revolution in France* was published in 1790. It was prompted, as his title makes clear, by the French Revolution, and its political purpose was to encourage a sense of the British character that would promote social stability. The French, he argued, had listened to the siren voices of reason, and it had led them to complete social breakdown and depravity – he alluded to stories that were then in circulation about the revolutionaries eating their own children and fornicating in the street. Although some members of what we today would call the 'chattering classes' – journalists and intellectuals – had seemed to be influenced by French thinking, the great mass of the British people had no inclination to be swayed by reason, and Burke saw this as a very good thing. He compared the *philosophes* and pamphleteers with grasshoppers making a noise in a field, while the great bovine mass of the population carried on regardless:

> Because half a dozen grasshoppers under a fern make the field ring with their importunate chink, whilst thousands of great cattle, reposed beneath the shadow of the British oak, chew the cud and are silent, pray do not imagine that those who make the noise are the only inhabitants of the field; that of course, they are many in number; or that, after all, they are other than the little shrivelled, meagre, hopping, though loud and troublesome insects of the hour.²¹

Burke concludes by putting his trust in the sullen and sluggish British character, which will not act in accordance with a fashionable argument, but will do what it always has done, in its bone-headed way. This represents, for Burke, a way of acting in accordance with the sedimented wisdom of the ages, rather than flightily following a personal whim, or a recent idea, however closely reasoned.

Burke stressed the role of the monarch in governance, seeing the monarch's authority as rooted in 'the people', as opposed to the aristocracy. The monarch was one of the 'three estates' – the others being the two houses of parliament. This arrangement was admired as a model, because each 'estate' helped to keep the others in check.²² Before 'the people' in general could vote, the monarch was seen as representing their interests, which is to say the nation's interests. So the popular view of the king of England, in Burke's time, was quite different from that of the French people's view of their 'absolute' king, whom they saw as a symbol of oppression, whereas (according to Burke) the British people saw their king as an emblem of their rights and their liberty. He associated French culture with refinement, fashion, sophistication and the intellect, whereas British culture was plain and wholesome:

> The people of England will not ape the fashions they have never tried, nor go back to those which they have found mischievous on trial. They look upon the legal hereditary succession of their crown as among their rights, not as

among their wrongs; as a benefit, not as grievance; as a security for their liberty, not as a badge of servitude.[23]

Burke's assessment of the British character has been found to be enduringly useful in predicting the behaviour of the British public. It also provides a mechanism by which someone who identifies with this description can resist rationality. Intellectualism is seen to be foreign and untrustworthy, whereas prejudice and tradition may not be comprehensible, but they are seen to embody whatever it is that makes us who we are, which is to say British. Not every British citizen will identify with this description, but those who do not are heavily outnumbered by those who do.

It is Squire Allworthy's old-fashionedness, the fact that he does not seem to be in tune with the modern, that makes him seem trustworthy in Fielding's eyes and presumably in the eyes of his mainstream readership. Burke's is the first systematically articulated analysis of the value system of 'middle England', but we should not assume that middle England was newly formed in his day, or that it has subsequently been dismantled. It was to this constituency that the old-fashioned Tudoresque had the strongest appeal, whether in James Malton's day or our own.

John Ruskin reflects this view in an early essay on architecture, published in 1837-8 when he was eighteen, before he had lighted on Venice as the ideal model for architecture. His assertion that 'the only style of villa architecture which can be called English – the Elizabethan, and its varieties – a style fantastic in its details, and capable of being subjected to no rule' is substantiated by comparing it with the national character:

> First, it is a humorist, an odd, twisted, independent being, with a great deal of mixed, obstinate, and occasionally absurd originality. It has one or two graceful lines about it, and several harsh and cutting ones; it is a whole, which would allow of no unison with any other architecture; it

is gathered in itself, and would look very ugly indeed, if pieces in a purer style of building were added. All this corresponds with points of English character, with its humours, its independency, and its horror of being put out of its own way.

Again, it is a thoroughly domestic building, homely and cottage-like in its prevailing forms, awakening no elevated ideas, assuming no nobility of form. It has none of the pride, or the grace of beauty, none of the dignity of delight which we found in the villa of Italy; but it is a habitation of everyday life, a protection from momentary inconvenience, covered with stiff efforts at decoration, and exactly typical of the mind of its inhabitant: not noble in its taste, not haughty in its recreation, not pure in its perception of beauty; but domestic in its pleasures, fond of matter-of-fact rather than of imagination, yet sparkling occasionally with odd wit and grotesque association.[24]

This is juvenile work, which reflects received wisdom far more than would Ruskin's more original and influential texts, but where the Tudoresque is concerned 'received wisdom' is often to the point. It is what everybody knows, even if they are not quite sure how it is that they know it. It belongs with the thought-world of everyday life, and Ruskin follows Burke in putting the pursuit of domestic contentment at the heart of the national character. Fine style, elevated ideas, intellectual analysis, grace and beauty are all very well in their way, but there is something untrustworthy and foreign about them. For the British, and for the Tudoresque, the received wisdom is that the important qualities are independence to the point of obstinacy, pragmatism and a sense of humour. The British keep calm and carry on, more or less whatever happens or whatever anyone says.

A *hybrid* Renaissance

Tudor architecture was sometimes seen as Gothic, sometimes as the beginning of the Renaissance in Britain. The fifteenth-century Italian Renaissance had an influence on the cosmopolitan elite in Tudor England, but its reception was complex. British builders were working in a flourishing medieval tradition that gave the mindset through which the new influence was understood. This tradition had evolved over the centuries – from the eleventh to the sixteenth – producing various different architectural styles, which nowadays are grouped together as varieties of Romanesque and Gothic. The tradition did not suddenly stop when it came into contact with Italian architectural ornament, but made sense of it in its own terms: familiar with the profusion of ornament on the facades of the great cathedrals, ignorant of the colonnaded discipline of the temples of ancient Greece. The versions of classical ornament that found their way into sixteenth-century Britain were thoroughly hybrid, mixing classical detail with a Gothic sense of composition and features (such as 'strap work') that were acquired from Flemish designers along the way. Inigo Jones is usually credited with the first examples of a 'pure' Italianate style, at Greenwich from 1616, under James I. This version of classicism, drawn more directly from Roman sources and codified by Serlio and Palladio in their illustrated books, came to be seen as authoritative, leaving the sixteenth-century versions looking under-informed and old-fashioned.[25] By the end of the eighteenth century, however, that was no longer a problem. There are versions of this hybrid Gothic-informed style, such as William Wilkins's Tregothnan, Cornwall, which dates from 1816 (illus. 9). The battlements and pinnacles (some of which turn out to be chimneys) are medieval in their inspiration, but when used in conjunction with the square-headed window openings, with the windows taking up such a large proportion of the wall surface and using the occasional Tudor arch and linen-fold panelling, the effect is Tudoresque. The genealogy for this building would take us back to Richard Payne Knight, whose own house at Downton Castle,

9 William Wilkins, Tregothnan, Cornwall, 1816. A Picturesque house in the country, by an architect well-known for his classical buildings, mostly built in towns.

Herefordshire, built in the 1770s, was invariably seen as a classical and medieval hybrid.[26] The Gothic tracery in its square-headed windows was added in the 1860s, and there is no Tudor character to be inferred here, but the house set an example for John Nash, who developed the irregular picturesque massing in a variety of styles in various projects, including his own house on the Isle of Wight, East Cowes Castle (1798), and Luscombe, Devon (1800). Tregothnan is a particularly striking example of Wilkins's picturesque Tudor manner, which he had developed by way of the earlier Dalmeny, West Lothian (1814), where the same architectural moves are seen in a slightly different cultural context and therefore categorized as Baronial. In Wilkins's case the influence from Knight was direct, since the two of them were working together on a publication for the Society of Dilettanti, and his earlier archaeologically informed Neoclassicism (such as The Grange, Hampshire, 1809) one of the purest expressions of the Greek Revival, was supplanted by the vigorously variegated Picturesque.[27] For his more urban designs, such as the National Gallery and University College in London, however, Wilkins continued in classicizing mode.

Another early example is Warleigh Manor in Bathford, Somerset (1815), by Neale Webb, a less significant architect, and a less grandiose dwelling than Tregothnan, with a smaller scale but equal intricacy. The house has the mood of something from the reign of Henry VIII and makes much more cautious use of the chimneys, turrets and towers, no doubt reining in the liveliness of the silhouette by considering the cost it would incur.

So Tudoresque buildings were being built in the early years of the nineteenth century, but in the 1830s they turned into a craze. Elizabethan architecture looked uniquely British and independent-minded, and it represented the olden days, which could be evoked, maybe even resurrected, if sociable practices such as hospitality were re-enacted. The stylistic impurity was seen by C. J. Richardson, for example, to be 'productive of highly picturesque and pleasing effects',[28] and if that was achieved by being somewhat ignorant of Roman models, then that suited the national sense of independence down to the ground.

Part of this valuing of hybridity was a consequence of scholarly advances in antiquarianism. At the beginning of the eighteenth century all the not particularly classical styles were collectively labelled as 'Gothic', which meant in effect 'barbaric', and so it could include exotic styles alongside versions of medieval architecture, even including the Romanesque, which had clear classical antecedents. During the eighteenth century there was a good deal of progress in understanding and analysing British medieval architecture. The earlier eighteenth-century sense of the 'Gothic', characterized by gloom, ignorance and superstition, still survives in 'Gothic horror' and pale teenage Goths. In 1805 Richard Payne Knight, who was a philhellene and not a medieval specialist, still saw Gothic as an indiscriminate jumble of different styles.[29] He advocated mixing architectural styles, on the grounds that some of Claude's finest pictures showed mixed styles to good effect, so he did not condemn Gothic architecture for its impurity, but he did think it futile to search for the purest Gothic.

The problems of understanding English medieval architectural styles were considered to be more or less solved by Rickman in 1817, who confirmed the multiplicity in medieval architecture, but also made sense of it.³⁰ C. J. Richardson drew attention to the same hybridity in Tudorbethan architecture, valued its picturesqueness, and suggested that what it lacked in authoritative knowledge could be compensated for with inborn national genius:

> An age and a country, that could produce a Bacon and a Shakespeare, was not likely to prove contemptible in architecture. With all those minor defects which we may allow to exist in the immortal works of our great bard, we yet recognise in those works an irresistible strength of spirit, that defies criticism, and strikes dumb the critic; and although England was not fortunate enough to find at this juncture a Shakespeare in architecture, yet can we point to many examples of the art, even at that period, fraught with much of the true Shakespearian spirit, poetic invention, and majestic grandeur.³¹

Richardson's praise of Bacon and Shakespeare is conventional enough in the nineteenth century, but he is clearly associating them with the Renaissance, rather than the Middle Ages. He puts a distance between their period and supposed medieval darkness when he says that the great patrons of the Elizabethan age could little 'tolerate the gloomy mansions which had hitherto sufficed for their paternal dwellings'.³² The great enthusiasm of the 1830s was not for cottages, but for the grander Tudorbethan mansions and manor houses. Their decorative details in timber and masonry were recorded, published and used as models by architects.³³ The style was not seen as universally applicable but, taking a cue from Knight, it was seen to suit the landscape, and domestic architecture.

> For the parsonage-house, the rural and sequestered villa, amidst coppices and garden-grounds, the Elizabethan style is not only admissible, but in accordance with the *genius*

> *loci*: its quaint gables, fantastic pinnacles and pendants; its intricate parapets and grotesque carvings, connect themselves intimately with surrounding scenery, and form a picture far more readily and agreeably than uniform symmetrical objects. So far let the Elizabethan be followed; but may no morbid passion for novelty lead to its introduction into civic architecture: still more should we deprecate and deplore its adoption in important public buildings: for such edifices, there is no style of design so appropriate, so convenient and so consistent, as the stately and symmetrical Greek, so far modified by the Roman and Palladian styles, as to suit the complex purposes of modern civic architecture.[34]

So for civic institutions the authority of classicism trumped the picturesque qualities of the Tudoresque, but for an image of settled domesticity old-English manor houses were unbeatable. They were comfortable, could be composed freely, so as to allow the convenient arrangement of rooms, and did not have about them any lingering taint of fanatical piety, which the Gothic could still evoke in a domestic context.[35] Francis Goodwin, a relaxedly eclectic architect, in 1834 published a book of 'designs for cottages, lodges, villas and other residences in the Grecian, Italian and Old English styles of architecture'. He just did not see the point of Gothic houses:

> To say the truth few things can be more despicable in their way, than some of the Gothic castelled mansions and villas that have been sent forth to the world, upon paper. Essentially anti-picturesque in every respect, betraying utter ignorance both as regards composition and detail; and equal clumsiness and want of judgement in respect to ordinary comfort, such articles of manufacture – for designs, they cannot be termed – are calculated to bring architecture into contempt, being apparently

intended as Byron rather oddly phrases it, when speaking of a sister art, 'to impose upon the nonsense of mankind'.[36]

The 'sister art' here is painting, and Byron was explaining how he had problems with religious art, feeling it to be some kind of imposture – confusing aesthetic appreciation with piety. Goodwin's implication is that he finds Gothic too redolent of medieval superstition. He does not make it clear whom he had in mind when he dismissed the Gothic. Had he been writing a few years later the prime suspect would have been Pugin, whose *Contrasts* was published in 1836, and *True Principles* in 1841.[37] Perhaps it was James Wyatt, who had been working at Windsor Castle, or more aptly Robert Smirke, whose symmetrical Eastnor Castle was completed in 1820, but that was a real building, not a paper design. There are certainly designs in P. F. Robinson's output that would deserve Goodwin's censure. He was ultra-eclectic in his approach, and published his drawings for Greek, Roman, Gothic and castellated mansions and cottages, as well as building the Egyptian Halls in Piccadilly and the Swiss Cottage in St John's Wood.

Robinson enjoyed picturesquely mixing styles, and published images of model villages where each building was in a different style. It is no great surprise to find that he turned his hand to Tudoresque buildings – 'the style of old England'.[38] His take on any style was superficial, without any of the antiquarian enthusiasm or moral conviction of its more serious adherents, but his book *Domestic Architecture in the Tudor Style* (1837) is the only one of his publications to present designs in just one style, which suggests a greater than usual level of commitment to it.[39]

One of Robinson's buildings, once an industrialist's mansion, now university offices, shows his handling of the Tudoresque as a variant of Gothic. Pinnacles and crockets enliven the silhouette, but the execution is sketchy, without the antiquarian detail that a more obsessive architect or client would have thought necessary (illus. 10). It is a no-nonsense reworking of the pattern established by Dalmeny or Tregothnan, looking every bit as romantic in the architect's drawing,

Reviving a Tradition

10 P. F. Robinson, a plate from *Domestic Architecture in the Tudor Style* (1837). Compare with illus. 4: practical Picturesque Tudor.

but quite perfunctory in its execution. Robinson's commercially minded operation would certainly have made sense to his commercially minded clients.

Informal domestic Tudor

Napoleon's defeats at Trafalgar and Waterloo made heroes of Nelson and Wellington, and made for a mood of national self-confidence that seems to have continued until 1914. Prosperity returned, buoyed by industrial manufacture, and by the 1830s there were major public monuments once more under construction – such as the National Gallery, the British Museum and then, after the disastrous fire of 1835, the New Palace of Westminster. The question that drove these building projects was not 'how can we achieve these things at minimum cost?', but 'can we make them splendid enough to outdo the French?' In well-to-do Tudoresque homes the preoccupation is with comfort, rather than with political imperatives or with show, and although the old manor houses feature strongly in illustrated books, it seems to be the example of Endsleigh's cottagey modesty, rather than the would-be prodigies, that is held up as the way ahead. In 1834 Goodwin said that

> for buildings upon a moderate scale, hardly any style is so well calculated to produce important character and striking effect with comparatively little finish of detail. Decision and expression in outline, bold transitions and contrasts, will go far towards securing those qualities, independently of the last mentioned one. This is more especially the case with regard to buildings of the cottage class, that is those where the family physiognomy which marks the examples of the Elizabethan period is retained, but divested of its formality and stateliness, and applied to homelier materials and purposes. Here form, rather than studied detail or beauty of workmanship, is to be considered, for what has been observed above – namely, that the mere outline of Gothic architecture would be crude and offensive – hardly applies to this subordinate branch, or rather descendent of it.[40]

In contrast with the Gothic, which was felt to be overly pious, the Tudoresque does not have to try too hard, especially where cottages are concerned. They represent 'the Tudor or Elizabethan in their undress'.[41] The detail is not too important, and its picturesque irregularity makes it readily adaptable if an extension is required.[42] Indeed, many Tudoresque houses are extensions or remodellings of older buildings, and as a style it could embrace and enjoy irregularities of composition as 'characterful', where a more formal classical style would have needed to mask them, or iron them out, which could only add to the cost of the project, and might eliminate rather than enhance elements of the older building's charm.

Goodwin makes the Tudoresque sound so attractive, undemanding and effortless that any alternative for 'off-duty' buildings would surely have to be an affectation and a waste. A decade later, John Claudius Loudon presented in his *Encyclopaedia* the '*beau idéal* of an English villa', making much the same recommendation:[43]

> There are many reasons which lead me to give a preference to the mixed style of Architecture, called the old English style, for a gentleman's residence in the country. For instance it is more picturesque and ornamental; it accords best with rural scenery; and as it admits of great irregularity of form, it affords space for the various offices and conveniences necessary in an English country house. It is also better suited to our climate than the Grecian style, which requires porticoes, projecting cornices, and windows of moderate size . . . all of which circumstances tend to make the house gloomy, and intercept the light. The old style, also, allows more variety of ornament upon the roof, such as the stacks of chimneys, gables, pinnacles, turrets and other things of importance to the general effect of a building to be seen at a distance: whereas in the Grecian style which requires perfect symmetry of form, and the prevalence of straight lines, the offices and chimneys are commonly excrescences offensive to the eye of genuine taste. For these and other reasons, therefore, I should erect a villa in the old English style, and in that ornate manner of it called the Elizabethan, as being most adapted to the habits of refined and peaceable times.[44]

Loudon's thought was not innovative in 1846, clearly echoing Goodwin and Richardson in his reasons for this preference, but the idea has clearly been established that the best mode of domestic life is old-fashioned and, when in England, is best housed in an old-English dwelling. It was probably by this time absolutely the mainstream view. For those with the means to develop that idea, Loudon is full of suggestions:

> An English hall admits of much picturesque embellishment, such as a carved oak roof or ceiling, either flat or semi-circular, enriched with highly wrought bosses or coats of arms; a music gallery across the end, supported by pillars or a carved screen; a chimney piece reaching to the cornice of the roof, and a carved wainscot covering half the height of the walls.[45]

This continued to be the dominant and unexceptional view so far as domestic architecture was concerned, even when the Gothic Revival seemed to predominate for institutional buildings, after the New Palace of Westminster put the style so firmly on the map (1840–52 and continuing). Its planning and the building operations were organized by Sir Charles Barry, who ensured that the building worked, but he enlisted Pugin for the Gothic detail that makes such a powerful visual impression. Pugin's loving detail in the stonework, the furnishings and the wallpapers give the building its air of sumptuous stability. He was a fanatic. His primary focus was church-related architecture, but he saw religious activity informing every aspect of a life, and was a particularly fervent convert to Catholicism.

Pugin personally avoided making use the term 'Gothic', because of the pejorative associations in its background, and advocated pre-Reformation 'pointed or Christian' architecture, as much because it was an expression of piety as for its aesthetic value. In his view the problem with his contemporaries' designs was that in their search for old England they had not gone back far enough.

> There is a great reviving taste for ancient domestic architecture, but a vast many pretended admirers of old English

beauties, instead of imitating the Tudor period, when domestic architecture was carried to a high state of perfection, stop short at the reign of Elizabeth, the very worst kind of English architecture; and strange to say, these unmeaning conglomerations of debased forms have been classed into a regular style, and called after the female tyrant during whose reign they were executed. The only reason I can assign for the fashionable rage for this architecture (if so it may be called) is, that its character is so corrupt, mixed, and bad, that the anachronisms and anomalies so frequently perpetuated by modern architects are made to pass muster under the general term of Elizabethan; and certainly I cannot deny that the appellation is very appropriate when applied to corrupted design and decayed taste.[46]

Pugin's position is extreme and idiosyncratic, distorted by his partisan 'spin'. He makes a categorical distinction between 'Tudor' and 'Elizabethan' styles, approving the first and condemning the second. His reason for excluding Elizabeth from the ranks of the Tudors is that he refuses to be swayed by the arguments that did not persuade Thomas More and Mary Tudor. Henry VIII on this view had only one child, Mary, who was suitable to rule. Her younger half-brother Edward had been the son from Henry's marriage to Jane Seymour, which happened soon after Mary's mother Katherine of Aragon's death, so although Edward was technically legitimate, he was a Protestant and not in Pugin's view a viable monarch. He came to the throne at the age of nine and died at fifteen, naming Lady Jane Grey as his successor. Mary, when she dispatched Jane Grey and came to the throne, understandably remained loyal to the Catholic Church and tried to root out Protestantism in England with multiple executions by burning. Mary's mother had been Spanish; Mary herself married Philip II of Spain (an uncrowned King of England). British Protestants thought that she was being influenced by the Spanish

Inquisition and called her 'Bloody Mary'. The Catholic Church never recognized Anne Boleyn as Henry's wife, and so their daughter was illegitimate and also obviously a villain, since when she took the throne she reintroduced Protestantism. While the general view, as we have seen, was that Elizabeth's reign was a golden age, in Pugin's eyes it was tyrannical and corrupt. The Tudors in his version of history perished with Mary. In the 'fashionable rage' for Tudoresque buildings the architects of Pugin's time have not, in Pugin's view, gone back far enough, but have stopped just short of them, seduced by the bastard-daughter-of-a-whore Elizabeth, rather than finding the late pre-Reformation work that for Pugin represented the ideal combination of religious splendour and genuine piety. His stance involved reopening arguments that one might have thought had been settled by the time that Elizabeth was allowed a coronation.

William James Audsley and his brother, George Ashdown Audsley, moderated this position when they said (in 1868) that 'next to the Gothic, the Elizabethan is unquestionably the most important and suitable style for modern houses'.[47] This is appreciation of a sort, but it clearly leaves Elizabethan architecture as second best. 'Everything which can be done in Elizabethan,' they said, 'can be executed in Gothic with far more grace, beauty and truth.'[48]

Pugin laid claim to Merry England for his cause, but located it firmly before the break with Rome. He also claimed that in those days the aristocracy actually lived on their estates, rather than spending 'the season' in London, or travelling abroad:

> Every person should be lodged as becomes his station and dignity, for in this there is nothing contrary to, but in accordance with the Catholic principle; but the mansions erected by our ancestors, were not the passing whim of a moment, or mere show places raised at such an extravagant cost as impoverished some generations of heirs to the estates, but solid, dignified, and Christian structures, built with due regard to the general prosperity of the

family; and the almost constant residence of the ancient gentry on their estates rendered it indispensable for them to have mansions where they might exercise the rights of hospitality to their fullest extent. They did not confine their guests, as at present, to a few fashionables who condescend to pass away a few days occasionally in a country house; but under the oaken rafters of their capacious halls the lords of the manor used to assemble all their friends and tenants at those successive periods when the church bids all her children rejoice, while humbler guests partook of their share of bounty dealt to them by the hand of the almoner beneath the groined entrance of the gatehouse. Catholic England was Merry England, at least for the humbler classes; and the architecture was in keeping with the faith and manners of the times, at once strong and hospitable.[49]

The Audsleys also stressed the populist aspect of 'our national styles', meaning Gothic and Tudor:

It is unquestionably to the revival of our national styles that we must attribute the great progress which has been made in our day in all branches of architecture and architectural art. It has restored us those styles whose flexible nature renders them equally valuable for the rich and the poor: for whilst the Lordly Palladian could not shrink to the humble proportions of a cottage, and the Greek appeared both out of place and ridiculous in anything of less pretension than the temple-like hall or church, the Gothic and Elizabethan styles rejoiced alike in their innate beauty and fitness whether exhibited in the labourer's cottage, the elegant villa or the mansion of the nobleman.[50]

The fact that these styles could be adapted for use at any level of society was clearly something to recommend them. Different classes of people remained, housed in different classes of dwelling (cottage, villa, mansion), but they could feel that they were all parts of the fabric of the same society. The cosmopolitan and often-absent aristocrats who would come to visit with their fashionable friends could have seemed as distant and otherworldly for ordinary decent folk as do present-day celebrities. Architecture could articulate this sense of separation, or could try to overcome it.

Modesty

There has always been a degree of freedom in the design of buildings in Britain, and a national style has never been imposed by law. Various arbiters of taste have, at various times since the rise of commerce, encouraged and condemned particular ways of doing things, for reasons of dignity and decorum, or morality. Pugin and Ruskin wrote books to promote their views; earlier, Lord Burlington had held salons; later, there were planning committees. Particular styles of building come to seem particularly characteristic of an era, so that, for example, when we think of a 'Georgian country house' a Palladian mansion comes to mind, and seems to represent the idea quite adequately. If we look to the dwellings of the super-rich, who made money often in the East India Company, and who built new houses rather than inheriting the ancestral home, then a much wider range of architectures comes into view. The pre-eminent example was the Brighton Pavilion, built for the Prince of Wales, who was not fabulously rich but was allowed to live as if he were, running up huge debts. No one who wrote about architectural taste ever wrote in favour of exoticisms as things to be encouraged on principle. If they are mentioned, they are seen as an extravagant indulgence, to be condemned. There was nevertheless a continuing appetite for them, which meant that they were built, along with a range of other less sensational styles.

The lack of a consensus about architectural style becomes more apparent as the number of people who commissioned buildings increased. Nineteenth-century industrialists who made great fortunes did not necessarily share aristocratic tastes, although, if they could, they sometimes wanted to look like aristocrats.

If the eighteenth century's architectural sensibility, despite its eclecticism, seems to be adequately epitomized in the Palladian house, the nineteenth century does not seem to have an equivalent. Eclecticism seems to be its distinguishing characteristic. If the question is 'where did the eclecticism come from?', then the answer is that it was always there, whenever there was enough money being made outside the class of people who had grand ancestral seats. So why was it that the Palladian house did not continue as the dominant model through the nineteenth century? It could have conferred on its proprietor an air of gentlemanly decorum and respectability, even if the money that supported it came from manufacture rather than the management of an estate. The answer to that question was given in 1864 by an architect, Robert Kerr, Professor of the Arts of Construction at King's College, London, looking back with lofty hindsight on the work of the previous generation. He pointed out that however attractive it might be for other reasons, 'the chief consideration which brought the Elizabethan Mansion into fashion was the obvious superiority of its plan',[51] and he pointed to a change in architectural manners since the eighteenth century:

> It may also be easy to remember here that a marked change had been effected, irrespective of all else, with regard to the fastidious question of *Display*. It was a sort of inherent virtue in the Palladian style that stateliness was so easy of accomplishment; it was also its vice that pretentiousness was so readily encouraged. The natural result was a reaction towards simplicity; and one which has not yet become exhausted; for at this moment, not withstanding all the facilities which we possess in inexpensive decoration, it

must be looked upon as a rule that an English gentleman will desire to avoid obtrusiveness even at the sacrifice of a good deal of that importance which properly belongs to the rank, wealth, education, and character of his class. That this consideration, therefore had its due weight in the establishment, in place of the more majestic Palladian, of the more modest Elizabethan, we may safely consider to be the fact.[52]

The level of exuberance with which to put one's wealth on display was, in other words, significantly diminished after the various revolutions overseas. The best examples of Tudoresque dwellings from Kerr's time, where grandiose accommodation was presented modestly and decorously, were designed by George Devey, whose early work for Lord De L'Isle at Penshurst began in 1850. He did restoration work in the

11 George Devey, Alterations and refurbishment at Penshurst Place, Penshurst, Kent, 1850 onwards – the blend of old and new.

12 George Devey, Betteshanger, Kent, 1856. Although appearing to blend old with new, this was in fact all new work.

village and at Penshurst Place, which was substantially a Tudor building, but with earlier elements, including a medieval great hall (illus. 11). Devey mixed styles and construction methods in his designs in a much more sophisticated way than P. F. Robinson had done, but with a similarly Picturesque agenda, trying to make the new buildings seem at ease in their surroundings by having been built and adapted piecemeal over centuries.[53] They never did look like new buildings, and even when a Tudor wing looks a little too well preserved to date from before the nineteenth century, one might overlook the fact that the medieval castle whose walls it seems to be bringing back into use is a complete fiction and that the masonry walls were built by the same contractors as the black-and-white adaptations, or the Tudoresque brickwork (illus. 12).[54]

Devey's buildings are self-effacing in their way, not by being inconspicuous but by seeming always to have been there. The visitor is not dazzled by the artistry, because by sleight of hand the artistry conceals itself, and one is inclined to accept the idea that the proprietor has inherited the property, rather than commissioned it. The argument is made without the proprietor having to say anything, but in an aristocratic context it is a powerfully persuasive argument of entitlement. The question of architectural style need not be discussed, because the really important buildings are already there and seem always to have been there. Where did they come from? Old England. That is all we know and all we need to know.

Chapter Three

Tudoresque Paternalism

Fatherly concern

'Paternalism' is a modern word for an ancient practice, where a person in authority takes on the responsibility for others' well-being.¹ The model is the traditional role of the father in a family – providing for and protecting his family – the 'paternal' role. A relation is 'paternalist' when it moves outside the realm of ties of blood and marriage into the world of politics and social obligations. Traditionally, the aristocracy has felt obligations to the poor, for example, and these obligations have often transferred to more abstract institutions, so that it is a charity or a branch of government that performs the role. The good side of paternalism is that it sees that people's needs are met. The bad side of it, which means that a system is condemned rather than neutrally described when it is called 'paternalist', is that the necessary consequence of having a 'father' figure is that one also has a 'child' figure, so a paternalistic system tends to infantilize the people it is helping. Sometimes one would rather not have the help than accept it on the terms on which it is offered. There can be something humiliating about it.

It involves accepting the authority of the paternal figure to take decisions on one's behalf. One might be prepared to accept assistance from a noble lord with a good reputation, less inclined to feel indebted to a disreputable neighbour or a 'godfather' figure, but in both cases there would be an adjustment of one's sense of self, from being an independent free agent, to being under the protection of the authority figure. The help comes with condescension, which one might welcome if one genuinely admires the person who bends to help, or might resent if the donor seems unworthy.

The proverbial paternalist figure is actually a woman, Lady Bountiful, who first appeared on the stage in 1707, in George Farquhar's *The Beaux' Stratagem*. She was philanthropic and self-deluding, and is a comic presence in the unfolding plot. Nowadays she is invoked with a roll of the eyes when the opportunity to condescend seems to have become the motive for making a generous gesture.

Conversely, the social obligations could be resented. Sir Joseph Banks, in a misanthropic moment, said: 'this is the day of our fair, when according to immemorial custom I am to feed and make drunk everyone who chooses to come, which will cost me in beef and ale near £20'.[2] He was expected not only to provide the entertainment but also to participate, and to be seen to be enjoying it: the convincing paternalist understands and shares his clients' pleasures. Whether the social role is enjoyed or resented, there is no doubting that it is there.

In an aristocratic society the social roles and obligations were tied to inheritance and title, but as great industrial fortunes came into being, their proprietors could take on responsibilities that had previously been aristocratic, and lower down the social and financial scale there was and continues to be fluidity, as the markers that identify gentry, yeomen, tradesmen, professionals and labourers are variously taken up or repudiated in people's dealings with one another. Housing was among the most important of such transactions.

Elizabeth I was often presented as a bountiful figure, her rank being beyond question and her condescension so clearly understood that she had no need to signal it for herself, but could act with apparent simplicity. One of her contemporaries describes a public appearance:

Now came the Queen dressed in black on account of the death of William of Orange and the Duke of Alençon; on each side of her curly hair she wore a pearl of the size of a hazelnut. The people standing on both sides fell on their knees, but she showed herself very gracious, and accepted with an humble mien letters from rich and poor ... Then the Queen returned as she had come and went to her room, and when on her passing the people fell on their knees, she said in English: 'Thank you with all my heart'.[3]

She was not the original of such behaviour, but became a model for it, setting an example for her high-ranking subjects. At a local level in the provinces this was the inhabitant of the manor house, the great hall of which would be known to everyone in the parish as the site of festivities of the kind that Joseph Banks seemed to be continuing in the eighteenth century.[4] 'This true noble hearted fellow', said Donald Lupton in 1632, of the rural squire,

> is to be dignified and honour'd, wheresoever he keeps his house ... he always kept his greatnesse by his Charity: he loved three things, an open Cellar, a full Hall and a sweating Cooke: he always provided for three dinners, one for himselfe, another for his Servants and one for the poore.[5]

This is the popular image of the old-fashioned squire – a species that Lupton believed might already be extinct when he was writing. Banks, in his private correspondence, could admit to falling a long way short of this ideal, but significantly less was expected of him (just one feast a year). The squire as a 'type' seems to have a greater presence in seventeenth-century literature than he had before, which suggests that by then he had become an emblem of a tradition. These 'emblems' become significant when the traditions they represent seem to be on the point of dying out. Earlier, the tradition would just have seemed to be part of the fabric of life, but in its dying days it was fetishized and artificially sustained into the future by self-conscious re-enactment (such as Banks's fair), which can be taken to be acts of Tudorism. John Selden in 1654 clearly consigned such figures to the past when he said that:

> The hall was the place where the Great Lord us'd to eat (wherefore else were the halls made so big?) Where he saw all his servants and tenants about him. He eat not in private, Except in time of sickness; when once he became a thing cooped up, all his greatness was spoil'd. Nay the King himself used to eat in the hall, and his Lords sate with him, and then he understood Men.[6]

Such figures may have belonged in the past, but the literature firmly put the model in view. There is pervasive reinforcement of the idea that no matter how far particular modern-day aristocrats might fall short of the ideal, nevertheless the institution of the aristocracy is valuable. Even a semi-fictional folk hero like Robin Hood, who was working to set right the wrongs of an unpatriotic king, turns out on closer inspection to be an aristocrat himself; and Disraeli's Sybil – a representative of the poor – is an impoverished aristocrat (whose family was dispossessed of its lands by Henry VIII's Reformation).[7]

Festivals of altruism

Just as the Victorians invented the idea of Christmas as the great festival of the family, so in the eighteenth century there was a desire to 'resurrect' festivals of what we might call 'social cohesion'. The Glorious Revolution of 1688 had demonstrated that the aristocracy could not ride roughshod over public opinion, and encouraged a sense of responsibility and paternalism – *noblesse oblige* – that resulted in the feasts and jollities that Joseph Banks felt obliged to continue. Of course, he was not alone, but perhaps the most interesting thing about what he said in his note was that his family's feast was an 'immemorial custom'. This was doubtless how it felt, but it is unlikely to have been going on for long in historical terms. It would not have gone back to the late medieval times that the hospitality evoked, and is more likely to have been begun by Banks's father at a time shortly before Banks himself could remember. Lady Buckingham and Elizabeth Montague of the Blue Stockings Society promoted the idea of 'harvest dinners' in the 1770s and '80s, with country dances and spit-roasting of oxen being used to evoke 'ancient English hospitality', bringing landowners and tenants together in the name of tradition.[8]

George O'Brien Wyndham, 3rd Earl of Egremont, held annual parties at his Petworth estate, to which he invited his workers and tenants. He was well aware of his political agenda, and upheld the privileges of the propertied.[9] His tenants were dismayed by his agricultural reforms, which introduced farm machinery that put many of them out of work, so the Petworth fête was conceived as a way of presenting him as generous and open: bountiful. His domestic arrangements, with various mistresses and their children living together at Petworth, certainly makes him seem like an old-fashioned *seigneur*, of the type who would become invisible under Victoria. In old age in 1835 he commissioned a painting of the event from William Frederick Witherington, and the fête continues as the town's 'day out' (illus. 13).

It is a genuinely popular event, as it was from the outset designed to be, but it was clearly a means of appeasement, rather than a gesture of absolute altruism. It gave Lord Egremont the opportunity to condescend, and thereby to confirm his high social standing. He did not undermine the effect by allowing that to show. The Petworth fête connects with, and grows out of the same culture as, publications such as Malton's *British Cottage Architecture*, which was mentioned earlier, and it is worth going back at this point to make it clear that the rural poor were really very poor indeed. Nathaniel Kent, back in 1775, before the American Declaration of Independence and the French Revolution, had said:

The shattered hovels which half the poor of this kingdom are obliged to put up with, is truly affecting to a heart fraught with humanity. Those condemned to visit these miserable tenements, can testify, that neither health nor decency can be preserved in them. The weather frequently penetrates all parts of them: which must occasion illness of various kinds, particularly agues; which more frequently visit the children of cottages than any others, and early shake their constitutions. And it is shocking that a man, his wife, and a half a dozen children should be obliged to lie all in one room together; and more so, that the wife should have no more private place to be brought to bed in. This description is not exaggerated, offensive as it may appear. We are all careful of our horses, nay of our dogs, which are less valuable animals: we bestow considerable attention upon our stables and kennels; but we are apt to look upon cottages as incumberances, and clogs to our property, when in fact, those who occupy them are the very nerves and sinews of agriculture. Nay I will be bold to aver, that more real advantages flow from cottages, than from any other source; for besides their great utility to landed property, they are the greatest support to the state, as being the most prolific cradles of population.[10]

Kent's suggestions were consistently humane, but there is an insistent awareness that providing decent conditions for the rural poor stood a better chance of being adopted if he made arguments that appealed to landowners' interests. A well-run estate with a decently housed population would be more productive and would produce a greater income than one where the workforce was unhealthy and demoralized or inclined to revolt. The poor were, if properly treated, an economic resource, rather than a liability.

Treating the poor well could be portrayed as altruism and benevolence on the part of the lord of the manor, but it was in his

13 William Frederick Witherington, *Fete in Petworth Park*, 1835, bringing the whole community together.

interests too. The dominant culture, however, was aristocratic and cosmopolitan, and in the literature it is the image of the benevolent nobleman that comes to the fore. This changed over the course of the long eighteenth century, as the middle classes became significantly larger and more confident, and found their way into print.[11] The symbolic marker of the result of this gradual change was the Reform Bill of 1832, which extended the franchise, but this was a way of dealing with problems that were already evident to Nathaniel Kent in the 1770s. Their urgency was intensified in political debate by the revolutions in America and France. 'The people' might have been like quiet cows in the shade, as Burke suggested, but the air was filled with the chatter of the grasshoppers, which made the possibility of revolution seem real enough.

Before 1832 paternalist ideas could usefully conceptualize the management of a private estate as being like the governing of the nation, but in miniature. Paternalism did not provide a clear role for the prosperous, well-educated people who did not have landed estates, but who made their money by their skills, usually in the towns – they were not really part of the picture and until 1832 did not vote. The special understanding that was imagined to link the people with the monarch was also in operation on a smaller scale, linking the tenants with their landowner. In looking for ways to demonstrate this link, architects kept finding elements of the Tudoresque.

For example, at Henbury, near Bristol, John Harford commissioned John Nash to build cottages for retired workers from his estate. Blaise Hamlet was the result, built in 1810–11 (illus. 7). The houses are grouped round a green with a pump, and they present a picture-perfect image of the vernacular tradition flourishing under benevolent patronage. Many elements of the buildings are plain and cannot be tied to any particular period of architectural history – the thatched roofs and leaded lights are non-specifically old English – but the chimneys were deliberately Tudoresque, designed by John Nash's assistant George Stanley Repton (Humphry Repton's son). The cottages needed chimneys, which were, as was usual in cottages, the most solidly constructed part of the building. The walls to keep out the weather could be made of timber or earth, but the chimney had to contain and withstand the fire in the hearth, and to rise up high, so as to produce a good draught in the fireplace, and therefore had to be built in masonry. Its solidity could be exploited by making it also support roof timbers. It had become the habit of eighteenth-century designers to suppress the appearance of the chimney, making it low key, placing it where it, along with the roof, would be masked by a parapet, or being made to project from the roof's ridge, where it could be made effective without being much higher than the roof. At Blaise Hamlet the chimneys were made emphatic, in brick, with Tudoresque chimney stacks becoming an important unifying feature in the varied compositions of the irregular cottages. The architect wrote to Harford to explain that 'these kind of chimney stacks are frequently seen in old cottages – and generally in old Manor Houses and buildings of the reign of Queen Elizabeth and invariably produce a picturesque effect'.[12]

Harford felt his paternalistic responsibilities keenly and genuinely, and did not strain to make a great show of what he had done. Nash had no such qualms, and images of his designs circulated widely in engraved prints. Their picturesque aspect was appealing, but it could be taken too far. Lord Ongley let it be known that he wanted the women cottagers at his quaint new village, Old Warden in Bedfordshire, to wear red cloaks and tall hats, in order to harmonize with the red doors and windows of their cottages (designed by P. F. Robinson in a variety of styles from 1830).[13] Here the way the cottages were managed must surely have left the cottagers feeling patronized, and daily aware of the compromise to their free-born liberty involved in accepting His Lordship's beneficence.

Sir Thomas and Lady Baring were less eccentric when they stipulated that their charitable gifts would go only to people who were decently pious.[14] This was intended as an encouragement to good citizenship and morality, but it clearly involved paternalist guardianship of the villagers' morals. There was an expectation that the tenants would, in their dealings with the lord of the manor, assume the role of the old-English peasant, and come to see themselves as part of a timeless old England. There was a trade-off to be made: accepting subjugation in exchange for domestic comfort. Since the alternative might be starvation, accepting the inconvenience of occasional kowtowing was no less than accepting the truth of one's situation in the world. John Harford's son said that 'his father loved to stroll around the "sweet little village" he had built, and that he met there in every Cottager the beaming expression of gratitude to a kind benefactor'.[15]

The Old English manor house

The paternalistic relationship between benevolent landowner and happy tenant was unconsciously rehearsed in various ways, which would be naturalized as custom and ingrained as habit. When they seemed to confirm the proper order of society, then they could be experienced as pleasurable events. The fashion for Tudoresque designs in the 1830s coincided with the newly enfranchised middle classes' new sense of their standing in society: a moment when they could with some conviction expect to take on some of the ways of behaving that had previously been reserved to the nobility. The Tudoresque mansion designs were specifically British, rather than cosmopolitan, and therefore reflect middle-class rather than aristocratic antiquarian influence on their production. They were also presented as a way to establish good old-English relations between the rich and the poor, and that could now include the newly rich, who might build a new Tudoresque mansion partly as a way to have a comfortable place to live, and partly in order to be able to 'lord' it over such guests as could be persuaded to assume the inferior position as the recipient of such hospitality. The transaction was complex, with elements of pleasure, envy, gratitude, resentment and admiration in the mix. The quality of the entertainment, the charm of the host, and one's sense of being patronized by or conferring social standing on an *arriviste*, could attract and avert potential guests. It was a prerequisite to have an appropriate setting for the event, and the more old-fashioned it looked, the more legitimate the occasion would seem to be.

The most important work in popularizing such a view was a series of lithographs by Joseph Nash, starting in 1839 and eventually making four volumes of images of *The Mansions of England in the Olden Time*.[16] Nash was interested in medieval as well as Tudor buildings, and his method was to show real historic buildings (interiors and exteriors) populated with imaginary historical characters. They include images of domestic contentment, and also livelier scenes. Nash described his project as being:

> a set of views of the Picturesque Architecture of the Mansions of England . . . [to show them] in a new and attractive light; not, as many of them now appear, gloomy desolate, and neglected, but furnished with the rude comfort of the early times of 'merry England', or exhibiting the more splendid luxury and elegant hospitality of later periods: in short, to represent 'the stately homes of England' glowing with the genial warmth of their firesides, and enlivened with the presence of their inmates

and guests, enjoying the recreations of past times, or celebrating the festivals of our ancestors. Thus not only the domestic architecture of past ages, but the costumes and habits of England in 'the olden time', are brought before the eye; and in attempting this, the artist has endeavoured to place himself as a visitor to these ancient edifices, whose fancy peoples the deserted halls, stripped of all movable ornaments, and looking damp and cheerless, with the family and household of the 'old English gentleman' surrounded by their everyday comforts, sharing the more rare and bounteous hospitalities offered to the guests, or partaking of the boisterous merriment of Christmas gambols.[17]

The aim was to show how appealing these buildings, now more or less ruined, once were as places to conduct a life, and while domestic apartments are shown in repose, the great halls are in party mood. Old England is presented in a wholly positive light, as a time and place where different classes lived in harmony, with the old-English gentleman very much in charge. Nash's lithographs point to a world of warmth and merriment that attaches to the post-medieval world, and not to feudal castles, and the theme of hospitality again comes to the fore, for example, in the 'Christmas Festivities at Haddon Hall' (illus. 14). The scene looks noisy and chaotic, but the people are having a good time, from the musicians in the gallery to the mummers on the floor of the hall, the men wrestling with a crocodile and the little monkey on the loose, who seems to catch the free-for-all spirit of the occasion, which also finds expression in the amorous advances being made to the left of the fireplace. This is an image that projects back into the olden days a topical concern – the revival of Christmas festivities – that is particularly associated with Dickens's *A Christmas Carol* of 1843. In the home it was to become the great festival of the family, but in the workplace some of this atmosphere persists in the office party, employers mixing with

Tudoresque

14 Joseph Nash, 'Christmas Festivities at Haddon Hall', from *The Mansions of England in the Olden Time* (1839). High life and low life in the great Tudor hall, establishing social bonds.

employees, the relaxing of conventional inhibitions and so on. It is a temporary state of affairs, before the proper order is restored after the holiday, but going through it enables all the participants to see the others as fully human.

The point with these reanimations of the past was to see that there was continuity with the present, avowedly so as to make history human and comprehensible, but also making it possible to identify with old-fashioned patterns of behaviour and adopt them in the present.

Richard Brown, in his *Domestic Architecture* of 1842, suggested that there was increased freedom in Tudor times, citing David Hume, who had explained that Henry VII's policy

> consisted in depressing the barons, and elevating and promoting men of new families, who were more dependent

upon his will. The nobility, therefore now, instead of vying with each other in the number and courage of their retainers, which had hitherto been the case, by degrees acquired a more social and laudable emulation, endeavouring to excel in the splendour of the mansions, stables and equipage; while the common people, no longer retained in vicious idleness by their superiors, were now obliged to learn some calling or trade, thus becoming useful both to themselves and to the state.[18]

Both Nash's and Brown's comments make clear that they set Tudor buildings in a paternalistic context, and the cultural connotations meant that the architecture was not only expressive of Englishness, but also of social inclusion, encouraging a more liberal and interactive relation between the ruling elite and the common English populace. Tudoresque buildings did not elide the differences between rich and poor, but brought them together under one roof in a way that a Neoclassical mansion did not. This version of 'Merry England' is one where the ruling class maintains its position not by hereditary right, or by the exercise of coercive force, but by popular demand. It is a democratic updating of the old class divisions, based on mutual respect, and enacted through hospitality, which could most clearly be made visible in a festive great hall.

One nation

The 'Young England' club was formed in the early 1840s – a group of Tory MPs, Lord John Manners, George Smythe and Benjamin Disraeli among them. Disraeli is the best known: he went on to become prime minister, and popularized his views through his novels.[19] The club's romantic outlook idealized pre-Reformation feudalism, seeing it as a great age of paternalist philanthropy, destroyed by Henry VIII's confiscation of monastic and ancient aristocratic lands. In 1841 Manners published the lines:

Each knew his place king, peasant, peer, or priest
The greatest owned connexion with the least;
From rank to rank the generous feeling ran,
And linked society as man to man.[20]

Disraeli harnessed the enthusiasm for the Gothic Revival, embodied in the New Palace of Westminster, to propose a reconciliation between the rich and the poor. This is dramatized most emphatically in *Sybil; or, The Two Nations* of 1845, the two nations in question being the rich and the poor, who live on the same land in modern England while knowing nothing of one another, having completely different cultures.[21] The outlook was like Pugin's, vehemently anti-Elizabethan, but Disraeli made a symbolic reconciliation by staging a happy marriage between the character Sybil, a representative of the poor, and a member of a newly rich family, whose wealth was made in industry. The reconciliation suggests that the new rich can become legitimate aristocrats if they treat the poor benevolently, and Sybil herself, although poor, turns out to be an ancient aristocrat whose family was impoverished by Henry VIII. The new would-be aristocrat had to learn to take pleasure in giving to the needy, like the 'fine old English gentleman' in Henry Russell's popular song:

> He kept a brave old mansion
> At a bountiful old rate
> With a good old porter to relieve
> The old poor at his gate
> Like a fine old English gentleman,
> All of the olden time.
>
> . . .
>
> When winter cold brought Christmas old,
> He opened house to all,
> And, though three score and ten his years,
> He featly led the ball;
> Nor was the houseless wanderer

Then driven from the hall,
For, while he feasted all the great,
He ne'er forgot the small —
Like a fine old English gentleman,
All of the olden time.[22]

Sir George Gilbert Scott, a committed Gothicist, said in 1857 in his *Secular and Domestic Architecture*:

> Providence has ordained the different orders and gradations into which the human family is divided, and it is right and necessary that it should be maintained . . . the position of a landed proprietor be he squire or nobleman, is one of dignity. Wealth must always bring responsibilities, but a landed proprietor is especially in a responsible position. He is the natural head of his parish or district – in which he should be looked up to as the bond of union between the classes. To him the poor man should look up for protection; those in doubt or difficulty for advice; the ill disposed for reproof or punishment; the deserving, of all classes, for consideration and hospitality: and all for a dignified, honourable and Christian example.[23]

This further reinforces the idea of aristocratic identity that was gaining ground, with Queen Victoria leading the way, using the moralistic outlook that came to be associated so firmly with her reign, to put a distance between the good modern aristocracy and the self-indulgence so evident among her forebears. Aristocrats were expected to acknowledge their responsibilities, and behave more like the respectable middle classes than they had during the Regency, while those of the prosperous middle classes who engaged in appropriately paternalistic philanthropic activity could gain the social prestige of aristocrats.[24] Thomas Escott, writing in 1879, said that:

> The great merchant banker of today is an English gentleman of a finished type. He is possibly a peer, and an active partner in a great City firm; if he is not a peer the chances are he is a member of the House of Commons. He is a man of extensive culture ... There is, in fact, but one standard of 'social position' in England and it is that which is formed by the blending of the plutocratic and the aristocratic element.[25]

This suggests that Disraeli's symbolic marriage of ancient aristocratic virtue and modern money had been made a persuasive fact of life in Victorian England. Ancient title, unaccompanied by the means to be bountiful, looked merely anachronistic, and the introduction of county and borough councils in 1888, soon after followed by urban and rural councils, meant that the gentry no longer had to run things or administer justice.[26] There were individuals who continued, quaintly, to play the role of the village squire, but in the absence of the means to offer employment or public amenities, it meant little, except to those who chose to cling on to it for an identity.

Victorian Tudoresque villages

The invention of the Tudoresque cottage in the late eighteenth century, and its deployment for housing the rural poor during the time of the wars with France, was driven partly by a concern for the state of the poor, and partly by fear of civil unrest, which had a patriotic aspect, in reminding the poor that they were not French and should not be influenced by French fashions in government. By the middle of the nineteenth century a different set of forces was in action. The poor were still in evidence and still needed help, but now philanthropy was a means of acceptance into the ranks of the aristocracy, or at least to a seat in the House of Lords. Once established, the fashion for cottage-building became ingrained as a competitive social practice, perhaps driven by a desire for social advancement, but nonetheless beneficial to the community.[27] From the 1830s the houses of the rich were more likely than in the past to adopt a self-consciously old-fashioned British style, sometimes because they were built by people with a less cosmopolitan culture than the old aristocracy, with its fondness for France, Italy and Greece. With the rise in the number of people who could afford to build mansions, there was also a desire that the houses should not look as new as the money that built them. It was socially better if they seemed always to have been there, since the olden days. This was not a new tendency – it was there in Henry Fielding's description of Squire Allworthy's house – but it was now within the reach of more people, so it was desired that some new buildings as well as the old ones should be able to show this kind of good character. If the houses of the rich were to have an old-fashioned, old-English, often Tudoresque character, in the houses that the rich built for the poor that character seems to have been even more pronounced. The variety of architectural styles in P. F. Robinson's designs, such as that for Old Warden, Bedfordshire, was there in order to suggest a gradual piecemeal development over a long time, mixing buildings in old-fashioned Gothic and Tudoresque styles with exotic Swiss-style novelty. The result was – or was intended – to seem more settled than the more 'rational' type of model village, such as that at Milton Abbas in Dorset (built in 1770), where the cottages were identical and set at regular intervals in a row.[28]

One of the most concerted adoptions of the Tudoresque was made by the Rothschild family when it settled in England. Their fortune was founded in banking, initially in Germany, and their background was absolutely cosmopolitan, with branches of the family in positions of commercial power across Europe. Nathan Mayer Rothschild came to England in 1798, working in Manchester and then London to establish the family's business interests, moving his family into Tring Park near Aylesbury in 1833. The villages around became known for their 'Rothschild Tudor' cottages, built philanthropically for the workers of various estates, including more than 200 houses in Tring alone, with others at Mentmore, Wing and Wingrave. They

15 William Huckvale, Cottages at Wingrave, Buckinghamshire, 1870s. Rothschild Tudor.

typically had white rendered walls, black timbers and tall Elizabethan-style chimney pots.[29] Their architects included William Huckvale and George Devey, and many of the buildings date from the 1870s (illus. 15). Cottages at Wingrave often have memorial plaques bearing Hannah de Rothschild's monogram and the date. After the death of her father in 1874, she was reputedly the richest woman in Britain, not necessarily excluding the Queen.

Hannah grew up at Mentmore Towers, built by her father from 1852 in the high Elizabethan style of Wollaton Hall, with Joseph Paxton as the architect (illus. 16). She became a countess when she married Lord Rosebery in 1878, with the Prince of Wales in attendance and Benjamin Disraeli to give her away – in the absence of any male members of her own family, who disapproved of her marrying a Christian.[30] (Coincidentally, Rosebery inherited that other Tudoresque pile, Dalmeny.) Her cousin Nathan Mayer Rothschild II (who, like her, had a grandfather in Nathan Mayer Rothschild I) inherited the family's baronetcy, and he was elevated to the House of Lords as the 1st Baron Rothschild in 1885.

The scale of the family's philanthropic work was amazing, as was the consistency of their commitment to varieties of the Tudoresque in their building projects. The family saw themselves as the equals of the crowned heads of Europe, and like royalty had a habit of marrying their more or less distant cousins. If at times their playing the role of the paternalistic squire seems anachronistic, in their cases there were so many people dependent on them that the role was quite authentic.[31] The private gentry had generally been made irrelevant by the introduction of district councils, but Tring Urban District Council owed so much to the Rothschilds that their role continued to be very visible, even in the days of the welfare state. The family built up a powerful rapport with the local community, doing the things, like racing horses, that the gentry were traditionally expected to do; but they worked hard to achieve that rapport, having to work against the prevalent low-level anti-Semitism that tended to exclude them. If life near Aylesbury seemed to have a particularly old-English quality to it, it was because the Rothschilds were initiating

16 Joseph Paxton, Mentmore Towers, Buckinghamshire, 1852. The Rothschilds' principal English seat.

events that belonged securely in that tradition, enacting, as it were, scenes from Joseph Nash's lithographs:

> Baron Mayer de Rothschild gave a substantial supper at the Anchor to all the labouring men who hold houses or cottages belonging to him. Hitherto they have been entertained at Mentmore, but this year they have been spared a long walk, and spent a most pleasant evening in their own village. Mr E. Hart presided at the supper table, which was well furnished with good old English fare: a noble round of beef, plum pudding etc. All the men appreciated the baron's kindness in remembering them. Several cottages have lately become the Baron's property . . . and the poor men may fully expect an improvement to their dwellings.[32]

At Wing, Leopold de Rothschild, who lived nearby at Ascott House, built a Tudoresque village hall. When it was opened in 1906 by his cousin Lord Rothschild, who was described in a local paper as the local people's 'honoured squire', he presented the hall as a place that would help the village to flourish as a community:

> The hall is . . . to be used for Theatricals, for dancing, concerts, and for games of all kinds. Those who have given you this room hope it will be the centre of village life, and that I trust also. I am sure that the presence of a Room like this, a well-organised room in the midst of a village does more than anything to lift the spirit of the inhabitants and to cement that good feeling and understanding which ought to exist between all the members of one parish.[33]

The gift, from the Rothschilds to the community, re-enacted the already-established relation of squire to villagers, and it also presented an image of village life that drew on the pre-industrial idea of the village as a self-contained community, which was possible when the

17 Attributed to George Devey at Wing, Buckinghamshire. A double house (semi-detached) displaying the Rothschild crest between the gables

inhabitants were involved mostly in agriculture. Perhaps the Rothschilds were already as aware as the Saxe-Coburgs of the tensions across Europe that would erupt in 1914, but the gift of a mechanism to promote social cohesion seems astute. At the opening, Walter Rothschild – the Liberal MP for Aylesbury and Lord Rothschild's son, who would later inherit the title – said that he was pleased that the hall had been built locally:

> I take this opportunity of saying how proud I feel, as the Member of this division, and I am sure you will also feel most proud, that this beautiful Hall which has been erected in memory of our great friend, should have been designed by the talent of one of yourselves, and that it should have been built by the united efforts of a local builder and of yourselves in the persons of local workmen. I am sure this is a refutation of those who say that the British workman is deteriorating and the foreigner is ousting us everywhere. I think it is one proof from you that you

all desire still to show that the Englishman wishes to be well to the front in every domestic and foreign affair.[34]

The village hall, built in Tudoresque black and white, not only expresses Englishness, it also embodies it, in promoting local life and in being the product of local life, albeit with the support of cosmopolitan money. Walter makes a point of the Englishness of the enterprise, and mentions threats from abroad, dismissing them but planting them in his audience's mind. The 'great friend' here was Charles Coates, a local man without wider reputation, and in claiming him as a great friend Walter is claiming that he too is part of the village community, so the hall has not been dropped in by a remote government, but can lay claim to local authenticity. It is a language of embeddedness, laying claim to Walter's, if not the Rothschild family's, indigenous roots, which he certainly had, even though he also had an international perspective on them. Walter Rothschild was involved with the family bank, but was also a keen zoologist, who, in order to show that it could be done, trained a team of six zebras to pull his carriage round London – a dashing and exotic sight when they did so. Their black-and-white stripes echo the family's out-of-town Tudoresque, which was the means of continuing or reviving the old-English squirearchy, which saw them dealing with royalty in part of their lives, and with national and international politics and finance, but looking for acceptance and security in the local culture of their fiefdom.

Industrialists' Tudor

The nineteenth-century Rothschilds were exceptional in various ways, set apart not only by their wealth (which was already well established in the family before it arrived in England) but also by their foreign ancestry and their Jewishness, which combined to make them English outsiders working for integration. Those of their contemporaries who had indigenous roots and made their own fortunes from industrial manufacture tended to see themselves differently – as yeomen who had prospered through Nonconformist Christian morality and hard work. They had a different experience of life from the aristocracy, and different expectations. They placed a higher value on temperance and thrift, and had less time for sumptuous display. Samuel Smiles codified their attitudes in his book *Self-Help*, published in 1858:

> Men great in science, literature, and art – apostles of great thoughts and lords of the great heart – have sprung indiscriminately from the English farm and the Scotch hillside, from the workshop and the mine, from the blacksmith's smithy and the cobbler's stool.... Take, for instance, the remarkable fact, that from the barber's shop came Jeremy Taylor, the most poetical of divines; Sir Richard Arkwright, the inventor of the spinning-jenny and founder of the cotton manufacture of Great Britain; Lord Tenterden, one of the most distinguished of Lord Chief Justices; and Turner, the greatest among landscape painters.[35]

The architectural productions for self-made men could be varied, and as a group they would be best characterized as independent-minded. But they often drew on the Tudoresque, either buying an old manor house for their own use or building a new one, and encouraging their workers by housing them in black-and-white yeomen's cottages. For example, at Leigh in Kent in 1870 Samuel Morley, a rich hosiery manufacturer and Nonconformist, bought a Georgian house called Hall Place. It was not large enough for his needs, so he demolished it and replaced it with something *more* old-fashioned, designed by George Devey in the style of an Elizabethan manor (illus. 18).[36] He also started to build Tudoresque cottage-style houses in the village (illus. 19), and after his death in 1876 his son, Samuel Hope Morley, continued, employing Ernest George and Harold Peto as his architects.[37] These houses were given to the workers on Morley's estate, and he was inducted into the House of Lords as the 1st Baron Hollenden in 1912. The architectural style underscores the paternalistic relation, aggrandizing the

18 George Devey, Hall Place, Leigh, Kent, 1870. This was Lord Hollenden's house.

19 George Devey, a house at Leigh, Kent, 1870, formerly on Lord Hollenden's estate.

philanthropist and making the beneficiaries clearly subservient. They would also no doubt have been comfortable and profoundly grateful, but that cannot be inferred so directly from the buildings.

There are similar stories elsewhere, and we will return to them in later chapters, but in passing we can notice the Congregationalist Mander family in Wolverhampton, producers of paints and printing ink. The workers' dwellings on the Manders' estate have a clear Tudoresque character, as does the house that Theodore Mander built, Wightwick Manor (illus. 20 and 21). Again philanthropy proved to be an effective way to demonstrate social commitment, and Mander's baronetcy was conferred in 1911. The soap business of another Congregationalist, William Hesketh Lever, flourished in Tudoresque style at Port Sunlight in Cheshire, built for the workers from 1888 onwards (illus. 22).[38] Lever for his own dwelling bought a house, Thornton Manor, which seems to have originated in the 1850s, but which he extended and made thoroughly Elizabethan after 1893, with John Douglas as his architect (illus. 23).[39] He was the Liberal MP for the Wirral (at the same time that Walter Rothschild was representing Aylesbury for the same party) and joined the House of Lords as Baron Leverhulme in 1917. Again, George Cadbury, a Quaker, in 1890 bought a house, New House, in Northfield, near Bournville, the workers' village that he founded. The house had been built in the 1820s, but he remodelled it in Elizabethan style and called it Northfield Manor (illus. 24).[40]

There is enough repetition here to show that it is a pattern of behaviour. The philosophy driving the development of the communities was impeccably liberal and nurturing, but the architecture expressed a paternalistic relation of squire and employee, even as the employees were encouraged towards self-help. The use of old-English style in these developments made the community look settled and established, and suggested continuity and tradition where in fact there was new money and social change. The Tudoresque cottages compare favourably with the grim minimal terraces that were constructed for the less fortunate employees of more exploitative industrialists in the

20 Edward Ould, workers' dwellings on the Manders' Estate, Wolverhampton, 1887–8.

21 Edward Ould, Wightwick Manor, Wolverhampton, 1887–8. Sir Theodore Mander's house.

Tudoresque Paternalism

22 Workers' dwellings at Port Sunlight, Cheshire, from 1888.

overleaf: 23 John Douglas, renovation and extensions to Thornton Manor, Port Sunlight, Cheshire, 1893, for Lord Leverhulme.

fast-growing cities. In those cases the employer would live in a completely different part of town in a house that had no relation to the workers' housing. The employer and the worker moved in separate worlds, had different pleasures and aspirations, and understood little of one another – or so Disraeli would lead us to believe.

The paternalistic developments shown here all make the same architectural moves in housing the workers in Tudoresque cottages and the bosses in Tudoresque manors. This expresses the fact that they are all in the same architectural world, despite some physical distance between the cottages and the manors, and despite the disparities of rank, which are plain for all to see. It is a socially responsible vision, expressive of the social bonds that were real enough and supported by genuine philanthropy, guided by moral conviction and eventually recognized in enhanced social status. It is not exactly egalitarian, but

24 William Alexander Harvey, remodelling of Northfield Manor, Northfield, Birmingham, 1890. George Cadbury's house.

the underpinning of Samuel Smiles's idea of self-help suggests a recognition of social mobility that involves a change of role perhaps, but not a fundamental change of character. One can move from a cottage to a manor house without changing one's soul, whereas to move to a Palladian mansion might seem to express something altogether more deracinating. For the hard-working self-made man the aspiration to embody the virtues of an old-fashioned squire would be manageable with good grace, and offer the prospect of comfort and cheer, where attempts to affect aristocratic manners might shiver apart in strenuous affectations.

Chapter Four

Tudoresque Self-Reliance

Independence: four acres and a cow

The poorest members of British society have never been in a position to influence architecture. They have lived as vagrants, or in squalid hovels, in cottages provided by wealthy landowners, and in the twentieth century in accommodation designed by architects and provided by the welfare state. The transition from the old feudal order to twenty-first-century popular democracy was a gradual process, because changes in the legislature do not always produce a corresponding social change, especially where the lower middle classes are concerned. It is they above all who embody Burke's image of the great herds of quiet cows, chewing the cud in the shade of mighty oak trees.[1]

This is the population of Middle England, who are not in the seats of power and have no ambition to think avant-garde thoughts. The general aim is to be allowed to live a quiet, contented life, raising a family and maintaining some level of social standing in the eyes of the local community. The attitudes that are ingrained at this level of society over many generations are not shaken off overnight. The image of a simple and contented domestic life, subsisting on one's own efforts, has one of its most powerful underpinnings in legislation enacted under Elizabeth I.

In an agricultural economy it is very evident that with a parcel of land at one's disposal there is no need for a salary: it is possible to subsist on what the land produces – money comes into the picture when there is a surplus to sell, and specialist goods or skills to buy. In 1577 the Reverend William Harrison promoted the idea of giving a peasant an acre of ground and a cow as a strategy to deal with poverty:

> The inhabitants of many places of our country are devoured and eaten up and their houses altogether pulled down or suffered to decay little by little, although sometime a poor man peradventure doth dwell in one of them, who, not being able to repair it, sufferreth it to fall down and thereto thinketh himself very friendly dealth withal, if he may have an acre of ground assigned unto him whereupon to keep a cow or wherein to set cabbages, radishes, parsnips, carrots, melons, pompons [pumpkins], or suchlike stuff, by which he and his poor household liveth as by their principal food, sith they can do no better.[2]

The idea gained ground, and in 1589 a law was made stipulating that no cottage should be built unless it could be provided with at least four acres of ground.

> For the avoydinge of the great inconvenience whiche are founde by experience to growe by the recetinge and buyldinge of great numbers and multitude of cottage ... are dylie more and more increased in manye part of this realme: be it enacted by the Quenes most excellent Majestie ... and the commons in this psent Parliament assembled and by the authoritie of the same ... [that] ... noe pson shall within this Realme of Englande make buylde or erect, or cause to be made buylded or erected, any manner of Cottage for habitation or dwelling ... unless the same pson doe assigne and laye to the same cottage or Buylding fower acres of Grownde at the least.[3]

When this provision worked, the results for the cottager were definitely good. The yeoman who could subsist on such a smallholding and produce a small surplus would be available for seasonal work, but had an independent means of support and a self-reliant character. Much of the land in England was unclaimed by its inhabitants, but their number increased from 2.26 million in 1525 to 4.1 million by 1601.[4] Problems followed from the act because there were many extant cottages without so much land attached, and when parishes were unwilling or felt themselves unable to make such provision for newcomers, they were left to wander, homeless and without any means of support.[5] Nevertheless, the law remained on the statute books until, long neglected, it was repealed in 1775.[6]

Reason can tell us that we have a right or a duty, but custom tells us that we will face social exclusion if we insist upon it. So when the Bill of Rights of 1689 (immediately after the Glorious Revolution) implied a new understanding of the individual in the social order, it did not mean that all individuals had the new conception of themselves, since habits of respect for established authority and ancient institutions still had a firm grip. It was a time for radical thought among the more educated, however, and John Locke, writing in 1690 and, taking up the language of the Bill of Rights, thinking about the basis of land-ownership, said:

> As much land as a man tills, plants, improves, cultivates, and can use the product of, so much is his property. He by his labour does, as it were, inclose it from the common. Nor will it invalidate his right, to say every body else has an equal title to it; and therefore he cannot appropriate, he cannot inclose, without the consent of all his fellow-commoners, all mankind. God, when he gave the world in common to all mankind, commanded man also to labour, and the penury of his condition required it of him. God and his reason commanded him to subdue the earth, i.e. improve it for the benefit of life, and

therein lay out something upon it that was his own, his labour. He that in obedience to this command of God, subdued, tilled and sowed any part of it, thereby annexed to it something that was his property, which another had no title to, nor could without injury take from him.

Nor was this appropriation of any parcel of land, by improving it, any prejudice to any other man, since there was still enough, and as good left; and more than the yet unprovided could use. So that, in effect, there was never the less left for others because of his enclosure for himself: for he that leaves as much as another can make use of, does as good as take nothing at all. No body could think himself injured by the drinking of another man, though he took a good draught, who had a whole river of the same water left him to quench his thirst: and the case of land and water, where there is enough of both, is perfectly the same.[7]

The premise is that everyone has a right to land, just as one has a right to food and water. Indeed, in this agricultural economy, the land is food – the means whereby sustenance is produced – so to have a little piece of England is to have the means of survival. Locke's model works so long as there are not too many people, or too little land: it presupposes that there is as much land as can be worked by the people who live on it.

This language of natural rights could be used in connection with common land, and Locke's radical position was to see all land as fundamentally common land, which was at odds with the established and continuing practice of land ownership under the law. In fact, throughout the eighteenth century there were many Acts of Parliament that took parcels of land out of common ownership and made it the private property of a landowner, who was also often a Member of Parliament.[8] During George III's reign by this means more than 3 million acres were 'filched from the people'.[9] Nevertheless, the holder of small property had rights, as William Pitt (the Elder) said in 1763:

> The poorest man, may, in his cottage, bid defiance to all the forces of the crown. It may be frail, its roof may shake; the wind may blow through it; the storm may enter; the rain may enter; but the King of England may not enter; all his force dare not cross the threshold of the ruined tenement.[10]

This image of 'the poorest man' is optimistic, since there were people who, as Nathaniel Kent made clear, were without even this level of accommodation, but it was true in law, and how the householder felt it to be.

The repeal of the Elizabethan cottage law brought it to wider notice again in the late eighteenth century, and it was known to and discussed by the Board of Agriculture in the 1790s. One of its members, Robert Beatson, for example, said:

> The cottage Law of Queen Elizabeth, which required that four acres of land should be attached for ever to each cottage, precluded the necessity of commons. This statute has been repealed. Four acres of land were too much for the spade, and too little for the plough, and therefore it was wise in the legislative authority, at a time when pasture gave place to tillage, to abrogate this law. Yet, perhaps, it would have been more advisable merely to have lessened the quantity of land required for each cottage, than to have dropped this provision altogether.[11]

Another adviser, Thomas Barker, alluded to the Elizabethan law when he said: 'I believe the cow-pasture and ploughing land to each cottage is four acres. I wish, and I have often said so, that parliament would make it a rule never to grant an inclosure, without a close laid out for the benefit of the poor.'[12]

The provision of the age of Elizabeth, the golden age of the cottager, had the combined merits of giving the humble citizen a stake in the land, making him disinclined to revolt, and made him self-sufficient, which meant that he was not a problem for the landowners. On the other hand, he did have land, which was desirable to others more powerful than himself, and it was in too small a parcel to be able to benefit from modern improvements in agricultural productivity, so it was agued that it was better for the nation to have these plots managed as part of a great estate. The image of the independent smallholder survived, not only in John Locke's imagination, but also in political discourse. It had a powerful revival in the 1880s, when 'three acres and a cow' was coined by Eli Hamshire and used as a slogan by land reformers such as Jesse Collings and Joseph Chamberlain, while Arthur Lloyd wrote a popular song that helped to spread the word.[13] The reduction of four Elizabethan acres to three Victorian acres reflected perhaps the increased population, but also the improved efficiency of cultivation. In 1910 G. K. Chesterton used it emblematically to allude to the simple desires of ordinary folk, forever thwarted by those in power: 'The great lords will refuse the English peasant his three acres and a cow on advanced grounds, if they cannot refuse it

25 Arthur Penty, Aldersyde, York, 1896. The house of Ernest Leetham, who had pioneering steam-powered flour mills in York, Newcastle, Hull and Cardiff.

Tudoresque Self-Reliance

26 Arthur Penty, Arcade House, Hampstead Garden Suburb, from Raymond Unwin's *Town Planning and Modern Architecture in the Hampstead Garden Suburb* (1909). Architecture for social reform.

longer on reactionary grounds. They will deny him the three acres on grounds of State Ownership. They will forbid him the cow on grounds of humanitarianism.'[14] And it crops up again in the 'distributist' tracts inspired by Chesterton and his ally Hilaire Belloc, which circulated during the 1920s. The outlook is in some aspects closely similar to John Locke's equation of property with the ability to use it productively. The crucial idea in distributism is a redistribution of property – not capital, but land – so as to restore the citizen's ancient contact with the land, which had been ruptured with the Industrial Revolution. It took its inspiration from a papal encyclical of 1891, *Rerum novarum*, and had a wide readership in England and America through Belloc's and Chesterton's advocacy, and their followers', as in Arthur Smith's *Three Acres and Employment* and the architect Arthur Penty's *Post-Industrialism*.[15] Penty grew up in York and took over his father's architectural firm there. He argued for the revival of medieval-style guilds, but his buildings were more often Tudoresque than Gothic (illus. 25). He was fired with enthusiasm for the Garden City idea, and designed some important buildings for Hampstead Garden Suburb, working with Parker and Unwin (illus. 26).[16]

At some point the idea of an independent smallholding with a cow stopped being a specifically Elizabethan reference, but the attitude of independence and self-help has a strong line of continuity from the Elizabethan law into the modern suburbs. Tudorism has deeper roots than the adoption of a Tudoresque style, congruent though that may be.

The lower middle class

In retrospect, one can see the origins of the lower middle class in the tradesmen and townsfolk of the Middle Ages, who were neither serfs nor servants, but that is not how they were seen at the time. They emerged in the second half of the nineteenth century as commercial society became more urban and more complex. They were clearly identifiable as the 'white collar workers', with less self-determination and social status than the already well-established 'professional' middle class (lawyers, doctors, bankers, civil servants). This lower middle class was employed to manage and serve in clerical and administrative roles in retailing, banking, accounting, advertising and trading.[17] Its culture was quite distinct from that of the working classes, who would be employed in industry, but it can be difficult to document. George and Weedon Grossmith's novel from 1888–9, *Diary of a Nobody*, is a rare and therefore particularly valuable insight into the attitudes of a representative of this class, Mr Pooter is the story's narrator and its protagonist. He is a clerk in an unspecified city firm, acutely aware of his status, given to pretension and to gaffes that the novel's readers were expected to recognize as such, since they are the basis of the novel's humour. The character is obsessed with his rented house (The Laurels, Brickfield Terrace, Holloway, in north London), but shows a lack of judgement. For example, he decides to paint the spines of some books, a washstand, sundry items of furniture and the bath all in the same red, which pleases him but not his wife or the servant – the maid's view being dismissed as 'an example of the ignorance of the lower classes in the matter of taste',[18] which is exactly how the reader is invited to view Pooter's own judgements. The books whose covers are painted are the family's edition of Shakespeare, evidently second-hand, since the binding is worn out, which can be taken in such a drawing room to be an unread token intended to signify high culture and Englishness. The important thing to notice, though, is that although the reader might be being invited to sneer at Mr Pooter, and although he would dearly love his judgements to coincide with those of the upper middle class or with those of the aristocracy, in fact he is very contented with his house and with his judgements. In his own eyes the painting of the furniture is 'an extraordinary improvement' and he is 'delighted with the result' of painting the bath. He does not feel answerable to anyone else for his tastes (not even his wife, though she asserts a view). He knows that it is the right thing to do because he is happy with it.

This class came into its own with the social upheavals around the First World War, with the decline of the industries that had boomed and led the world during the nineteenth century.[19] Again, there was the example of revolution overseas, this time the Russian Revolution of 1917, giving an uneasy feeling that Communism might resolve the nation's problems.[20] The young soldiers returning from the trenches in 1918 did not necessarily find employment. The nation ground to a halt with the General Strike of 1926, and then after the Great Crash of 1929 there were years of depression. The futile but symbolic Jarrow March of 1936 is the most potent emblem of the desperation faced by the unemployed. Two hundred able-bodied but unemployed men walked 240 miles to Westminster over the course of a month, sometimes with their MPs, who ensured extensive press coverage; but no government representative would see them and they returned home empty-handed.[21]

The great housing initiative of the inter-war years was the 'homes fit for heroes', designed to help soldiers returning in 1918 to face an uncertain future in the country for which they had sacrificed so much, relieved to be alive, but economically in a bad way, and possibly in a mood to be persuaded by Bolshevism.[22] In exactly the same way as the Board of Agriculture 120 years earlier, the prime minister, David

Lloyd George, saw that the provision of decent housing would be a way to persuade people that there was no need to resort to revolution. This time, though, the costs would not fall on the aristocratic landowners, but would be met from central taxation, the cost being justified by the need to maintain civil order: 'the money we are going to spend on housing', said the Local Government Board's Parliamentary Secretary, 'is an insurance against Bolshevism and Revolution'.[23] The working classes enjoyed a higher standard of living than they had before 1914, but the middle classes fared better still and were actually given more state support, as the political establishment sought to keep Bolshevism at bay. The suburbs prospered.[24]

The adoption of electricity to power industrial machinery enabled manufacture to spread away from the coalfields, which had been important for the rise of the first wave of steam-powered industries in the nineteenth century.[25] The arrival of electricity in the home stimulated new industries that produced the household appliances that it powered: vacuum cleaners, refrigerators, cookers, gramophones and wireless sets.[26] And the motor car, which before the war had been available only to the rich, went into mass production and was widely available during the 1920s, its use growing rapidly as the demand for it was met from new manufacturing plants in the Midlands and Oxford. It began to change settlement patterns, since the journey from home to work, already stretched by the railways, no longer needed to follow the tracks, but could allow houses to develop on land that could be reached only by road. Therefore, despite serious problems and social disquiet, houses were being built rapidly and to a high standard, on land that had not previously been viable.

In 1939 one third of the country's houses had been built in the previous twenty years.[27] The new houses were out of town and had more space about them than the dense developments of the industrial cities, and generally made for a much higher standard of living than the previous generation could have achieved.[28] They were mostly built privately and sold, with an element of public subsidy supporting 25 per cent of them.[29] They had gardens, usually with a vegetable patch –

haunted by a dim memory of subsistence, but now used really as a means to have a few good fresh vegetables at low cost, rather than as an absolute necessity. They were nowhere near the three-acre-yeoman size, but they always had a garage, which was usually a practical requirement, and the car soon became established as a component in the suburban dream. J. B. Priestley described these houses' inhabitants in his *English Journey* of 1934, where they represent the new face of England – the popular consumers of mass-produced commodities, this England of 'filling stations and factories that look like exhibition buildings, of giant cinemas and dance-halls and cafés, bungalows with tiny garages, cocktail bars, Woolworths, motor coaches, wireless, hiking, factory girls looking like actresses, greyhound racing and dirt tracks, swimming pools and everything given away for cigarette coupons'.[30]

Priestley saw that the old England of aristocracy and old industry was making way for a newer culture of cinemas, dance halls, cafés and bungalows. This consumer culture promoted a sense of individualism, with the consumer making the decisions, not feeling answerable to anyone else for his or her tastes, least of all to the state.[31] The highest aspiration of such individualism was a privately owned detached house in the suburbs. It was also its inhabitants' largest investment – they put everything they had into it – but for many it was an achievable aspiration: two million houses were built without state assistance in England in the 1930s, and the population climbed towards 40 million.[32] The important thing about these new houses for the people who lived in them was not that they were being bribed away from preparing for the revolution that would better serve their interests, but that at last they could achieve what they had wanted all along and for so long had been denied.

Class struggle?

In the language of class struggle these houses express the expansion of a class that could afford a decent privately owned house. The rise in wages, and a shift in the balance of power between the classes, was such that those in control at last felt obliged to provide more or less what had been held as an aspiration for three centuries. 'Four acres and a cow' was finally delivered to the masses, but as a tenth of an acre and a car. This could be seen as a victory for the lower middle class, or a fracturing of the working class, that duped part of it into thinking of itself as middle class and turned the members of this appeased class into counter-revolutionaries. The standard of living, however, was a real improvement, and the likes of Mr Pooter had been thinking of themselves as middle class long before this actual improvement in their conditions.

The war of 1914–18 was important in making things shift. The mass slaughter, by means of which warfare was then conducted, meant that a generation was under-populated with young men, and attitudes changed. The survivors were treated with more respect than previously, not only because of their scarcity but also because their officers had learnt new respect for them as they faced death together.[33] They were heroes, and deserved decent homes. The proliferation of new houses expressed the fact that many more people than ever before were given to feel that they had a stake in the land – their own little piece of England.

The 'default' choice of architectural style for these houses was Tudoresque, because it seemed unpretentious and traditional. Clearly it was British, which was important at this time when people had recently been expected to die for their country, while the modernism that was around and available as an alternative was seen as Germanic and had little impact outside avant-garde circles.[34] It was not off-limits in the suburbs, but was confined to horizontally proportioned windows, or a curved wall here and there, and 'Englished' by being recuperated within a cottagey frame that took the radicalism out of it.[35]

The main alternative to Tudoresque cottage style was neo-Georgian, which could have been more pretentious, if it implied a miniature villa, but a Georgian-cottage style would fit well enough the ethos of the suburbs being described here.[36] The colonial-style bungalow (in Britain by definition a single-storey dwelling) also came into vogue, often itself Tudoresque, with verandas learnt from India, now providing shelter from summer showers rather than tropical glare or monsoons.³⁷

The important thing about these houses was that they had become affordable for the lower middle class. *Ideal Home* magazine, which catered for this readership, was encouragingly practical, and repeatedly stressed the fact that a house was no longer to be seen as out of reach. It published pictures of some glamorous buildings, to which its readership might aspire in their dreams, but most of the time the dreaming was reined in so that the aspirations remained achievable. The ideal homes covered in *Ideal Home* were small compared with the mansions we have seen in earlier chapters, but larger than the smallest cottages, and unelaborate in their detail. They were usually their owner's only dwelling, so they had to be adaptable as seasons changed and families grew. There was much discussion about labour-saving equipment and domestic economy, and the presentations continually stressed that such houses could become reality and need not remain a dream:

> The house of which illustrations are shown this month [illus. 27], [has] about it an unmistakable English air: something indeed, entirely indigenous to the country, yet at the same time the treatment is original and is the outcome of certain definite arrangements in the planning of the house.
> The prevailing thought in the mind of the designer of the house under consideration has been economy.³⁸

Such houses would feel at home in the old English countryside, but for practical reasons the Arcadian vision of rolling hills and woodland was compromised into a suburb.³⁹ The hedgerows of the countryside, which stopped wandering livestock, became the clipped privet that gave privacy from the neighbours. These were definitely not agricultural cottages, but dwellings for people who were employed in a

27 A small country house, from *Ideal Home* (May 1920), unmistakeably English, and affordable.

town, and who valued the town's facilities – the goods and services, schools and hospitals – but who dreamed of living in the countryside, with its fresh air, space for children to play and stress-free ambience.[40] It was the popular realization of the Garden City that had been imagined in 1898 as a theoretical idea by Ebenezer Howard, and promoted by the Metropolitan Railway between 1915 and 1932 as 'Metro-land'.[41]

If these buildings are ever to be understood sympathetically, we need to note that there were two desires at work here. One is the desire to bask in an air of settled well-being that seems to be implied by an old-fashioned exterior and a well-tended garden. The other is the desire to have the most up-to-date facilities both inside the building and available outside. In principle, these facilities can be invisible: they just have to do their job. If they are not in use then they can be put away. The settled old-fashioned ambience, however, is absolutely a matter of appearance and display, demonstrating continuity with the immemorial rural past, looking beyond the recent trauma of war:

> This is a good parcel of English soil in which to build home and strike root, inhabited from of old, as witness the lines of camps on the hill tops and the confused mounds among the woods, the great dyke which crossed it east and west, the British trackways, the Roman road aslant the eastern border, the pack-horse ways worn deep in the steep hill sides, the innumerable field paths which mark the labourer's daily routine from hamlet to farm.
>
> The new settlement of Metro-land proceeds apace; the new colonists thrive amain.[42]

This is from the Metro-land guide for 1927, encouraging leisure-travellers to explore the railway, and also encouraging settlement along it. There is a spirit of adventure with these 'new colonists', but they are venturing into a richly historic landscape, and if indeed they did 'thrive amain' then they flourished in a self-consciously archaic way, connecting with the olden days.

Das englische Haus

In 1904 Hermann Muthesius had said that the characteristic thing about the English was the importance they attached to owning their own home:

> The Englishman sees the whole of life embodied in his house. Here in the heart of his family, self-sufficient and feeling no great urge for sociability, pursuing his own interests in virtual isolation, he finds his happiness and his real spiritual comfort.[43]

This contrasted profoundly with urban life as Muthesius knew it in Germany, with its 'outside pleasures, the hubbub of the metropolitan streets, [or] a visit to the *Bierkeller* or a café'.[44] There is already a well-developed sense of the household as a self-contained family unit, with its privacy and detachment from the throng. George Orwell pointed out that the supposed ownership of the house was a sleight of hand on the part of the mortgage lenders:

> Building societies are the cleverest racket of modern times ... The really subtle swindle ... is the mental one. Merely because of the illusion that we own our own houses and have what's called a 'stake in the country', we poor saps ... are turned into ... devoted slaves for ever.[45]

This portrays the importance of home ownership to the ordinary British citizen, and also the idea of property ownership being a 'stake in the country', which is accurate about people's feelings, but technically at odds with the relation to the state. The lower middle classes did not have a vote until 1918, when property restrictions were removed for men over 21 (mainly in order to avoid disenfranchising returning soldiers).[46] Women who did not own property were allowed to vote after 1928.[47] So by the time Orwell was writing it was technically a recent possibility, for the first time in the nation's history, to have 'a stake in the country' without actually having a house. Nevertheless, the emotional import of the house continued to be ingrained as if this technicality had not been changed.

The house can absorb unlimited quantities of effort and attention, and the feeling that the inhabitants have for the house is so great that when circumstances allowed it, it was indulged to a remarkable degree. J. M. Richards pointed out in 1946 that while various Continental neighbours were proverbially known for being house-proud, in

> the English suburb the equivalent quality goes deeper than conscientious order and cleanliness. It is more positive, more creative, and, moreover, pervades both indoors and out, uniting them in a single world of its own making. The well-scrubbed floor is echoed in the well-mown lawn, the polished grate in the weeded gravel path, the Welsh

dresser with its rows of gleaming plates in the vegetable bed where the purple-sprouting broccoli is planted in equally meticulous rows, and each plant of the winter lettuce is carefully tied up with bass to keep even its outer leaves from dropping on to the damp or dusty ground. Care and cleanliness here recognise no difference between the house and its garden setting; Ewbank and Atco reign side by side.[48]

'Ewbank' and 'Atco' were the trade names of popular products. 'Ewbank' was a carpet sweeper, the vacuum cleaner's predecessor; 'Atco' was a lawnmower. The work being described here goes beyond being onerous and becomes a vocation for the woman of the household. At least that was the idea. When women's voices are heard on the subject of housework, it becomes clear that the investment of her self in her home was not always felt to be as rewarding as she had been led to believe before she married.[49] If she could afford it, she would have domestic help. Traditional masculine tasks included carrying heavy objects (like the coal scuttle), mowing the lawn, pruning bushes, cutting hedges and growing vegetables. Again, the better off would employ a gardener. Nevertheless, the important thing that was going on here was the investment of themselves in the place – not only their money, but also their time and attention. When they were here they were in charge, and no detail escaped their scrutiny and control. The *paterfamilias* was his own master, in his own micro-kingdom a micro-aristocrat.[50]

Ideas of individuality and self-reliance in the suburbs have their genealogy in the yeoman's smallholding and the peasant's tillage, finding expression in 'do-it-yourself' modifications to the dwelling, and the vegetable garden. The point of these activities might have a practical aspect. The home improvements might be made in the usually ill-founded belief that they added value to the house, and they could well have some utility. Their most important aspect is not their utility, but the feeling of self-reliance that they bring to the fore, which feeds a sense of independence and autonomy.[51] The vegetable garden might produce some edible food. It does not matter that with the expenditure of far less time and effort we could have bought some leeks at the grocer's; what matters is that we grew them ourselves; therefore, they are intrinsically special, even if they do not taste remarkable.

The sense of self-determination and individualism that develops through such a culture is certainly counter-revolutionary. What is really remarkable is that this sense is so deep-rooted that it can be sustained even in the face of the realization that the patterns of behaviour and achievements of the neighbours are closely similar. Indeed, not only the immediate neighbours, but also whole suburban swathes of the nation turn out to be doing much the same thing. This sense of independence is defended through the adoption of superficially eccentric hobbies, and by a profound unwillingness to cooperate with others. For example, the habit of growing vegetables on allotments – which had been vital for survival during the Second World War – also fed a spirit of wilful self-determination, which Lord Kennett in 1947 found revealing:

> We are passing some allotments, those patches of mother earth which give so much pleasure and peace of mind to some of her children who but for them would not see much of her. We notice the evidence which they give of our vehement individualism. On each patch there is separate erection of bits of board and old tins. It is a shed for the holder's tools. The allotments Committee had a plan to provide a row of lockers in a special structure at the entrance to the allotments. The lockers would have been neater and more convenient than the tumble-down sheds on the plots, and they would have enabled the holders each to have had a bit more ground. But the holders would have none of them. An Englishman's house is his castle, and his spade and hoe must have their castle too. It is part of the pleasure of the allotment.[52]

These practices continue into the twenty-first century, supported by the garden centres and DIY stores that are now to be found outside the centre of every town large enough to have a suburb. It would be stretching a point to insist that the practices are essentially Tudoresque, since their roots go back beyond the Tudor period; but they certainly continue the practice of reawakening in the modern individual the yeoman's sense of independence that was first enshrined in Tudor law, with the provision of a four-acre smallholding for each cottage. So it is apt that the most recognizable synecdoche of interwar England is a black-and-white gabled Tudoresque house.

Mock Tudor

One of the things that had recommended a Tudoresque cottage style was its simplicity, since there was never a requirement to use historically accurate detail, finely judged proportions or meticulous mouldings, as any classical style would, were it to be well done. There were nevertheless huge variations in the quality of Tudoresque cottage-style buildings, from the well-heeled upper-middle-class versions, which Osbert Lancaster would call 'stockbroker's Tudor', to lower-middle-class varieties that could make use of very perfunctory stylistic cues.[53] The periodicals of the era show not an absolute separation, but a difference in balance between their inclusion of different styles. *Country Life*, founded in 1897, sold to a mainly upper-middle-class market. Aristocrats were addressed in the editorials, and some of them certainly subscribed, but their numbers were insignificant. What was important for the readership was the feeling that they were keeping aristocratic company. *Country Life* regularly carried articles on architectural history and on new houses. The new houses were regularly Tudoresque, but equally often neo-Georgian. In *Homes and Gardens* and *Ideal Home* in the 1920s, these journals having been aimed at a more cost-conscious popular audience, Tudoresque designs clearly predominate, and an image of one was used as the cover of the latter's launch issue in 1919 (illus. 28). In their view of the world the Tudoresque was normal and pervasive, the style to be adopted without comment — it is the variations from it that might need to be explained, but on page after page Tudoresque designs are presented without their style being mentioned.

Oliver Hill was a well-regarded domestic architect who worked between the wars in a range of styles. *Country Life* published some of his Georgian-style designs, *Homes and Gardens* his Tudoresque work.[54] This would suggest that Georgian style was seen as smarter, but for the lower middle class it would have seemed too pretentious, while the Tudor cottage style had an air of authenticity. It also seemed to invite or allow more readily than a more 'sophisticated' style, the do-it-yourself adaptations and decoration that were, and continue to be, an important part of the culture.[55] *Ideal Home* was full of encouragement, pointing out that a house need not be an impossible dream, but could be built for a modest outlay, elaborating the benefits of a vegetable plot, or explaining to the housewife how rewarding she would find it all:

28 Cover of the first issue of *Ideal Home* (1919). Crystallizing a common-sense dream.

> Tudor and Elizabethan houses, whether as cottages or mansions, are an everlasting joy to the woman who is at once a housewife and an artist. For her they spell opportunity.
>
> Within them she can exercise her taste to a degree that perhaps no other style of architecture offers her. Without she can design her garden as a setting to the irregular beauty of the house.[56]

Clearly, the Tudor style was seen to be more flexible and adaptable than others, and this aspect of it makes it able more comfortably to accept the investment of time, effort and improvisation that go with the ideal of self-determination. It went without saying that one would *want* to make one's mark on the property. The idea that a particular style of house might be easier to maintain is never mentioned. Often the quality of the design and execution of the inter-war housing has been regretted or deplored.[57] The historical allusions referred fairly randomly to memorable bits of the past, sometimes with surprisingly fine execution of decorative detail in stained glass: images from heraldry, galleons, windmills or castles.[58] The straightforwardness of the construction made do-it-yourself adaptations more approachable. It is easier to do a porch with a more-or-less rustic character than something more polished. The new house as purchased was only the beginning, as *Ideal Home* readers were reminded: 'For each old house is a repository of history, not perhaps the history of kings but of Englishmen, to preserve and enrich which should be the effort of each successive owner.'[59] Each house therefore has a real history, which is legible through its fabric. It will not go back very far in a new house, but one can contribute to the archaeological record by investing one's self in that fabric, making adaptations to the house, and maintaining it. There is also an imaginary history, suggested in the allusions to old-English buildings, which suggest a kinship with the past. *1066 and All That* was published in 1930, and is an impeccable guide to the uncertain grasp of historical knowledge that was then in common circulation.[60] Its authors' 'method' of 'memorable history', however hilarious the results, was in fact the actual method employed by the designers of inter-war houses when it came to historical allusion.

It did not matter that before the nineteenth century the houses had not routinely been black and white. Now 'black and white' was the signifier that identified the magpie Tudor cottage. A book by Thomas Garner and Arthur Stratton, best known as Gothic Revival architects at the end of the nineteenth century, was republished in 1929. It was called *The Domestic Architecture of England during the Tudor Period*, and if designers of Tudoresque buildings sought to clarify their ideas by reading books, then this was the book they would have read. Its focus was 'traditional' Tudor domestic architecture, rather than work by famous architects for aristocratic clients, such as Joseph Nash had put before the public.[61]

> Beautiful and full of vitality as is the domestic architecture of the Tudor period, it is remarkable that the traditional work which then predominated throughout England should not hitherto have been adequately considered and illustrated. One of the chief reasons that makes this particular period of such supreme importance is that the house building is indigenous to the soil. It is as radical as the name with which it is shaped; it breathes the restful yet vigorous spirit of the time that gave it birth and without is characterised by a self-contained homeliness redolent of the life and customs of the Englishman of the day, and impossible to be either originated or imitated by his continental contemporaries.[62]

Ideal Home echoed these sentiments through the 1930s and after. Robert Symonds, an architect who was also an expert on English furniture, writing in 1952, said:

> The more we learn about English homes and habits of the past, the more we discover how practical and pleasant they were, even in quite early times.
> Man does not want much to make him happy, and the needs of past ages were fulfilled out of the conditions that obtained. And there was always a margin of culture and comfort, at least for the middle and upper classes.
> 'Merry England' of Elizabeth's day, in spite of the dark sides, justifies its title. Compared with the state of affairs

on the Continent, the Englishman was free from political despotism and he used his freedom to explore the world and extend his trade far beyond Europe.

The Elizabethan chronicler, William Harrison, gives a convincing picture of the ordinary Englishman's life in the second half of the sixteenth century.

Houses of yeoman farmers, town craftsmen, and other citizens of the middling sort, had roofs of thatch and walls of 'wattle and daub' – a type of house which aroused the contempt of visiting Spaniards. But, according to Harrison when they saw the kind and quantity of food which was being eaten inside these cottages, they were aroused to admiration and wonder. 'These English have their houses made of sticks and dirt, but they fare commonly so well as the King'.[63]

Symonds's own designs were not specifically historicizing in their style, but belonged to what he described as the 'Modern English Traditional School', looking for common ground between modernity and the craft tradition. In the passage here, the mention of 'citizens of the middling sort', with whom his readers would certainly have identified themselves, brings out subject matter from everyday life, which has traditionally been neglected by historians, who are more inclined to gravitate towards great events and important men than to pay attention to the unexceptional goings-on in unexceptional settings. Symonds here appeals to *Ideal Home*'s readers to notice that they have a heritage, to be proud of it and to connect with it.

A simple life

There is no particular need to trace an absolute origin for the idea of modest domestic independence, but it was enshrined in law under Elizabeth, and since then it has been a guiding aspiration for British domesticity, even though the practical realization has often fallen a long way short of the dream. It is a dream of authenticity, a simple life, ideally producing one's own food and living in self-contained domestic bliss, without interference from outside, and without the obligation to waste time and money on fashion or vanity, or go in search of high office. The vision was warmly embraced by Middle England, and has been in place for as long as there has been a sense of British folk and nation. It was this vision that enabled the emergent lower middle class to feel comfortable about itself and its achievements, but although it was genuinely popular it was not universally endorsed. George Orwell has been cited above, sounding a sour note.

Orwell grew up in Tudoresque houses, in a household that had aspirations beyond its means. He had been born in India, and his father remained out there, working in the colonial service, while his half-French mother returned to England with the children. Orwell went to Eton, on a scholarship, and was educated in an aristocratic outlook, but the experience predisposed him to the socialism that he went on to embrace. He described his family as belonging to the 'lower-upper-middle-class', which gave them an 'almost purely theoretical' gentility, since their income almost debarred them from membership of the class.[64] In his novel *Coming Up for Air* of 1939, the protagonist, George Bowling, returns to his childhood home of Binfield to reminisce over the 'good old days' of his childhood. There is some nostalgic warmth in the descriptions, but also disappointment. The Lower Binfield Estate is not what it once was; and both it and the Upper Binfield Estate are now covered with 'bogus Tudor' houses and other symbols of inauthenticity, brash consumerism and social decline. He finds the estate populated by a new breed of 'simple lifer' – securely upper-middle-class people whose lives are caught up in vegetarianism, folk music and nudism. He meets an inhabitant, who says:

> 'They talk of their Garden Cities. But we call Upper Binfield the Woodland City – te-hee! Nature!' He waved a hand at what was left of the trees. 'The primeval forest brooding round us.' . . .

He began to show me round the estate. There was nothing left of the woods. It was all houses, houses – and what houses! Do you know these faked-up Tudor houses with the curly roofs and the buttresses that don't buttress anything, and the rock-gardens with concrete bird-baths and those red plaster elves you can buy at the florists? You could see in your mind's eye the awful gang of food-cranks and spook-hunters and simple-lifers with 1,000 pounds a year that lived there. Even the pavements were crazy. I didn't let him take me far. Some of the houses made me wish I'd got a hand-grenade in my pocket.[65]

The £1,000 a year was a healthy income. Orwell said that his own family had about £400 a year when he was growing up, so the houses in the Upper Binfield Estate are being presented as belonging to a pretentious class, which is deluding itself into believing that it has found simplicity. If we look through Orwell to the delusions that he condemns, however, he sees himself as being in opposition to a mainstream that makes routine use of the Tudoresque. The inhabitants of the estate deliberately evoke the pre-industrial idyll of rural life, but without any of the hardships that would come from subsisting on a smallholding. This version of the simple life in the suburb is modelled on life in a *cottage orné*, with pseudo-aristocratic disdain for actual work. The resident's view excludes the income-generating part of life from consideration, in a way that no peasant ever could. It is a deluded view, but however unconvincing it might be, it is nevertheless a dream of autonomy, realized in the Tudoresque.

It is in conveying this sense of independence, of not being answerable to a higher authority for the arrangements in one's domestic life, that the Tudoresque cottage style has found its most persuasive role. It is important that the house should work efficiently, and that its facilities should be good. Le Corbusier said in the 1920s that a house was a *machine à habiter* – a machine for living – and drew the conclusion that it should therefore look like a machine.[66] The multitude of anonymous builders of the Tudoresque embraced the facilities offered by the machine, but declined to make the house look like anything other than an old-fashioned house. If critics sneered at them for doing so, then that was none of their business. When the Tudoresque houses went unchallenged, they were the image of stability and traditional comfort. When they were challenged, one found that the apparent repose was backed up by a bone-headed truculence that was already well recognized in the eighteenth century.

The four acres and a cow that gave practical independence to the yeomen under Elizabeth I did not continue in a very direct way into contemporary culture, and yet at some level it is understood. The increase in popular democracy somehow connected with the Tudor cottage as the most potent expression of its aspiration for a contented and independent domestic life. Somewhere far away beyond the privet hedge there are explosions, torture, floods, famine and miscarriages of justice, but here at home there is the immediate family, honey for tea and roses round the door; and so nothing really fundamental can be wrong. The little kingdom's horizons are close at hand, and beyond them life is complicated and out of control. The four-acres-and-a-cow recipe for happiness is to bring all the essentials of life within that limited horizon, and if we do not often manage to subsist quite so independently these days, we can nevertheless sustain its feeling of independent well-being on a daydream and borrowed money.

Chapter Five

Backstage Tudoresque

Spaces of escape

The dwelling has various roles. It shelters its occupants from the elements, keeps them and their belongings secure, and gives them the privacy that they feel they need. They are also places where guests are received, and on those occasions there is a display, as some things are thrown into prominence and others are tidied away. In large houses there is enough room for the separate functions to be given their own designated spaces, and Joseph Nash, for example, showed the Tudor great house with its hall *en fête* as an example of paternal hospitality (illus. 14). It is a stage on which to enact the rituals of hospitality, and it would not be used for the squire's family's ordinary meals, which would be taken off-stage in a smaller room that was less difficult to heat and where behaviour could be more relaxed. Such a dwelling was not a private house in the way we would now understand it, but had public functions, such as hospitality and the administration of justice, which for minor transgressions was in the hands of the local gentry (magistrates) rather than the courts. A stately home would need rooms suitable for regal entertainment and where the monarch on a royal progress could meet a stream of loyal subjects – not only those with whom he had business to conduct, but also the poor, who believed that he could cure their illnesses. In the twenty-first century such functions have been superseded, often migrating to public buildings and administered by public bodies. We are more likely to entertain in rooms that we use for everyday life, but in the nineteenth century, even in small houses with any pretensions to respectability, a front parlour would be sequestered from everyday use, so that it was in a state suitable for receiving visitors, and that practice continued, but with decreasing urgency, as the twentieth century progressed.

The place where the performance is at its most elaborate is at the dining table, where, whether it is a festive banquet in a great hall or a small dinner with friends, we find ways to display our taste and ingenuity, whether by a great indulgence of plenty or by refinement and novelty. Just as in the great palaces of the past one would be especially privileged if invited into the inner rooms – the bedchamber, the closet – so on a much smaller scale there is a suggestion of trust and esteem in being invited to an informal meal that is not matched by the invitation to act as a witness at a showy formal dinner. The latter is obviously and avowedly a display; the former is, as it were, an invitation to a real off-stage encounter, and that is now well established as an alternate display. We play these various roles in order to establish our position in society, partly so that society feels obliged to recognize our standing, but much more importantly, so that we recognize it ourselves. We need to persuade ourselves that we really are the people we imagine ourselves to be.[1]

When we are 'off stage' we have privacy and can be in the grip of whatever mood takes us, without it being a problem. We are 'performing' whenever we need to be polite, even if the performance is ingrained and unconscious, whenever we choose clothes that have an aspect that is not strictly utilitarian.[2] Even utilitarian clothes can be worn gesturally – the politician's conspicuously 'high-street' skirt, showing that she is in touch with the people, or her male counterpart's open-necked shirt to signal his engagement with 'modernity' – but the normal sense of clothes appropriate to the occasion can range from relatively straightforward choices for routine activity, to prescribed uniforms – the city suit, the academic gown – or outright spectacle (with ostrich feathers) for the monarch in a regal pageant or female Hollywood stars on a red carpet.[3] Identity is a performance, or more accurately a set of performances, since we all have more than one aspect to our identities, and we have the identities that we know how to perform.[4] We need to keep performing them if we want them to continue to be plausible to others and to feel authentic to ourselves. In establishing these identities we establish whatever power it is that we have to act in society.

Domestic space is a very important part of these performances, sometimes as a place to be seen, but more often as a place to rehearse or to disconnect temporarily and recuperate, preparing oneself to face the world, rehearsing to be the self that the occasion demands. These things are most visible when the self in question has a high status, when the disconnection between the performance of power and the domestic recuperation can be great.

In 1938 *Homes and Gardens* ran a notorious article about Adolf Hitler's mountain retreat, Haus Wachenfeld, showing Hitler relaxing at home, looking amiable and contented. It was a performance, of course, but it was a performance of being off-stage, far from the public person who had already, when the article appeared, invaded the Rhineland and Austria.[5] This is a striking example, not least because the house in question is in a traditional chalet style, which could be seen as a local equivalent of the Tudoresque in that Alpine region. It was embracing the idea of a 'simple life' as certainly as anyone on the Upper Binfield Estate.

The cult of nature begins when people start to feel that they are in danger of losing their connection with it, and worry that their innate vitality might be sapped by over-refinement. There are versions of it in the ancient world – the *Idylls* of Theocritus, Virgil's *Eclogues* – and it was an important part of eighteenth-century British culture. Joseph Addison set up the *Spectator* to spread something like the polish of a liberal education to people who had not had the benefit of the real thing. He wrote in an early issue in 1711:

True happiness is of a retired nature, and an enemy of pomp and noise; it arises, in the first place, from the enjoyment of one's self; and in the next from the friendship and conversation of a few select companions: it loves shade and solitude, and naturally haunts groves and fountains, fields and meadows: in short it feels every thing it wants within itself, and receives no addition from multitudes of witnesses and spectators. On the contrary false happiness loves to be in a crowd, and to draw the eyes of the world upon her. She does not receive any satisfaction from the applauses which she gives herself, but from the admiration she raises from others. She flourishes in courts and palaces, theatres and assemblies and has no existence but when she is looked upon.[6]

Addison's *Spectator* essays were repeatedly republished; they were and are routinely cited by other authors and were absorbed into the cultural mainstream, becoming part of the curriculum of the British Enlightenment. The pleasures of a sophisticated but modest rural retreat were best exemplified for an eighteenth-century British audience by William Shenstone, whose little estate, The Leasowes, near Dudley, he called a *ferme ornée*.[7] It was much visited as a place of refined taste. Its landscaping was admired and the fragments of poetry carved here and there planted evocative trains of thought in the visitors' minds. It worked for as long as Shenstone was there to animate it. A later visitor, Thomas Jefferson, who came after Shenstone's death, was disappointed, seeing nothing in it but a grazing farm with a path round it.[8]

Later in the eighteenth century a different sensibility developed, which saw nature less as a useful resource for contemplation, and more as a power to be worshipped. Again we might look to the ancient world for the roots of this idea, but in modern Europe its most persuasive prophet was Jean-Jacques Rousseau. He was an Enlightenment figure, but the tenor of his arguments, which were carefully reasoned, ran against the 'march of mind' that came to dominate the age. He is associated with 'Romanticism', which tends to be seen as a post-Enlightenment movement, but he made his name as a solitary man of letters before the 'age of Romanticism'. His early prizewinning essays at the Dijon academy – 'On the Progress of the Arts and Sciences' and 'On the Origins of Inequality' (of 1750 and 1752, respectively) suggested that all civilized progress was more or less bad, and that we would be better off in a state of nature.

> In fact, whether one leafs through the annals of the world or supplements uncertain chronicles with philosophic research, human learning will not be found to have an origin corresponding to the idea we like to have of it. Astronomy was born from superstition; Eloquence from ambition, hate, flattery and falsehood; Geometry from avarice; Physics from vain curiosity; all even Moral philosophy from human pride. Thus the sciences and the arts owe their birth to our vices; we would be less doubtful of their advantages if they owed it to our virtues.[9]

What Rousseau had in common with his more utilitarian rationalist contemporaries, the more orthodox Enlightenment *philosophes*, was the understanding that superstition and received wisdom had to be challenged whenever they were encountered and firmly set aside. He wrote music, and had a popular success with *Le Devin du village*, a one-act opera, which was presented at court to Louis XV in 1752.[10] Its rustic setting was matched by tuneful singing with only the simplest harmony. Rousseau's theory of the development of language imagined singing as a primitive mode of communication, prior to speech, and the aim was to be as unaffected as birdsong in the composition. Rousseau argued that:

> Before Art had moulded our manners and taught our passions to speak an affected language, our morals were rustic but natural, and differences of conduct announced

at first glance those of character. Human nature, basically, was no better, but men found their security in the ease of seeing through each other, and that advantage, which we no longer appreciate, spared them many vices.[11]

So in order to reform society from its contemporary disordered state, he argued, it is necessary to uncover the natural self that is innate in all of us, and to listen to what it tells us to do:

> O virtue! Sublime science of simple souls, are so many difficulties and preparations needed to know you? Are not your principles engraved in all hearts, and is it not enough in order to learn your laws to return into oneself and listen to the voice of one's conscience in the silence of the passions?[12]

Rousseau propagated a new sensibility, suggesting that a primitive 'noble savage' was intuitively and naturally more moral than the bourgeois citizens of civilized Europe. If he did not translate his ideas into architecture, maybe it was because Marc-Antoine Laugier was quicker off the mark, publishing his essay on architecture in 1752. He reasoned in a way that seems to be strongly influenced by Rousseau's method, arguing in the age of the Baroque for the retrieval of the absolute fundamentals of classical architecture, which he presented as being embodied in a radically primitive hut. The hut's corners were tree trunks, still growing in the ground, but the essentials of true architectural form were in place: the column, the beam and the slope of the roof, which could be monumentalized in stone and refined into the classical temple.[13] Joachim Winckelmann saw the noble savage's virtues as remaining intact in the civilization of ancient Greece.[14]

Rousseau's ideas had little attraction for farm-workers, but he was lionized by the aristocracy, and when he died his grave was set prominently and romantically surrounded by poplars on a little island in a lake in the landscaped park at Ermenonville, which belonged to his friend the Marquis René-Louis de Girardin, in whose house Rousseau had fallen ill and died. The body was later moved for re-burial at the Panthéon in central Paris, adapted as a national memorial from the former church of Ste-Geneviève – one of the few contemporary buildings that met with Laugier's approval.[15]

It was Rousseau's line of thought that prompted Louis XVI's queen, Marie-Antoinette, to build a rustic hamlet as a retreat from not only the oppressive formalities of court life at Versailles, but also from the Petit Trianon – a retreat in itself – in whose garden her hamlet sat. The *petit hameau*, designed in 1783 by Richard Mique, is a picturesquely contrived rural idyll, with cows and pigs, and a series of rustic-looking cottages, including a watermill and a well-appointed dairy. On the outside they looked dilapidated – just like real cottages – but there were substantial and comfortable rooms within, one room per cottage, more or less, where the queen's close circle could relax, sometimes with country dances.[16] The appearance was one thing, the use quite another. Functionally, it was a very different arrangement from an ordinary hamlet, where each of the cottages would have housed a whole family as their only abode. There is half-timbering here, but it is not a reference to anything Tudor. In France, this is recognized as *le style normand* and has a different set of connotations.

The *hameau* was part of a rural fantasy, not the means to live like an actual peasant, but it was a way in which Marie-Antoinette could set aside her regal identity and escape by role-playing peasants in amateur dramatics. She was not trying to empathize with the poor, but to find her own genuine feelings and cultivate her sensibility by disengaging from the rigidities of court ritual, using the simple life as the means by which to find personal grace.

Rousseau's influence was not confined to France, but found its way to Britain, where he was widely read by the educated classes, and very fashionable among aristocrats. William Wordsworth lived for a time in France, witnessed some of the events of the Revolution and was enthused with its spirit ('Bliss was it in that dawn to be alive, And to be young was very heaven!').[17] He more than anyone brought the Romantic sensibility to England. His poems in *Lyrical Ballads* (1798) dispensed with the eighteenth-century poetic conventions that populated the page with dryads and zephyrs, nymphs and classical gods, and in their place told stories of the trials borne by rural workers who heroically scratched a living from the Cumberland hills. He said that it was these hills, along with nature in general, that were 'the soul of all my moral being'.[18] Nature was charged with moral force, and the people who daily dealt with it knew plain truth. Wordsworth settled at Dove Cottage in Grasmere, and lived simply but with domestic help. He would have been horrified had anyone suggested that this was a *cottage orné*. In 1799 his friends Robert Southey and Samuel Taylor Coleridge wrote some doggerel mocking the idea:

[The Devil] passed a cottage with a double coach-house,
A cottage of gentility;
And he owned with a grin
That his favorite sin
Is pride that apes humility.[19]

A number of architectural pattern books were published in England in the wake of the French Revolution, with much greater frequency than earlier. It was not a suitable time for the great landowners to be embarking on ambitious schemes; their incomes had fallen because of the rise in taxes to pay for the war with France, and it plainly made sense to defer the start of a major building or landscaping project. This put architects out of work, and in the hope of finding it a few of them turned to publishing. The buildings that stood the best chance of being commissioned were modest ones, and several books included or were entirely composed of designs for cottages, which the Board of Agriculture was encouraging landowners to build.[20] James Malton's *British Cottage Architecture* was among them.

They were all aimed at landowners – the cost of a well-illustrated book would put it well beyond the reach of a labouring cottager – and some of them, like Malton, included designs that were intended for the landowner to build for his tenants, while others, with different accommodation indicated on plan, would serve as *cottages ornés*. The buildings might look similar, but they would function differently. The worker's cottage would ideally be attached to a smallholding, or if the estate was being run on modern lines, near agricultural fields with crops of livestock. It would have few rooms, and would accommodate a family the whole year round. The *cottage orné* would be used by gentlefolk with education and a poetic sensibility, who would visit for part of the year and would need accommodation for at least one servant. Their income would not be dependent on local work. The pattern of their lives might have something of the routine of the great landowners, with winters in the city and summers in the countryside, but they could be managing on a much lower income, so this cottage-like villa, rather than an ancestral pile in a landscaped park, was their summer home.

Thomas Dearn, a rural doctor, pointed out that 'under the sanction of fashion' even people of relatively modest means could enjoy the comforts of a cottage, since, he said, 'we have seen even royalty become the inmate and inhabitant of a cottage'.[21] His book, *Sketches in Architecture*, is not actually a pattern book, though at first sight it looks like one. The images of picturesque cottages are appealing, but no plans are included and Dearn himself was not looking for architectural work. He was drawing attention to the terrible living conditions of the rural poor, and the fact that something could and should be done about them. He sought to find a readership for his harsh truths by sugar-coating the pill for a genteel audience. Joseph Gandy published books of designs for cottages that explicitly sought to work to the Board of Agriculture's agenda, and seem to be in tune with Wordsworth's vision, but they drew some of their inspiration from French sources, rather than cultivating an old-English air, and seem to have had little influence.[22] Richard Elsam took the line of recommending the *cottage orné*, which probably met with more success:

To persons of a more refined taste and discernment the following designs of cottages are offered, not as models of perfection, but as Designs from which others may be contrived to answer most of the purposes required by persons anxious to construct themselves, small comfortable, genteel cottages in the country, at a moderate expense . . . The greatest recommendation to the Cottage itself should be, its making a lively appearance for to those persons who are desirous of partaking in a country life, as a relaxation from business.[23]

And he quoted here the passage from Addison cited above, to substantiate his point. The practice of contemplative reflection does not require buildings to do it in. In fact, as an activity it is more programmatically to be located in eighteenth-century gardens, which sometimes had a hermit to make that point.[24] Moreover, it is possible to be contemplative in a grandiose Palladian seat, and so one need not necessarily move into a *cottage orné* in order to feel close to nature. Nevertheless, it was a move that people made, and by doing so they were telling themselves as much as others that they were persons of sensibility.

At the time that Dearn was writing, Richard Payne Knight moved out of his country seat, Downton Castle, which he left to the charge of his married younger brother. Knight himself kept up his house in Soho Square in London, but for the summers moved to a cottage on the Downton estate, where he lived surrounded by trees, taking long daily walks and preparing his edition of Homer while trying to live as close as possible to nature, like an ancient Greek.[25] He was part of fashionable society, and may have influenced the Duke and Duchess of Bedford in their desire for a rural retreat (though since they employed the services of Humphry Repton in determining the site for it, they were not unduly swayed by Knight's opinion).[26]

Their site was immensely picturesque and chosen by Repton and the duchess for its views. The house could have been in the grandest and most palatial style, since the duke's property speculations in the West End of London were extensive and immensely successful;[27] but Repton recommended on Picturesque grounds that a farm building would be best suited to the scenery at Endsleigh.[28] In the event Jeffry Wyatt was employed in 1809, and he designed the large house that was required, but made its style that of a rambling cottage – or rather a group of cottages, some of them linked by verandas (illus. 8). The building's bulk was thereby diminished, and it offered comfortable facilities while looking as unimposing a building as possible. The overtly Tudoresque details include the chimneys, oriels and the pattern of stone mullions and transoms in the windows, while the general effect is generically old English, avoiding 'high style' but not too crudely vernacular.[29] The point was not so much to pretend to be poor, as to set aside the burdens of responsibility and to be close to nature. Even when seen from a distance, this dwelling could never have been mistaken for that of a peasant – it is much too substantial for that – but it looks equally unlike a stately home.

From 1824 Wyatt would also work for George IV on the castle at Windsor, which he thoroughly re-designed, 'restoring' its medieval style by giving it a completely new picturesque silhouette.[30] With the king's permission, he extended his name, making it 'Wyatville'.[31] Earlier, when George III's insanity and incapacity for government had led to his son George being declared Prince Regent, he had had John Nash renovate and extend a lodge on the Windsor estate, moving into it in 1815, when it was known as the Prince Regent's Cottage. This was while the king was confined in the castle, keeping him well out of the public eye. Wyatville made further extensions after 1823; by then it had become the King's Cottage (illus. 29). It had 90 acres of grounds attached, and its own dairy, which may have been used by the prince for role-playing the farmer, but George III was known as 'Farmer George', and that would surely have made the idea unappealing to the son.[32] In 1830 it was demolished by William IV (George's younger brother), but there have been subsequent buildings on the site, which is now known as the Royal Lodge.

29 William Daniell, view of John Nash's Royal Lodge (the King's Cottage) Windsor, Berkshire, 1811. A palace styled as a cottage.

Wyatville's building was again a sprawling, much-extended version of cottage style, following much the same formula as Endsleigh, so far as the architectural detail is concerned. It offered accommodation as comfortable as that at the earlier Brighton Pavilion – built for the same person, before he was Regent – but the architectural expression could hardly be more different. The Brighton Pavilion looks sumptuous and exotic, while the King's Cottage looks like modesty personified.

George's sister Elizabeth married in 1818 and moved to the Landgraviate of Hesse-Homburg – an independent country in those days, now part of Germany; but before she went, she also had a cottage at Windsor, of even greater modesty (illus. 30). It is supposed once to have been a cowshed, but had already been converted into a house by a previous proprietor, Richard Bateman – a friend of Horace Walpole, who credited him with introducing Sharawaggi (the supposedly Chinese taste in garden design) to England.[33] This was the Garden House in the grounds of his own house, which he at first called The Grove, but then changed it to The Priory – after Walpole's influence had led him to abandon his Chinese taste for the Gothic. In 1831 a guidebook to the area said of Princess Elizabeth's Cottage that:

> They who draw their notions of royal enjoyment from the tinsel of its external trappings, will scarcely believe the above cottage to have been the residence of an English princess. Yet such was the rank of its occupant but a few years since, distant as may be the contrast of courts and cottages, and the natural enjoyment of rural life from the artificial luxury – the painted pomp and idle glitter of regal state . . .
>
> The . . . cottage stands in the grounds of Grove House, adjoining the churchyard of Old Windsor. It was built under the superintendent taste of the Princess Elizabeth, second sister of the present King, and now known as the Landgravine of Hesse Homburg. To the decoration of this cottage the Princess paid much attention: it is quite in the *ornée* style; and its situation is so beautiful as to baffle all embellishment.[34]

30 Princess Elizabeth's *cottage orné* at The Grove, Windsor, plate from the *Mirror of Literature, Amusement and Instruction* (1831).

Elizabeth's cottage does seem to have kept an air of simplicity, and never had a reputation for great luxury within. Like Marie-Antoinette's hamlet, it gave her a space where she had some independence from the court and, perhaps more importantly, from her family, but the cottage was not a focus of activity for fashionable society. She flourished after her marriage, with the less formal manners of the Hesse-Homburg court, and her own more prominent position in it.

Another more self-consciously ornamental and sociable example was one designed by John Nash in 1810, the so-called Swiss Cottage at Cahir, County Tipperary, for Richard Butler, 12th Baron Cahir, 1st Earl of Glengall.[35] Stylistically, it is related to Nash's pseudo-vernacular work at Blaise Hamlet, here a deep overhanging thatch giving the cottage its rustic character, but with no evident Tudorisms – nor does it look particularly Swiss. In the absence of clear signifiers to the contrary, the white walls, low chimneys and deep thatch probably mean that Nash thought he was designing something like a traditional Irish cottage, but the local people, recognizing that it was no such thing, fixed on 'Swiss' as the appropriate characterization, meaning 'foreign'. It was designed as a retreat for Lord and Lady Cahir, but they entertained there and the cottage was equipped for that, with a kitchen and wine cellar in the basement. Hand-painted Dufour wallpaper from Paris decorated the salon with scenes of Ottoman Turkey, emblematic of luxury; and in the music room there is a double portrait of Lady Cahir, depicted once in smart fashionable dress, once in peasant costume, pointing to the roles she might choose to play there.[36] The enviable thing about the peasant was not the *poverty*, but the ability to connect with and to know one's own feelings instead of following the rituals of court or polite behaviour. Peasants were supposedly free to follow their passions, could marry for love, and in literary tradition they certainly made the best lovers.[37] The presence of a music room suggests that this was a space where feelings were cultivated. The double portrait confirms it.

> '... love's not suited to the city's strife,
> As ev'ry lover love's a cottage life.'
> 'Tis true, that love unmix'd with mad desire,
> The chaste devotion, and th'extatic fire,
> Flies far from cities and from courtly noise,
> To Contemplation and Reflection's joys.[38]

The polite cottage

If the *cottage orné* took root among a small number of people of means, who might have seemed eccentric, by the time that the pattern books were being produced, it was a well-established fashionable idea. James Malton said:

> When we consider the master [of a stately home] as mere man, there is found no consistency between the possessor and the thing possessed: the immensity of his demands, the attention he must necessarily exact of others, and a continual reliance upon them for the support of his dignity, more immediately renders him the dependent, than the lord of his servants.[39]

The country cottage could be a comfortable retreat not only for the aristocratic landowner, but also for people who made their money in towns. Their interest in a rural retreat was not so much in role-playing the peasant in order to find their true feelings, but in relaxation.[40] The countryside became a place of revitalization for the middle class – a class that had very limited significance for the countryside up to the eighteenth century, but which grew in size and mobility. The importance of the cottage for the person with a town-based workplace is as a restorative place for contemplation, where life can slow down and one can prepare to return refreshed to urban stress. In 1807 William Pococke recommended one of his *Architectural Designs for Rustic Cottages, Picturesque Dwellings, Villas etc* by saying:

From the size and accommodations of this Building, if built in an appropriate situation, it would make a desirable retreat for those who love
'The cool, the fragrant, and the silent hour
To Meditation due'.[41]

Pococke's quotation is from James Thomson's *The Seasons*, and the hour in question is soon after dawn, when the shepherd leaves his mossy cottage, 'where with Peace he dwells', to take his flock out to pasture.[42] The poem dates from 1744, and clearly owes something to Virgil's *Georgics*, so it is far from being a novel sensibility, but Pococke's proposition is that it could, with his help, be a practical possibility for someone with an educated outlook, a poetic disposition and ample but not unlimited means.

In 1818 John Buonarotti Papworth's *Rural Residences* made a slightly different point, suggesting that his clients would want not a real rural cottage, but something more refined:

> The *cottage orné* is a new species of building in the economy of domestic architecture, and subject to its own laws of fitness and propriety. It is not the habitation of the laborious, but of the affluent, of the man of study, of science, or of leisure; it is often the rallying point of domestic comfort, and in this age of refinement, a mere cottage would be incongruous with the nature of its occupancy.[43]

Super-scale cottages

A *cottage orné* could not convincingly be a powerful person's main residence, only a supplementary one. It could make a convincing retreat, but its proprietor would need an urban dwelling from which to retreat, and that would have been in a restrained, formal modern style, which we would call Georgian, in the eighteenth century, and then as the nineteenth century progressed in some other historicizing garb.[44]

Houses such as Endsleigh and the King's Cottage at Windsor had something of the character of a cottage, but the size of a substantial manor house. The Tudoresque old-English manor houses in chapter Three sometimes seem to have the elements of stately homes, in miniature, and sometimes seem to be more like cottages that have grown beyond a cottage's legitimate size. These different inflections suggest that their proprietors had different ideas of who they were – aspirant aristocrats or yeomen-made-good. The wealthy industrialists who built themselves houses that looked like Palladian stately homes fall outside the scope of this study, but they too were around (and indeed they are still with us).

Those who sought out the Tudoresque were best served by George Devey in the middle of the nineteenth century, and then later by Richard Norman Shaw and William Eden Nesfield, who launched their black-and-white old-English style in the 1860s.[45] There was a stylistic shift here, as the number of black-and-white gables in the country started to proliferate, but their significance is less as an architectural fashion and more as an indication of social change. These super-scaled cottages are tied to the proprietors' sense of themselves being 'of the British people', rather than aristocratic and cosmopolitan. The number of people who so identified themselves and who were in a position to build a large house increased hugely in the second half of the nineteenth century. They were mainly involved with industry, and the idea of the cottage represented to them much the same as it had to the people who inhabited *cottages ornés* – escape from the pressures of a more demanding part of life – but in this case escape from the stress of the workplace, rather than of the rigid formalities of court.[46]

The houses could be principal residences, and so they would be larger than all but the most exceptional *cottages ornés*, and when they were principal dwellings they would need to be within reach of the workplace. The distance of that 'reach' increased enormously from about the middle of the nineteenth century because of the introduction of the railways, piecemeal, which began to have an impact not only on the journey time between cities, but also on the way that a large industrial city worked.[47] With so much new money around, Britain, the 'workshop of the world', being able to produce novelty to order and the cities becoming sootier and foggier with each passing year, the daily escape to the countryside by train seemed profoundly necessary for those who could afford it. It also became more fashionable than ever to make houses look old-fashioned, as if they had always been there, to fit into their surroundings rather than to stand out. These 'old-English' buildings were likely to be sturdily built in masonry, but would be decorated with whitewash and dark applied timbers that implied a structural frame. Even an architect with rich clients such as Norman Shaw can be found using applied timbers to make the right visual impression, without worrying that it did not express the building's actual construction.[48] Such buildings could be flexibly planned, because irregularity was part of their charm, and it was no bad thing if the various parts seemed to have been built at different times, so long as they sat harmoniously together. Tile hanging might cover parts of the wall, and chimneys would be tall and emphatic, the general appearance inspired by farmhouses rather than stately homes.[49]

In the early 1860s such houses were rare, and more ostentatious styles were fashionable,[50] but this version of old-English style steadily gained ground. It did not have a strong aesthetic discipline, but was allusive in ways that were popularly understood, referencing a historically vague but powerful idea of the type of house that an Elizabethan yeoman farmer would have had. They were unpretentious, un-cosmopolitan and did not look new, which puts them close to defining in architectural terms the British character as analysed by Burke.[51] They were presenting themselves as the descendents of Elizabethan yeomen, albeit often with much more ample means at their disposal, but the means would be disposed with care, not with the sacrificial exuberance of an aristocratic leisure-class. They were proud of their hard work and sound character and wanted to distinguish themselves from the idle rich. Looking back to the 'paternalist' relations set up between the industrialists mentioned in chapter Three and their workers' housing, George Cadbury's and Theodore Mander's houses both clearly belong in this category of the palatial yeoman cottage.

Hammerfield, near Penshurst in Kent, designed by George Devey, was commissioned by the very popular Royal Academician Frederick Richard Lee, but then bought and re-named by James Nasmyth, inventor of the steam hammer (illus. 31). Nasmyth was Scottish, and his working life was based around Manchester, but as he approached retirement in 1859 he remembered a painting by his brother of 'a cottage in Kent', which had been the very image of domestic contentment. He went to Kent in search of something like it, and despite Hammerfield's substantial size, in his autobiography he consistently calls it his 'cottage in Kent', seeing it as the very embodiment of the 'place of refuge' that he sought.[52] He added various extensions to the house, which was already designed to look as if it had grown accretively over the years, artfully mixing Tudoresque and

31 George Devey, Hammerfield, Penshurst, Kent, 1859. James Naysmith, inventor of the steam-hammer, retired to this substantial 'cottage'.

32 George Devey, Ascott House, Wing, Buckinghamshire, 1874. A Rothschild palace styled as a cottage.

vernacular elements – black-and-white work, brick, tile hanging, variegated windows with timber or masonry mullions and transoms, and tall, emphatic brick chimneys.

Devey also designed Ascott House, at Wing, for Leopold de Rothschild (illus. 32). The Rothschilds, as was mentioned in chapter Three when their paternalism was discussed, had an extraordinary presence in this area and certainly played the role of traditional squires. Ascott is a large house by anyone else's standards, but in comparison with Mentmore, the family's main seat, it is a picture of modesty. William Gladstone's daughter, Mary, described it as a 'palace-like cottage'.[53] The interior was palatial. The exterior looked like a surprisingly disciplined Tudoresque village, with many black-and-white gables of a very small scale, given the overall size of the building. Like

Endsleigh and the King's Cottage at Windsor, rather than being a 'palace-like cottage', this is really a 'cottage-like palace', and in this respect it belongs firmly in the class of *cottages ornés*.

Experiments

Devey's output is remarkable, as he continued to work in a mainly Tudoresque style through the middle years of the nineteenth century, even when the Gothic Revival was attracting much more attention, and he was finding clients who wanted to buy into his vision of domestic architecture, which could accommodate them as squires or yeomen, or indeed as tenants. Norman Shaw and Eden Nesfield greatly admired Devey's work, and it is in their hands that the story of the Tudoresque made its next important developments among architecture professionals. Part of the importance of the Tudoresque, however, is the way that it keeps escaping the professional realm. Its capacity to evoke a tradition of self-reliance makes it attractive to autodidacts and oddballs. One such was Lord Sudeley, Charles Hanbury-Tracy, who in 1840 demolished his seventeenth-century manor house, Gregynog Hall, near Newtown in Wales, and replaced it with what at first glance might be taken to be a sixteenth-century building (illus. 33). The old manor had in it some sixteenth-century rooms, which were preserved, and the black-and-white framing passes as traditional in this area, but it is here pursued with unusual vigour, following the example of the decorative half-timbered exterior of Little Moreton Hall and the assertive massing of Kingston Maurward, built in masonry with projecting, tower-like wings. The main Hanbury-Tracy residence, by the time Gregynog was being worked over, was Toddington Manor in Gloucestershire, which Lord Sudeley designed himself and had built from 1819 onwards in an equally assertive Gothic style.[54] The designer's extreme independence of mind at Gregynog, however, is indicated not in the choice of style, arresting though that is, but in his decision to clad the house entirely in concrete panels – a decision that seems to be unprecedented.[55]

Concrete is so much associated with the architecture of the 1950s and '60s that one might have thought it was a new invention then. It in fact has a long history, but it was not always visible in the buildings where it was used. The ancient Romans used it structurally and usually covered it up with something more splendid, such as marble, but concrete is at the core, doing the hard work in holding up the aqueducts and vaults. The big difference between ancient and modern concrete is the introduction of steel. François Hennebique patented a system of reinforcement, which made it possible to build very strong structural concrete frames. His method was commercially available from 1890.[56] The cladding panels at Gregynog are not the mass concrete of the Romans, nor do they anticipate Hennebique's innovation. They were probably a premonition of a method that was made systematic and patented by W. H. Lascelles in 1875, of which more will be said below. Whatever their detail, they were highly

33 Gregynog Hall, Newtown, Powys, Wales, 1840s. Innovative concrete cladding, made to look rather startlingly traditional.

experimental – as were the workers' cottages here, which were built entirely in concrete. The panels cladding the main house were painted black and white, which are striking, but give an impression of an older and much less innovative building.

Another house that mixed technical innovation and stylistic conservatism a generation later was Richard Norman Shaw's Cragside (1869–85) for Lord Armstrong, who both built battleships and manufactured weapons in Newcastle upon Tyne, about 40 miles away. He illuminated the house with pre-Edison light bulbs, powered by an innovative hydroelectric scheme, making it the first house anywhere with electric light.[57] It was a domestic space, but also crucially a place where he could entertain business associates, often from overseas and of a rank in their government such that they could commission a battleship. They included the King of Siam, the Shah of Persia and the crown princes of Japan and Afghanistan. The house had a role as an unusually well-appointed hunting lodge, with facilities to entertain the hunting parties before and after the shoot. Stylistically, it is significantly more than an overgrown cottage. The building has suggestions of a castle in its positioning, its massing and in the crenellations above one tall bay window and again on its highest tower. But the battlements are hardly noticed because they are oversailed by roofs – on the tower by the black-and-white gable that is the house's most conspicuous identifier (illus. 34) – an arrangement that Shaw had already devised for Leys Wood (illus. 35). The rest of the detail is more suggestive of a manor house, but the setting is wrong for it as a manor house – there is no agricultural land in sight, just forest and a vast crowd of rhododendrons. Its style is English through and through, which no doubt played well with foreign visitors, but its setting seems to be taking it in the direction of Neuschwanstein (Ludwig II's ultra-romantic alp-top castle in Bavaria), rather than the idyll of old England and the village green.

Nevertheless, Armstrong and Shaw chose a Tudoresque style over the alternatives. In doing so, Armstrong elected to identify himself as bourgeois rather than aristocratic, the unembarrassed self-made

34 Richard Norman Shaw, Cragside, Rothbury, Northumberland, 1869–85. The first house anywhere with electric lighting, but with a traditional Picturesque appearance.

man, made distinguished by his achievements rather than his lineage. Given the company he was keeping, it would have been implausible to attempt anything else, and it would have been bad for his business if he had managed to pass himself off as a landed aristocrat. He was a magician with special powers. When twenty-first-century visitors see the electric dinner gong at work, they see a household appliance that seems unaccountably ahead of its time. When Armstrong's guests saw it, and when they telephoned one another in their rooms, they knew that they were in the home of someone who could do things that no one else on earth could do, and that he had made the astonishing house by using those special abilities in the commercial world. His clients were buying power in weaponry that would see off all known opposition: they needed to believe in his magic touch, that there was no one like him, and that they had to go to him if they were going to achieve their ends. It again connects back to the theme of the Tudoresque as an expression of self-reliance.

The theme of technical innovation was also to the fore in a book of designs for cottages by Shaw and Ernest Newton, published in 1878. The buildings were designed to be constructed using W. H. Lascelles's cement-slab construction. This system used a timber frame, with posts 3 feet apart, and iron-reinforced concrete panels 2 feet high by 3 feet wide and 1.5 inches thick (60 x 90 x 4 cm). The outer face of the panel was textured to look like tile hanging, and in 1878, when the system was launched to the wider public with Shaw and Newton's book, the timber was replaced by 'cement posts with iron in them'.[58] The designs used a Tudoresque old-English style, which seems to disguise the novelty that could have been on display.

In fact, there is a decent match between the constructional system and its expression: the frame that supports the concrete panels

35 Richard Norman Shaw, Leys Wood, Groombridge, Sussex, 1868. Battlements and half-timbered gables.

translates into the timbers that ornament some parts of the walls. There is, however, no doubt that the aim of the designs was to reassure, and they present the most traditional image of the cottage. The professional press thought this a failing. 'We should never wish to speak otherwise than respectfully of anything produced by Mr Norman Shaw', said *The Builder*,

> but we must confess that we fail to see the reason for thus imitating rustic buildings in a modern material, unless it be to believe that there is a charm in whatever is old-fashioned in building and something wrong about whatever is new. Our opinion is that here was a real chance for doing something new on the basis of a new material and method, which chance has been deliberately and almost perversely thrown away; for the very surfaces of the slabs are made in what is called by the builder a 'fish-scale pattern', to imitate the effect of wall tiling, and it is promised that the slabs may be stained with an indelible red stain with the same object.[59]

The Builder's sense that a new method of construction should generate a new style of architecture is associated with Eugène Viollet-le-Duc, whose discourses on architecture had been published in English in 1875, and who may in turn have been influenced by reading John Ruskin, who had made 'truth' one of his seven guiding principles of architecture.[60] Shaw's and Newton's designs are not by any means all rustic in character. They range in scale and complexity from very small cottages that compare with those proposed by Nathaniel Kent, so far as their facilities are concerned, labelled as being for workmen. Others, scarcely larger, have better facilities – a separate kitchen and living room, a housekeeper's bedroom associated with the kitchen, and water closets rather than the ash closets suggested for the smallest cottages (illus. 36). There are designs for small estate buildings, and then larger houses, a cottage hospital, and a final house that approaches the scale

36 Richard Norman Shaw, Middle-class Cottage Residences, plate from *Sketches for Cottages and Other Buildings* (1878). A design for a system-built concrete house, made palatable by the magic of Picturesque Tudor.

of the original Cragside – maybe half the size, but a substantial house for a rich client, and an unlikely use for such an untested building method – unlikely but not impossible, as the example of Gregynog makes clear.

Pioneers

The issue of craftsmanship, and making visible the means by which a building was constructed, became increasingly important in architectural circles as the nineteenth century progressed, and it came to seem that it would be the defining issue in the search for a new architecture that everyone seemed to be expecting. Such an architecture would be based not on historical allusions to old building styles, but on the inner logic of new materials. Some people thought that it had arrived with the Crystal Palace in 1851, but others – such as Ruskin – disagreed. The Arts and Crafts movement, which took its inspiration from Ruskin and his devotee William Morris, stressed the importance of the craftsman and craft skills, as opposed to the steam-powered machinery that was making the country rich. At first, it seemed to be steeped in medievalism, but in retrospect various architects of different stylistic persuasions have been grouped under this banner. One of the central ideas was 'individualism', as opposed to mechanical repetition, but another was 'collectivism', which Ruskin promoted using the idea of guilds.[61] Arts and Crafts architects gravitated towards vernacular traditions of building form, and allowed themselves plenty of stylistic freedom. In the 1890s there was a widespread idea of a 'Queen Anne' style, but her reign, 1702–14, was not long enough for a distinct architectural style to develop, and in fact the style is better characterized by its sophisticatedly relaxed compositions with clean lines and expanses of plain surfaces, and eclecticism.[62] Its decorative elements were limited in extent, and often floral – primroses, sunflowers, roses, lilies – with an element of geometric composition or stylization about them. There were often elements of the Tudoresque in the mix – a striped gable, a four-centred arch, linen-fold panelling. Tudorism was unproblematic for these architects, not a transgression.

Mackay Hugh Baillie Scott's work belongs securely in the Arts and Crafts tradition, and often drew on Tudoresque effects. Black-and-white work is pervasive in his designs, which were inventive and experimental in some ways while having a reassuring and traditional overall appearance. His house Blackwell, just south of Bowness on Lake Windermere, dates from 1898 and has the massing of a Tudor manor, with windows placed so as to be convenient for the rooms within, rather than following a rigid symmetrical arrangement, so the effect is gentle, considerate and slightly vernacular – taken further in that direction by the harling render. The runs of horizontally proportioned square-headed windows, divided by multiple stone mullions and transoms, are distinctly Tudoresque in character, while the house's most striking space is its central hallway, a large double-height living room, with overtones of a great hall, spectacular half-timbering and galleries running round two sides of the room at the higher level, from which small windows with leaded lights look down into the room.

Spatially, it has much in common with the double-height galleried living rooms of Le Corbusier's villas, 30 years later, but its dress is that of Joseph Nash's images of olden times, so it looks 100 years older (illus. 37).[63]

In fact, though, if we look at English architecture thirty years after Blackwell, it did not look at all behind the times. The great popular boom in black-and-white Tudor was just about to begin. In the *Ideal Home* in 1919 Henry Walker thought that 'the traditional houses of old England' were under threat:

> The oak timbered dwellings of our ancestors were coeval with the 'Wooden Walls of old England' and it is regrettable that they are fast disappearing in the devastating march of modern improvement. Many of these quaint magpies date back to the fourteenth century, at which

37 Mackay Hugh Baillie Scott, Blackwell, Bowness, Cumbria, completed 1900. Tudoresque work in an Arts and Crafts building, here evoking the idea of a great hall.

period the districts in which they stand were covered by extensive forests, the wood from which being the cheapest and handiest material available was utilised in the construction of the cottage and mansion. Nothing catches the eye of the traveller so readily as the beautifully chequered fronts of these old homesteads.[64]

Of course, black-and-white buildings from the fourteenth century were in short supply, and it was buildings from the Arts and Crafts tradition that had the greatest impact on normalizing the Tudoresque for British domestic buildings of the 1920s and '30s. A different influence was ascribed to them by Nikolaus Pevsner, whose *Pioneers of the Modern Movement* came out in 1936.[65] Its general aim was to show that 'the new style, the genuine and legitimate style of our century, was achieved by 1914'.[66] This 'genuine and legitimate' style was the Modern Movement. Pevsner presented the Arts and Crafts architects as 'pioneers' of modernism, which was not necessarily how they had seen themselves.

Charles Francis Annesley Voysey's work was included. He had specialized in domestic architecture for the middle classes and became fashionable. His most famous client was H. G. Wells, but Voysey's designs were not futuristic. They were marked by their good sense in the way of construction, and in their deliberate avoidance of decoration. They were carefully considered, so as to maximize the space and comfort available for a limited budget, and they drew on the forms of vernacular rather than elite architectures. His client-base dried up in 1914, but he lived, frugally, until 1941. His houses have something of the plainness of Gandy's cottage designs (illus. 38), but without their arresting gawkiness. Voysey's buildings look at ease with themselves and their settings, and do nothing to repudiate their 'traditional' overtones, but neither do they make specific historical references to earlier periods.[67]

In casting the Arts and Crafts architects as 'pioneers of the Modern Movement', Pevsner was suggesting that they shared the twentieth-century modernists' vision of what architecture should be like, but that in their day they could take things only so far. Voysey himself did not welcome this interpretation of his work, preferring to consider it a fully achieved realization of a different vision. He 'heartily disliked' Pevsner's modernism, and did not want to be seen as a pioneer of it.[68] For Pevsner, the crucial link from the Arts and Crafts to the Modern Movement was forged by Hermann Muthesius, whose study of the English house was published in German in 1904–5, commending to a receptive audience in Germany the practicality and objectivity (*Sachlichkeit*) of English domestic design. So, in Pevsner's account, the development of the twentieth century's 'genuine and legitimate style' began in England, but then after 1904 continued on the Continent.[69]

Pevsner's analysis has given Arts and Crafts architecture a place in the pedigree of modernism, and in the academic library, while the much more widespread influence on the British suburbs has somehow been seen as less than legitimate; but surely, given the overwhelming popular support for it, this should be the dominant narrative. Arts and Crafts houses began in an attempt to perpetuate craft skills, but houses produced in that way made them cost more than most people could afford, and while they remained an ideal to which to aspire, it was seen that by streamlining the process and lowering the specification, it was possible to produce something that looked broadly similar but was much more affordable. Corners were cut. The mass-market houses of the 1920s and '30s were inevitably less fine than were individually designed upper-middle-class pre-war houses, but the influence is genuine enough. The legacy of the Arts and Crafts movement is no less potent for having been vulgarized in the British suburbs as well as being refined on the Continent.

Even when people had money, their increased mobility during the 1920s meant that they did not necessarily want to spend it on the home. 'Few, even among the wealthier classes, desire great mansions,' said P. A. Barron in *The House Desirable* in 1929, 'for in these days of cars and world travel the range of our interests has widened. The home may be the centre of those interests but not the boundary.'[70] For the middle-class person, who had clothes made to measure ('I presume that you are not to be numbered among the people who buy their clothes ready made', Barron tells the reader),[71] the aspirations of the day were as much about mobility as possessions:

> The young wife who is not blessed, or cursed, with wealth does not pine for a double-fronted house larger than that of her neighbours. Her ideal may be described according to the taste and fancy of the describer, as: a cottage and a car, a bungalow and a Baby Austin, or a maisonette and a Morris minor. If she lives in the country she has no desire for three acres and a cow; she would prefer a quarter-acre and a Cowley.[72]

If the ideal arrangement is to build and still have enough money left to travel and see the world beyond the home, then it makes sense to choose the cottage rather than the stately pile as the model to emulate. Sir Banister Fletcher had said as much before the war, and of course it had always been true:

> In the general conception of a small house it seems desirable that one should think of realizing a large and roomy cottage rather than a cramped villa; that the limited sum available for such a building should be spent in floor space and elbow room rather than in lofty and necessarily smaller rooms.[73]

His presentation of 'Modern English Homes' included many Tudoresque examples, and many designed by the firm Banister Fletcher & Sons, which in his account seems to be the age's leading domestic architecture company. There are some designs from Baillie Scott, C.F.A. Voysey and Edwin Lutyens, who made lasting reputations, and some from others who did not.[74]

38 Joseph Gandy, design for a double cottage for agricultural labourers, plate from *Designs for Cottages*, 1805, reproduced in F.R.S. Yorke's *The Modern House* (1934). History can show us the way.

This outlook is markedly different from that of F.R.S. Yorke in *The Modern House* of 1934. One of the prominent images in the book's opening pages is of one of Joseph Gandy's designs, taking us back to 1805 and the point at which the old-English style was being invented (illus. 38). Gandy, it seemed to Yorke, had had an early premonition of twentieth-century modernism, but if Gandy was being prophetic, he was in a wilderness. His predictions had taken a long time to be heard, and meanwhile the country had been covered by buildings that seemed to have come from the pages of James Malton.

Yorke was born in Stratford-upon-Avon, which may have given him a particular aversion to imitations of Tudor. He presents an example of it as an exemplary horror: 'a small country house in Somerset', from *The Englishman's House* of 1871 (illus. 39).[75] This 'triumph of the picturesque' in all its 'splendid confusion' is the antithesis of all a modern house should be, and in the text and illustrations that follow, it quickly becomes clear that the modern house should follow the guidance offered by Le Corbusier in *Vers une architecture* – whose vision British architects have consistently found more compelling than has the British public.[76]

The lower-middle-class houses of the 1920s and '30s that made use of Tudoresque imagery did so in a much more level-headed way than the tortuous building illustrated by Yorke. They were sensibly

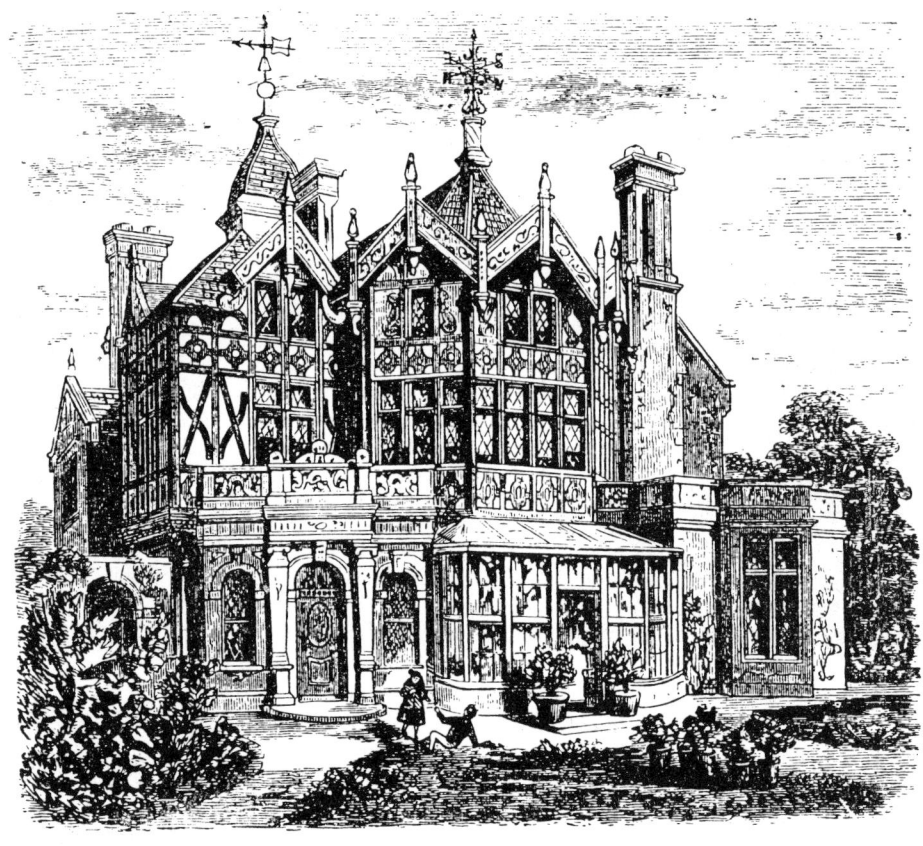

39 C. J. Richardson's 'small country house in Somerset', plate from *The Englishman's House* (1874), reproduced in F.R.S. Yorke's *The Modern House* (1934). What not to do, according to Yorke.

planned and their decoration was not elaborate, but it did seem to be necessary.⁷⁷ The markers of Tudoresque in a 1930s suburban building could be reduced to a few timber boards and some black and white paint. Some builders clearly enjoyed the visual effect of what they were producing (illus. 40), but others seem to have been aiming to produce the signification of Tudoresqueness at minimum cost (illus. 41). Once a pattern has been established, the more perfunctory additions can be dropped altogether without losing the general effect, but making everything seem a little meaner or under-dressed. The houses that are most prominent in illustration 42 have small

40 Douglas Smith and Barley, houses on the Hanger Hill Garden Estate, Ealing, London. Enthusiastically black and white.

41 Houses in Kingsbury, London. Working to a budget.

42 Houses in Fenham, Newcastle upon Tyne. Slow fade: the Tudoresque mood is established, but its signifiers are not repeated in every dwelling.

gables with applied timber that clearly designates them as Tudoresque. The other houses nearby, visible in the background, are identical, but without the gables. So the Tudoresque signification is 'understood' across the whole group. Sometimes there are streets that have no obvious Tudoresque detail, but because they are approached by way of a clearly Tudoresque street, they are seen as 'more of the same' and therefore subliminally register as Tudoresque. A suburb can settle into a Tudoresque 'mood', which seems pervasive and continuous, despite there being very few actual signifiers.

Tudoresque tokenism such as this has brought the style into disrepute among people in search of high-quality architecture; but it has not alienated the people of limited means whose higher priority is for a well-functioning home. These buildings were actually the *machines à habiter* that people between the wars could afford to buy and that met not only their utilitarian needs but also signalled their aspirations for independence and a settled place in the world.[78] In 1938 Osbert Lancaster remarked that sixteenth-century domestic buildings had little to recommend them, except that they were better than the medieval ones before them. At first, he went on, Tudor-style buildings were very expensive to produce, but 'so deep and so widespread was the post-war devotion to the olde-worlde that an enormous number of such houses were erected'. Then:

> the invention of new and cheaper methods of production brought it within the reach of the builders of Metroland. And today when the passer-by is a little unnerved at being suddenly confronted with a hundred and fifty accurate reproductions of Anne Hathaway's cottage, each complete with central-heating and garage, he should pause to reflect on the extraordinary fact that all over the country the latest and most scientific methods of mass-production are being utilized to turn out a stream of old oak beams, leaded window panes and small discs of bottle-glass, all structural devices which our ancestors lost no time in abandoning as soon as an increase in wealth and knowledge enabled them to do so.[79]

Anthony Bertram, also writing in 1938, argued that:

> Probably the popular love for the Tudor, whether genuine or bogus, is based on fear and a wish to escape. When I was broadcasting I had many letters that said quite frankly, 'the suggestion of those quiet old days gives us the restful atmosphere we seek in our homes.' This is self-deception, because of course the quiet old days were far from quiet, but it is not surprising. These are insecure and frightening times and I believe that economic depression and the fear of war are the chief promoters of the Tudoresque.[80]

Writing just after the Second World War, about the time just before it, J. M. Richards, who is best known as a propagandist for modernism, contributed a book on suburbia, *The Castles on the Ground* (1946), which is remarkable for its sympathy and understanding of the set of values involved. The illustrations were by John Piper who had illustrated Shell guides and then been a war artist, whose involvement with the project in itself suggests that the suburban dwellings he depicted were worthy of attention (illus. 43). Richards said:

43 John Piper, suburban street scene, plate from J. M. Richards's *The Castles on the Ground* (2nd edn, 1973).

> We well know the epithets used to revile the modern suburb – 'Jerrybethan', and the rest – and the scornful finger that gets pointed at spec-builder's Tudor with its half-inch boards nailed flat to the wall in imitation of oak timbering, though perhaps we should not criticize so fiercely the architectural idiom the suburb has adopted as its own if we understood the instincts and ideals it aims to satisfy, and how well, judged by its own standards, it often succeeds in doing so.[81]
>
> Nothing is to be gained, the instinct of the suburban resident tells him, by condemning the make-believe of spec-builder's Tudor when the thing that is most valued is its cosiness and familiarity, which makes it a secure anchorage in a changeable world.[82]

This image of the anchor is apt. With the advent of modernity in the sixteenth century there came an awareness of change, which intensified as the rate of change continued to accelerate. What began as a sense that there was progress threatened to engulf us as we became postmodern and entered the space of flows.[83] There is not an abrupt shift from one era to another, but a continuity of gradual acceleration, and the sense that the Tudoresque offers is not now explicitly the sense of an escape back to a golden age of Tudor monarchs, but something more like clinging to the wreckage of something we thought we once knew. There have been huge ruptures that have shaken the whole of society, with the two World Wars and who knows what else. There have been personal crises that leave us disorientated for a while, in search of bearings. The old certainties of empire and religion have

44 The Anchor Inn, Hutton, Lancashire. Clinging to the wreckage.

all gone, and in a multicultural society one is always aware that perspectives will shift and dislocate; an idea that seems innocuous to one generation seems poisonous to the next; and to hope for certainty anywhere at all seems to be a forlorn nostalgia. It is in this kind of world, where we are all at sea, that we reach out for an anchor; and however imperfect its styling, that is what the Tudoresque has to offer.

Chapter Six

Britannia *'Outre-mer'*

Travel

The surest way to develop a sense of national identity is to travel. Overseas, things are done differently, without the people feeling the need to explain why. They eat different food, speak different languages and build differently. Every interaction with a tradesman or a fellow passenger brings with it a reminder that one is not at home. The grander eighteenth-century tourists who travelled with a retinue of servants would have been sheltered from some of the inconvenience involved, because their servants set things up on their behalf. Travel was not to be undertaken lightly in the days before engines, telecommunications and cash machines, and a journey from Britain to Italy would take weeks. The educational 'Grand Tour', which savoured the culture of the places visited, would last a year or more, and the people who went on it came back changed. Normally they would not repeat the experience, but would carry a memory of the Italian countryside and the ruins of Rome with them as a nostalgia, waiting to be awakened by evocative buildings, landscapes and cultural tokens.

The most-often-aristocratic Grand Tourists inspired in their less-travelled friends and acquaintances an envy that turned to defiance. They sought out equivalent interests closer to home. These autochthonous interests could be portrayed as more patriotic and legitimate, even in the face of the clear ascendancy of Latin and Greek in schools and the continuing sense of superior cultural value that their adepts could and did claim.[1] The ancient languages were the core curriculum of schools long before science was taught in them. The well-educated British Grand Tourist could find himself, in some foreign parts, strangely at home: Joseph Addison's *Letter from Italy* of 1701 expresses a sense not so much of discovery but of recognition in a landscape that he already knew from reading classics:

> Me into foreign realms my fate conveys,
> Through nations fruitful of immortal lays,
> Where the soft season and inviting clime
> Conspire to trouble your repose with rhyme.
>
> For wheresoe'er I turn my ravish'd eyes,
> Gay gilded scenes and shining prospects rise,
> Poetic fields encompass me around,
> And still I seem to tread on classic ground;
> For here the Muse so oft her harp has strung
> That not a mountain rears its head unsung,
> Renown'd in verse each shady thicket grows,
> And ev'ry stream in heavenly numbers flows.[2]

'Numbers' here are 'verses' – everything is steeped in poetry. Back in Britain as the eighteenth century progressed there was a developing nationalist sense that there should be equal merit in British scenes. Landscapes were developed on the great estates with views and monuments that supplied the classical allusions that had previously been lacking – a statue of a classical figure, an evocative ruin or a vista evoking the tree-clad Tuscan hills – things that reminded the man who had travelled of his youth and his adventures in Italy.

The more sophisticated versions of this practice developed in the later eighteenth century to the point where the allusions were understood even without the apparatus of statuary and monuments, but could work by means of more or less natural scenery, using only indigenous plants.³ The Wye Valley and then the Lake District became places to visit for the sake of their natural scenery, and were seen in their different ways as 'Arcadian' – which originally referred to a region of Greece, in the central Peloponnese.⁴ Indigenous culture was elevated by being associated with ideal places overseas.

It may be coincidental, or there may be a relation of cause and effect, but as the British sense of power and self-importance grew with the development of the British Empire, the sense took hold that British antiquities must be as worthy of interest as those of foreign parts, and there was a concern to retrieve an indigenous British culture. Stukeley's inventive 'reconstruction' of the Druids was the most colourful example.⁵ It had limited application for daily life, but had a lasting impact on taste. In the 1830s, when John Claudius Loudon was travelling round Britain, he encountered an imitation of Stonehenge – which was then thought to be Druidic – at Alton Towers, along with Grecian and Gothic temples, and a pagoda. He found it remarkable that so many ruins and Druidical temples had been set up in the gardens of wealthy gentlemen.⁶

Where Druids were concerned there was always a play between the fantastical and the factual. The ruins of Stonehenge are real enough, but no one really knows what to make of them. The Druids were real also, but nothing much is known about them. Obviously, in the popular imagination Stonehenge and the Druids belong together, as surely as Robin Hood and Queen Elizabeth I, and so-called Druidic rites are still celebrated at Stonehenge, even now that we should know better.⁷ Ancient sites, such as Stonehenge and Glastonbury, have become strongly associated with mysticism. The induction of trance-like states with amplified music and large gatherings seems to have become the way of celebrating a feeling of primitive connection to the ancient earth.

For a time Gothic architecture was seen as indigenous, and it therefore found patriotic favour in the eighteenth and earlier nineteenth centuries, but as scholarly knowledge increased and the style's Continental roots became clearer, it became less effective in that role.

It still had its uses, particularly in signifying piety, but the varieties of 'old-English' style that had been developed at the end of the eighteenth century turned into the clearest way of signalling British identity. The search for an authentically English building style sought to improve on James Malton's intuitions in *British Cottage Architecture*. The demand was clear enough.

In 1825 Thomas Hunt published *Half a Dozen Hints, on Domestic Picturesque Architecture*, nine images of old-English domestic-style buildings 'indigenous to this soil'. He said that this style has 'been preferred to every other, admitting of greater variety of form and outline, and as being better suited to the scenery of this country, than the Greek Temple or the Italian Villa'.[8] The designs are recognizably Tudoresque (half-timbering, huge chimneys), but are self-consciously quaint in character, and highly wrought, making them very expensive buildings for their size, and providing modest facilities for dwelling (illus. 45). He followed this in 1830 with *Exemplars of Tudor Architecture, Adapted to Modern Habitations*, in which he presented designs drawing on what he called 'the beautiful, though long-neglected Architecture of my own country', to show that 'English Architecture is still the most applicable for English habitations'.[9] He explained why his designs look overwrought. He object was, he said,

> not to exhibit specimens of hovels and cheap structures, but to combine in one edifice as many Architectural features as can with propriety be blended: thus affording hints of what may be separated and used as occasion shall require. It may also be necessary to observe that when I had recommended this particular style of Architecture as an economical style, I have only wished to be understood that it is so as compared with the buildings of ancient Greece or Rome, and not with the monotonous and unadorned dwellings of our London streets, in which, unhappily, too few traces of art are visible. Would that the legislature could control the practices of modern builders, since Taste has

lost her 'empire!' – but that must always be a vain hope in a commercial and free country like this, seeing, as a modern traveller has shewn, that, even in Turkey, where grievances are more summarily corrected, such attempts are fruitless.[10]

So modern builders had been making two kinds of mistakes. One was to neglect art altogether, producing monotonous utilitarian buildings; the other was to copy non-indigenous precedents, importing ideas from ancient Greece and Rome, and being wasteful in the process, as well as unpatriotic. Repton's work for the Duke of Bedford at Endsleigh should be seen against this background.[11] It had been undertaken earlier, but it was guided by the same cultural predispositions, and perhaps the nationalist sentiment was felt more urgently while the Napoleonic threat still loomed.

Endsleigh was eventually designed by Wyatville, but Repton working with his son (John Adey Repton) had made designs for Endsleigh in 'Queen Elizabeth's Gothic', and for a carefully researched cottage at Aspley Wood, when 'his Grace expressed a desire to have a Cottage of the style and date of buildings prior to the reign of Henry VIII'.[12] The

45 Thomas Frederick Hunt, design for a gamekeeper's cottage, a plate from *Half a Dozen Hints on Picturesque Domestic Architecture* (1825). Avowedly a deliberately overdone confection, full of motifs intended for a more sparing use.

46 Humphry Repton, design for a cottage at Aspley Wood, plate from *Fragments on the Theory and Practice of Landscape Gardening* (1816). A design with carefully researched detail.

archaeological work was painstaking and the resultant design more ornate than would have been possible for an ordinary cottager of any era (illus. 46). The intricately carved barge-boards evident here would become a staple of the nineteenth-century builder's repertoire, and can be found in the larger houses of many Victorian suburbs. Their signification was Tudoresque, referring to the intricate Flemish-inspired carving to be found on well-appointed timber buildings of the sixteenth century; the touches of Gothic tracery suggest the earlier part of the century. The design was published, and its antiquarian aspect highlighted, so its appeal was not simply as an attractive picturesque design, but as an authoritative example of the national architecture, carrying a sense of obligation with its charm.[13] Part of its appeal was in its indigenous patriotic character.

Hunt, in his *Exemplars of Tudor Architecture*, similarly supported his designs by presenting himself as a scholarly authority on Tudor buildings, documenting his observations with many footnotes;[14] and even P. F. Robinson can be found using this technique of persuasion, basing one of his designs on East Barsham Hall in Norfolk, with its 'Enriched chimney-shafts which prevailed during the reigns of Henry the Eighth

47 P. F. Robinson, Design no 3, in *Designs for Lodges and Park Entrances* (1833). A designed supercharged with Tudoresque detail, owing much to Repton and Hunt.

and Elizabeth' and 'ornamental gable boards', which could be carved in oak or chestnut.[15] He regretted the disappearance of old buildings in timber and plaster,[16] but nothing quite prepares one for the confection that Robinson proposes as the result of all this nostalgia (illus. 47).

John Claudius Loudon compiled an authoritative compendium of architectural knowledge in his *Encyclopaedia of Cottage, Farm and Villa Architecture*, published in the 1830s, saying:

> Half-Timbered cottages are very picturesque objects, and seem particularly appropriate to a woody country . . . As Ornamental objects in parks they are very desirable, both on account of their beauty and their historical interest; carrying back as they do, the mind to the time when not only all the better kind of cottages in the central districts of England were built in this manner, but as Holinshed informs us, most of the houses of the landed proprietors. A cottage built in the half-timbered style, in those parts of England where stone is the building material, or in Scotland where this is also the case, is not appropriate to the scenery

of the country; but it has a strikingly ornamental effect in another point of view, that is, from its rarity and its contrast with the local cottages.[17]

The presentation of the knowledge in this *Enyclopaedia*, with its mass circulation and dictionary-like authority, marks the codification of the accepted version of the Tudor cottage as a national style. The need to signal a building's British identity has seemed more pressing at some times than at others. It is perhaps to be expected when the country is at war with a foreign power, and foreigners seem dangerous: the indigenous population is wary of visitors at such times, and assertive of British ways. It is also very evident when the British build overseas, for example in the international exhibitions that followed in the wake of the Great Exhibition of 1851. The British pavilions in Paris and Chicago adopted vigorous black-and-white Tudorism in 1878 and 1893 respectively (illus. 48 and 49); and in Paris in 1900 copied a Jacobean building (illus. 50).[18] The building of 1900 was designed by Lutyens, and was built with a steel frame supporting moulded concrete panels that reproduced the appearance of The Hall at Bradford-on-Avon, Wiltshire – continuing the alliance of conservative taste and innovative technology that is clearly part of the Tudoresque ethos.

Even in 1937, at the Cité Universitaire, the Collège Franco-Britannique had some Tudoresque detail, but was modernized by its horizontally proportioned windows (illus. 51). This is a very different case, however, because the architects of the building were French (Pierre Martin and Maurice Vieu), and they were trying to evoke the atmosphere of an Oxford college, which might go unrecognized.

The type of the college building, though, is an important and specialized example of Tudoresque influence, since the prestige and primacy of Oxford and Cambridge are recognized around the world, and there have been many attempts to make imitations in educational institutions, especially in the USA. The treatment of buildings at Harvard, Yale, Princeton and many other places evokes a link to academic tradition by using courtyards, arches, Tudor-style windows and masonry.

48 British pavilions at the Exposition Universelle, Paris, 1878. Promoting British style to the world in Europe.

49 British Government building, distant view, at the Chicago World's Fair, 1893. Promoting British style to the world in America.

50 Sir Edwin Lutyens, British pavilion, Exposition Universelle, Paris, 1900. Technical innovation, British style: a reinforced concrete reproduction of a Jacobean building for Parisian visitors and exotic foreigners, including a Scotsman.

New buildings at Whitman College, Princeton (2002–7), by Porphyrios Associates, continue in this vein, reflecting not only the Princeton tradition, but also the practice's earlier work at Magdalen College, Oxford (1994–8), and Selwyn College, Cambridge (2003–5).

The Collège Franco-Britannique was convincingly up to date when it was built, and its use of Tudoresque motifs, which were

51 Pierre Martin and Maurice Vieu, College Franco-Britannique, Cité Universitaire, 1937. Connecting with the tradition of the Tudor colleges in Oxford and Cambridge.

absolutely characteristic of its day, were readily understood to signify the building's part-British provenance. It was built after, and close to, the subsequently much more celebrated Pavillon Suisse by Le Corbusier (1931–3). Le Corbusier's design, rigorously thought through and highly innovative, came to look 'normal' three decades later, so in retrospect it looks prophetic, while the Collège Franco-Britannique's building looks as if it missed the point. When it was built, though, the future was not clear, and it looked like a sensibly up-to-date building.

At more recent international exhibitions and world fairs the Tudoresque has been avoided in favour of attempts to be eye-catchingly modern, rather than identifiably nationalistic. The aim is to represent the nation as a place for business, which is looking to the future, and this sits at odds with the Tudorism that in fact continues to be the way to signal the national identity overseas. When the equivalent thing happens in the East, or even in North Africa, it is called 'orientalism' – the former colonies of the north European empires being represented as exotic and picturesque, which is beguiling in itself, but leaves a lingering impression of them as places where serious progress cannot be made – and the consequence is that they may be taken less seriously than they should be as players on the international stage. This is therefore a charm that should be resisted, or at least to be indulged with caution.[19] This is the danger that faces the United Kingdom, which still wants to present itself as a nation with a future, capable of technological innovation and a prosperous future. However, that is not necessarily the role that the rest of the world has in mind for it. For example, in Walt Disney's Experimental Prototype Community of Tomorrow (EPCOT) near Orlando, Florida, various parts of the world are represented, including England, which is represented predominantly by Tudoresque buildings (along with Peter Pan and Mary Poppins) and has absolutely no modernism in sight at all.[20]

British architects spent significant effort in establishing the character of old-English Tudoresque, and succeeded in identifying it as a national style, so it would be illogical to complain if people overseas listened, and when they want to signify that a building has a British character, to adopt a Tudoresque style. Nevertheless, although the British public has continued to feel comfortable with occupying Tudoresque dwellings from the 1930s and before, and commissioning new Tudoresque designs, or buying them newly built from commercial house builders, the British state has been uncomfortable with the country being represented as old-fashioned in any international context. Since the 1930s Tudorism has fallen out of favour in official commissions for identifiably British buildings overseas, in favour of various representations of modernity, some more convincing than others. The British pavilions by Nicholas Grimshaw at Seville (1992) and Thomas Heatherwick at Beijing (2010) were particularly eye-catching.

While the official state culture promotes the idea of Britain as a place to do business, popular culture has a different agenda and different priorities. British dwellings for individuals have often used the Tudoresque, wherever the dwellings happen to be. They are to be found around the world wherever there have been British settlers, whether the settlements have been a matter of individual emigration or of state-supported colonization.

In these instances the decisions about building style are taken without officialdom being involved, and the design may not be skilful, but the gestural links back to old England are well understood. 'Elite' versions are more artistically accomplished, but carry the same sentimental charge. Their number is vast, and again, as in the UK, it would be impossible to catalogue them. So many of the individual examples are mediocre that it would soon become a dispiriting task. Therefore, in what follows various examples of different uses of the Tudoresque are presented, in order to show the range and adaptability of the styles.

Exclusions

The taste-directing elites may now have doubts about whether Tudor-style buildings adequately represent Britain on the global stage, but the British people recognize especially black-and-white Tudor as familiar. In fact, it is generally recognized around the world as British, and used to signify as much. There can be confusions, however, since timber-framed domestic architecture was to be found right across Europe both during and after the Middle Ages. The basic discipline of erecting a heavy timber frame and then infilling the walls as non-structural panels is much the same wherever it is used. There are local traditions that vary the proportions, the way the joints are made and the frequency of the diagonal bracing members, but the general effect is much the same. Reported sightings of Tudoresque buildings in forested regions of France, Switzerland, Germany, Hungary and Austria invariably turn out to derive from local traditions that owe nothing to the Tudors. The thing that they have in common is that they are, if they date back no further than the eighteenth century, vernacular-revival styles, connected with some sense of regional or national identity, and they have sometimes been developed for use with larger buildings than the vernacular cottages in which they originated.

Of all these styles the closest to the black-and-white Tudoresque is the Black Forest cottage style, which is to be found not only in Germany but also in the USA, where it is associated with the folk stories collected by Wilhelm and Jacob Grimm. The buildings that show this influence most clearly have a quaint and fantastical character, with deliberately crooked roofs and twisted chimneys. They have an air of theatrical contrivance about them, which is not there in the originals back in the Black Forest, where the constructional logic wins through.[21]

These buildings are not Tudoresque, because they make no reference to the buildings of Tudor England and have a different set of associations for an observer. They may look very much the same, however, and there can be some ambiguity. It is possible for a single building to have more than one architecture:[22] it can be understood in different ways, and for one observer it might connote British tradition, for another the Grimm folk tales. There are examples of Tudorism that are just as theatrical in character as the 'storybook-style' houses. Rather than just adopting an old-fashioned style, the designer has gone out of the way to make the building appear not only older than it is, but also in a worse state of repair, with crooked floors and a sagging roof line. These buildings have to be classed as eccentricities, belonging with the little houses that have drawbridges and battlements, or gardens populated by a disturbing number of gnomes. They are 'folk' versions of buildings that express impulses that would immediately be taken seriously if they were realized with more professional skill and more substantial budgets. But orthodox householders of any stripe want their buildings to be sound and in a good state of repair, and to go about things so as to give a different impression must be seen as an affectation.

There is a suburb of New York City – fifteen minutes from Manhattan by train – called Forest Hills Gardens, in Queens. Many of

Britannia 'Outre-mer'

the houses there are black and white, making unequivocal allusion to British suburban architecture. The architectural set piece that greets visitors-by-rail on their arrival stylistically might seem at first sight equally reminiscent of German work, on account of its roof forms (illus. 52).[23] In this case, however, it is clear that the important precedent is Arthur Penty's work at Hampstead Garden Suburb, where he was working for Parker and Unwin in 1908.[24] This was illustrated in Raymond Unwin's books *Town Planning in Practice* and *Town Planning and Modern Architecture at the Hampstead Garden Suburb*, both published in 1909 (illus. 26).[25]

Forest Hills Gardens was promoted as the first 'Garden City' in America, master-planned by Frederick Law Olmsted Jr, whose name is familiar because it is the same as his father's, and he in turn is best known for laying out Central Park. Olmsted Jr's reputation is now almost entirely, but not deservedly, eclipsed by his father's, but the Forest Hills development attracted a great deal of attention because it was an experimental idea. Olmsted's architect was Grosvenor Atterbury, and their client was the Russell Sage Foundation, set up by

52 Grosvenor Attenbury and Frederick Law Olmsted, Station Square, Forest Hills Gardens, Queens, New York City, 1911. Architecture for social reform in America (see illus. 26).

Sage's widow, Olivia, whose benefactions were self-effacing but equalled those of the Rockefellers and Carnegie.[26] The aim at Forest Hills was to set up a community that would run on the lines of Bournville or Port Sunlight, which were seen as 'small floral paradises' for factory workers.[27] There were doubts about whether so co-operative an endeavour could work in America, but the experiment was designed to show how it could be done. The charity underwrote the development costs, and then ran the development so as to produce an income for the charity, improving living conditions by building, and then using the income for other good works, such as the alleviation of tuberculosis. Some house plots were sold off individually, so the dwellings do not have an institutional taste coordinating them.

The most innovative architectural composition, around the arrivals square by the railway station, included such facilities as shops and a 150-room, nine-storey hotel – the tallest building in the development. The various groups of buildings around Station Square were designed with a concrete structural frame that follows the pattern of the old timber frames in traditional vernacular construction. Instead of being painted black and white here, which would have made its Tudor character emphatic, the grey of the concrete contrasts gently with the over-burnt terracotta infill. The construction was innovative, but the appearance traditional. On the social plane radical innovation was similarly tempered by the conservative aesthetic, with traditional picturesque compositions, lawns and public parks. It enabled the production of a public realm far better than that in the surrounding area, where market forces drove the development.

The Tudoresque can make real radicalism possible, by making it palatable to the paying public. It can give a reassuringly traditional appearance to new ways of doing things, and new ways of living. A more startling architectural style might have *looked* more radical, but could have undermined the take-up of the scheme, which would have prevented it from having the good influence that it did have: it was because it did *not* look too daring that it was able to attract the urban workers' hard-earned savings.

Swanky houses

The Tudoresque is particularly well represented among the revivalist styles employed in one-off houses for the fabulously rich in the USA. There are many examples, and houses in this category are of fine quality, so it is tempting to dwell on them, but in truth they all do much the same thing: the old-fashioned house gives an air of settled decorum and aristocratic entitlement, even though the money that paid for it was newly made.

In the west there is the Doheny mansion, Greystones, in Beverly Hills (illus 53): built between 1925 and 1928 with money from Edward Doheny's oilfields, and designed by Gordon Kaufmann (who would give the Hoover Dam its Art Deco styling). It was intended for Doheny's son (Edward Jr, or Ned), who lived there for only six months before being murdered by his secretary.[28] Nevertheless, the house looks sober and distinguished, a fine stately building that has an air of permanence partly because of its style, partly because of its masonry construction – an extravagance in this part of the world. For comparison, the Hollyhock House, which Frank Lloyd Wright designed for Aline Barnsdall, is not far away, and was also built with oil money. It is much better known to architects, though the Doheny house has been used in so many films that it has surely been seen (but not recognized) by more people. Wright's design is earlier, dating from 1921, and is less traditional and more vulnerable to decay.

The Lovell Health House, by Richard Neutra, and also in Hollywood, dates from 1928. It established a pattern of steel-framed house with whole walls of glass, which seems in the rest of the world to set the style for twentieth-century life in Los Angeles. In the Hollywood hills, however, there were far more 1920s mansions that made use of Tudoresque styles, sometimes grandiloquently, sometimes in overgrown cottages that started to sprawl. They do not all survive – the building plots are prone to redevelopment – but, for example, Fatty Arbuckle, Theda Bara, Marion Davies, Bette Davis, Carole Lombard, Robert Montgomery, Eleanor Powell, James Stewart, King Vidor and Lois

53 Gordon Kaufmann, Greystones, Beverly Hills, California, 1925–8. Stately West-coast glamour.

Wilson all chose to live in Tudoresque homes, while Charlie Chaplin's studios recall his British roots in their architecture. Some of his studios' buildings are still standing, even though in its current incarnation Kermit the Frog has taken over as the studios' main star (illus. 54). Their roadside location makes them accessible in a way that the houses are not. The houses are sequestered behind banks of trees, and their gateways offer little to uninvited visitors beyond the promise of an armed response.

In California, the territory's Hispanic past has had a more powerful influence on the architecture, and the Tudoresque is not the most frequently found style, but it is nevertheless a presence, no doubt selected initially by people who have chosen to identify with their British past. Chaplin rented a house (6147 Temple Drive) that was in a decent low-key Tudor style, but then commissioned a house in a style that he described as 'California Gothic' (1085 Summit

Drive). Marion Davies left her Tudoresque cottage-style home in the hills for a palatial beach house, bankrolled by William Randolph Hearst and designed by Julia Morgan (his architect at San Simeon). Buildings are caught up in people's projects of self-invention and reinvention. The contrast between Marion Davies's two houses makes the little cottage-style house look sweet and innocent, while the society hostess who put on such a show at the beach house looks like a fallen woman.

On the east coast there are innumerable grandiose houses with a Tudoresque character, especially on Long Island and in upstate New York — Tuxedo Park, for example. Images of the Sassafras estate on Long Island have circulated since it was rented to film stars in 2009, and it well represents the type. It dates from 1987, and evokes the 1920s as much as the sixteenth century, but with up-to-date technology.

54 Mendel Meyer and Gabriel Holler, Jim Henson Studios, formerly Charlie Chaplin Studios, Hollywood, California, 1917. Chaplin recalling England. Kermit recalling Chaplin.

The most complete, sustained and developed example of the Tudoresque ideal in America is Stan Hywet Hall, in Akron, Ohio. It dates from 1913 and was built for Frank Seiberling, founder of the Goodyear Tire and Rubber Company. Seiberling's pattern of behaviour was exactly the same as that of the philanthropic industrialists mentioned in chapter Three. He treated the Goodyear workers well, and gave generous support to local charities. The house's name was supposed to mean 'hewn stone' in old English, and over its door there is a Latin motto, *non nobis solum* (not for us alone), which signals the anticipated hospitality that would be on offer here, putting the proprietor in a lordly relation to his guests. Subsidiary buildings are in a half-timbered 'cottage' mode, but the main house is in brick and stone, with elaborately carved timber.

The architect was Charles Sumner Schneider, an employee of George B. Post's firm, and the care that went into the design was remarkable. Seiberling had already decided that he wanted a Tudoresque design before he chose his architect, and in 1912 Schneider travelled round the UK with the Seiberlings in order to make detailed studies of old manor houses. It was Mrs Seiberling and her daughter who spent more time with the architect, since Mr Seiberling had other business to attend to. She was an accomplished musician, who had sung for President Taft at the White House, and Stan Hywet's quality no doubt owes much to her influence, as well as to her husband's generosity. They were guided in England by Sir Walter Tyndale, a well-known illustrator, who had published pictures of Sussex and Wessex manor houses, and he took them to Ockwells Manor in Berkshire, Compton Wynyates in Warwickshire and Haddon Hall in Derbyshire, which were particularly important in working up the design.[29] Ockwells, which Nikolaus Pevsner described as 'the most refined and the most sophisticated timber-framed mansion in England',[30] also surrendered a harpsichord for Stan Hywet's music room, after Mrs Seiberling had charmed its owners with a rapt performance of a Handel aria.[31]

The aim was to live like an old-English aristocrat, and the house's detail supports the evocation of the grand manner of the olden days,

Britannia 'Outre-mer'

55 Pargetted panels above a shop window in Bronxville, Westchester County, New York. Fine Tudoresque detail in a high-quality environment.

with large fireplaces, exposed timbers, much timber panelling (some of it salvaged from England) and a mixture of antique and traditional furniture.[32] The pattern for this behaviour was well established in England, but it is unexpected to find a native of Ohio adopting an old-English model and realizing it so well in so many of its aspects. The quality of the architectural detail here, for example, is finer than Lord Armstrong allowed at Cragside. What the Tudor style permitted was a setting that could be grand without being too pretentious, welcoming rather than aloof. The Seiberlings were able to act out to perfection the role that Fielding ascribed to Squire Allworthy, the Tudoresque giving architectural support of style, authority and good character to a self-made millionaire who was not short of personal charm and goodwill.

Seiberling would surely have entered the peerage if had done what he did as a British citizen, but for people with less wealth at their disposal a baronial home was out of the question, and the half-timbered cottage was a more feasible model. There are so many of them that selecting an individual example seems arbitrary, but there is a particularly pleasant enclave at Bronxville, Westchester County, which has been within commuting distance of Manhattan since the railway arrived there in 1844.[33]

Bronxville is not exactly an ordinary community, but it manages very successfully to be what many other places aspire to be. It was already well established by 1915, when it was described as 'the most desired residential village near New York City'.[34] It grew rapidly and consolidated its character during the 1920s: a property advertisement placed in *House and Garden* in 1925 said that 'to be able to call Bronxville one's home is to have one's social status definitely and pleasantly established'.[35] *Desperate Housewives* has taught us to look with some irony at this kind of environment, since the maintenance of social standing in a good neighbourhood can entail certain sleights of hand and low cunning in order to keep up a perfect appearance. But there is no doubt about it: the appearance here *is* perfect. It matters as a place not just because it is a good place to live, but because it is the kind of place that so many people would like to live.

The houses here are not unified in style, but Tudorism predominates. The tone is set by the shops in the high street, which have pargetted panels with fine low-relief decoration (illus. 55). The quality of the public realm is high, with sweeping lawns and many mature trees giving a settled ambiance as well as dappled shade in the central residential streets. The buildings also aim to look settled, and the Tudoresque buildings, from various decades from the 1890s to the 1930s and later, embody that aim. There is a prominent church and a prominent Tudoresque high school, and doubtless there are problems, but they do not find expression here, where all seems to be serene and well balanced. There is a story that during the Great Depression, when many of the residents had financial difficulties, the village rallied round and made a supportive network that meant that people did not have to move away.[36] The downside of such a tight-knit community is that outsiders are excluded, but for those who find

56 Tudor Village, Queens, New York. Modest dwellings aspiring to the settled tranquillity of Bronxville.

their way in, the idyll of the American suburban village remains surprisingly intact here.

Aspirations

For the rest, which is to say for nearly everyone else, there is more modest accommodation. Tudor Village in Queens poignantly announces its aspiration in its name: it would love to be Bronxville, but there is not enough money for that, not here. This is entry level for the American dream. Corners have been cut, but crucial signifiers are in place (illus. 56). The houses are smaller, packed closer together, and the planting is less park-like. There is a token patch of lawn and a garden path, a brick facade, leaded lights in the windows, and rough stucco evocative of pargetting over the ground-floor windows. The roof is flat, except for a small mansard at the front, which makes it possible to introduce a miniature gable over the upstairs window. There is no applied half-timbering, and the Tudor signification might be doubted were it not for the settlement's name, and the advertisements that were produced to sell the houses from 1926 onwards when they were new. Most Tudoresque houses around the world were built by or for people who had a background in Britain, if not in their childhood then in an earlier generation of their family. The architect here, David J. Levinson, was originally from Lithuania.[37]

Tudor Village is particularly interesting because its houses were sold to people from a more varied range of backgrounds, but to begin with they were predominantly of English, German and Irish descent.[38] There was an influx of Italian immigrants in the 1950s.[39] The village, if it is a village, is a short commute from Manhattan, and close to the sea, near Ozone Park and Jamaica Bay, and although it seems modest after Bronxville, for most of the people who settled there it was a move up in the world. The Tudorism here is to be recognized as a signifier of elite status. It is elite status on a budget, and therefore not as elite as it is possible to be, but it was necessary to have secure employment in order to settle here, and during the 1930s jobs disappeared, property prices fell and mortgages became difficult to pay. It was possible for the dream to fade. The houses were built on sandy soil that was formerly farmland, tailing off into salt marshes along the coast. The neighbourhood's sense of stability and permanence is helped along by the Tudor associations, which here surely suggest some kind of kinship with settlements like Bronxville rather than with anything more antique and remote. The signification may seem sketchy, but it was enough to work its magic and raise the residents' self-esteem.

Apartments

The sketchiness could be taken much further. Originally, the timbers of a Tudor cottage would have been structural, but in nearly all the revived Tudoresque work the timbers are no more than boards fixed to

57 Sherwood Terrace, Yonkers, New York. Robin Hood's forest is evoked in the name, a castle in the massing, and domesticity in the black-and-white gables.

the surface of a structural wall. Some buildings in Queens, instead of applying actual timbers, merely signify them with a line of brick in a contrasting colour, suggesting the line where a timber could have been. The effect looks mean, but boards need painting, and the line of bricks is maintenance-free. The important thing to notice here is that somebody thought the gesture worth making: the effect of the lines of brickwork was, in somebody's eyes, an enhancement of the bare block that was worth the trouble of the work it entailed. In this case the association seems to be with a development such as Sherwood Terrace (in Yonkers, New York). It is a group of apartment blocks, whose massing on a slope overlooking the admittedly low-key Bronx River gives it the presence of a medieval fortification (illus. 57). The brickwork is modelled into castellated turrets at some corners, and relieved by applied half-timbering here and there. There are 'Tudor' arches over the entrance doors and the general effect is like an inflated version of Stokesay Castle in Shropshire, where late medieval half-timbered apartments project from a fortified structure with a great hall. The name also references Sherwood Forest where Robin Hood lived with his Merry Men, and old England is firmly evoked – supported by popular entertainment, Douglas Fairbanks having played the role of Robin Hood in 1922. The building's associations for its first owners remain unclear, but as it is approached from Mount Vernon West station it has a prominence and presence that would have made it appealing, and its treatment has given the cue for other smaller-scale Tudoresque developments in the area, including some just across the road.⁴⁰

This type of apartment block takes its cue from Hudson View Gardens, on Manhattan, built on high ground overlooking the Hudson River – a majestic expanse of water, with cliffs on the opposite bank, though the view of it has been compromised by later development. The whole area was developed by Dr Charles V. Paterno, who gave up

59 Tudoresque building on Fifth Avenue in Midtown Manhattan, New York. A survivor overshadowed by newer developments.

58 George F. Pelham, Hudson View Gardens, Manhattan, New York. Battlements and gables in a smart apartment building.

196

Britannia 'Outre-mer'

medicine for property, and made a fortune. He built an extravagant house on the waterfront here, in 1906, Paterno Castle, which looked like a toy fortress. In 1923 he joined forces with another important developer, Frederick F. French, and employed George F. Pelham, already a prolific designer of Manhattan apartments, to produce a housing co-operative, Hudson View Gardens (illus. 58).[41] There are approximately 350 apartments here, so it is a significant development, and has many of the qualities of a village. The name suggests a suburb, and the open square in front of the building, together with the expansive views, made it a respectable but affordable alternative to a commute.

The choice of architectural style seems also to suggest an out-of-town location, and might on those grounds have seemed appropriate to the site at the time, but the Tudoresque was pervasive in a way that we tend to forget now that so many of the buildings of that era have been demolished for redevelopment. One survives on Fifth Avenue in Midtown Manhattan (illus. 59) and there is the perennially chic Pomander Walk, which dates from 1921 – a miniature street of tiny houses based on the stage set of a play that had been a Broadway hit. Reading it on the page it is impossible to imagine why, but a hit it undoubtedly was. It was set in the London suburb of Chiswick, and the Tudoresque scene evoked Chiswick for a New York audience.[42] The story is that the development was supposed to be temporary, but its charm saved it and its prices escalated, and now it has landmark status and is protected.[43]

Whatever the particular reason, Pelham's stylistic choice would not have seemed odd at the time, but it was developed with flair and originality. There are hints of crenellation here and there, as if to acknowledge the presence of the castle in the view, but the overall effect is not fortress-like. It is rather gentle and benign, and contrives to seem calm in a place that more often has a defensive or formal character. In the 1930s Paterno decided to demolish his house, and developed another co-operative, Castle Village: a row of five tower blocks designed by George F. Pelham II, the son of the architect of Hudson View Gardens. The towers, built in 1938, have Tudor entrance

60 Tudor City, Manhattan, New York. Prodigy apartments in high Tudor style (see illus. 1).

porches and panels of historical ornament close to ground level, as if to soften the modernity of the rest of the design. They seem to be the final vestiges of the vanished castle.

Tudor glamour

The common ground between Tudor and Gothic is used in the most high-profile and spectacular of Tudoresque developments, Tudor City, which looked to Robert Smythson houses rather than cottages for its style-cues. It is on Manhattan, across the road from the United Nations headquarters – a site of some prominence, and this is not a reticent building, but a row of twenty-storey apartment buildings with smaller blocks abutting them, twelve blocks altogether, and a huge neon sign on one of the roofs proclaiming its name: Tudor City (illus.

60). From the United Nations side it looks rather blank. From here the buildings connect together so that there is a continuous run of undecorated wall with small windows, each of three buildings running the length of a city block from 40th to 43rd Street. From the city side the blocks break forward and are expressed as a run of nine towers, looking over a park that establishes a 'ground level' several storeys above the street. The towers are finished in brick with Tudoresque stone finials and carved decoration around their entrances, including Gothic arches and tracery, and the Tudor City website explains that the place takes its name 'from England's Tudor Dynasty (1485–1603), a Golden Age of Arts and Letters'.[44] The remark accurately locates the building in the popular imagination, as making reference to an elite (English kings and queens) and to a 'golden age', here of sophisticated cultural accomplishment – the age of Shakespeare.

The Tudor City development dates from 1925–8, another speculation on the part of Frederick F. French. It reached completion at the time when the foundations were started for the Chrysler Building – a taller and more celebrated building, in an Art Deco style – both of them, along with the Empire State Building, products of the boom that ended with the catastrophic crash of 1929. Tudor City was designed a little earlier than these other buildings, but that alone does not account for the disparity in styles.

The Chrysler and Empire State Buildings were aiming to look as modern as possible, in their different ways, and each was the tallest building in the world – for only eleven months in the Chrysler Building's case – which guaranteed them some attention. Some 5,000 people live in Tudor City, and they chose to do so despite the site being initially unprepossessing. It was at the edge of Manhattan (while the other buildings are more central), and when it was built there were slaughterhouses between these apartments and the river. They were demolished in the 1940s to make way for the United Nations building, but they were very much part of the surroundings when Tudor City was designed and when it was first occupied. The design sought to glamorize the place as much as it could, making it respectable by adopting a style that made strong links with British royalty in order to overcome the repellent qualities of the place. Nearly all the apartments look west, back across the island, into the city, and many of them now have views of the Chrysler Building, which is not far away. Had the building been developed after the United Nations, then undoubtedly the blocks' more exposed facades would have been given a more elaborate treatment, and the view of the river would have been enjoyed rather than suppressed.

In fact, all the Tudor detail is on the westward facades, and it includes an inscription carved in stone above one of the entrances to Tudor Tower. In Gothic letters, which takes a while to decipher, it says on one side 'on this site in MDCCCXXVII [1827] stood F .B. Winthrop's summer home', and on the other: 'and here in Anno MDCCCLXXVIII [1878] was Paddy Corcoran's Roost'. Francis Winthrop belonged to a family of prosperous New York merchants, but his house is lost to view.[45] When he moved to this site he would have been attracted by the place's natural beauties – views across land and water – but over the following fifty years the area declined, and came to be known as Hell Gate.[46] It was then that Paddy Corcoran lived here. He was one of the most notorious criminals – leader of the 'Rag Gang'. The point of the inscriptions is to give a sense of history. The style of lettering is deliberately archaic, and the Gothic arch and tracery used here are ecclesiastical in their origins – not specifically Tudoresque, but generically old-fashioned. It seems odd to be evoking the earlier presence of a notorious criminal on the spot, but the two inscriptions work together to give a sense of progress from being undeveloped countryside, to a place for feral pioneering competition, and then – now – a site of well-established civilization and cultural accomplishment.

The uses of Tudor

The various ways in which Tudor references have been used here range from being a national identifier for England or the UK, to being a signification of elitism and glamour, or a means of softening a building to make it feel more like home. It is not always possible to separate out these different aspects of Tudorism, and they can shift if the culture changes. The examples from the USA have gravitated towards Manhattan, where there is a particularly rich and varied supply of them, but they are not confined to the region or the country. The suburban houses especially are reproduced around the world where formerly British people have settled, and it would have been possible to fill the book with images of houses from across the USA, Canada, Australia and New Zealand. Without some clues from beyond the building, it would have been impossible to guess where the photos were taken. The plants in their gardens would give more information about their locality on the globe.

These are never the buildings in the most extreme conditions, where stones, logs or corrugated iron are pressed into service to make dwellings, but in places where there is time to give some thought to decorum. If one has grown up surrounded by Tudor-style buildings then a dwelling that has no more than its undecorated walls and roof seems to be somehow unfinished, and curiously under-dressed. Some painted boards at the gable and roses round the door make everything more seemly. In America, especially in the hands of the fabulously rich, the imaginative world that the Tudoresque brought with it could lend stability and authority to new property, without making it seem brash or overbearing. One of the advantages of its always having looked old-fashioned is that when it is done well it never looks *arriviste*, but as if it has somehow always been there.

Chapter Seven

A Global Brand: Beyond the Tropics and Back Again

Home from home

Joseph Addison could travel to Italy and feel at home there. Settlers in temperate climes, especially when the local population did not produce monumental buildings, could believe that they had found another Eden that was just waiting for them to harvest its bounty. In the East, where there were large indigenous populations, some impressive buildings and sometimes a difficult climate, it was more difficult to feel at home. There were compelling reasons for British subjects to go to the tropics. Huge fortunes were made there, which translated into political influence back in Britain, but dwelling there was a challenge. The British presence in India began under Elizabeth I, who granted a Royal Charter to a 'Governor and Company of Merchants of London trading with the East Indies', which eventually developed into the East India Trading Company.[1] Its reach was so pervasive that if the Indian context was clear, then it would invariably be called just 'The Company'. It competed with commercial Dutch and Portuguese activity in the region, and increasingly took on military and administrative roles, both to protect its trading activities and as a commercial service that suited the local rajas. The Company became the government, and at the point where it became clear that it was answerable to the British monarch rather than the rajas, the British started to claim it as an imperial possession. Queen Victoria adopted the title Empress of India in 1875.

The climate was always a problem for European visitors, who found it difficult day by day, and believed that it made them age faster than they would have done in a cooler place.[2] One way to thrive in the climate was to learn from the locals, and the bungalow was developed, from the *bangla* – a Bengali hut – with a large curved thatched roof to keep out the rain and, if it is thick enough, to insulate against the sun's heat. The roof should oversail the building's walls and be supported by poles at its edges and corners, to make a peripteral veranda. This has the effect of casting the walls into shadow, which stops them overheating. The building materials – bamboo and grasses – are perishable and need to be renewed on a regular basis, maybe by starting again with a new structure. The European adaptation of the pattern used more durable building materials – bricks for the walls, tiles for the roof – and the veranda space could be partly enclosed to make a more compartmentalized plan, better suiting European expectations of a dwelling, with small rooms at the corners that were usually used for sleeping or bathing.[3]

There were two distinct styles for this 'European' bungalow. The first type of bungalow aggrandized itself with the Neoclassical elements associated with the houses of the aristocracy, so the dwellings took on a Palladian aspect with the verandas turning into loggias. These were preferred by the higher-ranking administrators. The other principal type developed the bungalow's 'cottage' aspect, often keeping the *bangla*'s thatched roof and using plastered brick piers rather than classical columns around its verandas.[4] This suggests something unpretentiously homely, but the effect could be dismaying. James Gray arrived in Bombay in 1852 and was disappointed with his first sight of the bungalow that had been provided for him. He had expected 'Oriental pomp and magnificence', and was pleased by the 'elegant equipage with turbaned attendants' that took him to the bungalow. But he must have felt a sense of disappointment close to panic as the realization dawned that he was expected to live in a single-storey building with an overhanging thatched roof, which he thought looked like a cow-house.[5]

However, we must admit that the similarity to the cow-house extended no further than the exterior; and our drooping spirits began to revive as we stepped direct, without any intervening hall or passage, into a large and elegant drawing room, supported upon pillars of faultless proportions, and furnished with every modern luxury that either taste could suggest or wealth command.[6]

There was a certain want of decorum in the abruptness of the transition from inside to outside, but a fine finish within. Moreover, the place was clearly well arranged, to suit the needs of inhabitants with high expectations for comfort. Each person had a suite of rooms (bedroom, dressing room, bathroom), at least one of which opened on to the veranda – the value of which Gray came to realize:

> [The veranda] is considered indispensable in the construction of even the poorest abode; not only as affording protection from the intolerable glare of the sun during the day, but as presenting an agreeable family resort, when the refreshing evening breeze tempts every one to exchange the heat and lights of the drawing room for a delightful 'réunion' in the open air.
>
> Here, too, conversation flows on more unrestrainedly than beneath the blaze of the numerous lamps, rendered necessary by the extensive dimensions of a Bombay room.[7]

Even habitually reserved people have been known, he says, to become eloquent on the veranda. He makes the point that his description refers specifically to the bungalow, and not to the generality of English residences around Bombay, which were lofty and spacious, with *portes cochères* large enough to take to carriages abreast.[8] He also remarks on the lack of privacy that a new arrival feels in a Bombay house, because of everything being as open as possible to promote the movement of air through the building, so the bedroom is a less-closed place of personal retreat than an Englishman would expect, leaving him with the feeling of being expected to sleep in a 'magnified bird-cage'.[9] This comfortable but externally less pretentious style of bungalow, like Gray's, was built in greater numbers, while those in classical dress would have carried greater prestige and would be seen to be used appropriately when high-ranking officials occupied them.

Gray was relieved to find classical columns and a level of social pretension that suited him on the inside of the house, even though the exterior offered nothing. Nevertheless, whether classical or not, the bungalow was seen as *pukka*, having reasonable levels of comfort and status, and they were used on occasion by later governors and viceroys.[10] The imperatives for this tropical architecture are climatic, not stylistic, though that was often forgotten when an idea of the bungalow was brought back to the British suburbs. It should have verandas, which can shelter from the rain as effectively as from overbearing heat, and open up the interior to outdoor space, but often it is used as an all-purpose word for a single-storey dwelling, without awareness of its Anglo-Indian pedigree, so completely has it been naturalized into the culture. Gray's observations make it clear how unsettling life could be during the period of adjustment after arrival. Obviously, in such circumstances the British reach for the Tudoresque.

The Himalayan village of Shimla (formerly Simla) in northern India is far from unique in using old-English style, but it is the purest and most sustained example of Tudoresque development in the Subcontinent. The British ruling elite developed it as a hill-station retreat from Calcutta's and Delhi's oppressive heat and then from 1864 established the place as a seasonal capital that was in use as the seat of government from March to November.[11] Beyond the houses often having verandas, the buildings here owe nothing to the indigenous culture to which one has necessarily adjusted by the time one reaches this out-of-the-way spot. The spectacular views of snow-capped mountains, the climate, the dense vegetation that it produces and the wildlife – especially the monkeys – make it clear enough that these buildings are not in the Home Counties; and yet the buildings have been transplanted from that far-away land. It seems utterly surreal: the buildings dislocated, as though carried here by a genie, from a place that from here looks fanciful and exotic.

The town hall has a black-and-white gable and oriel windows; the prominent library has a masonry lower floor with black-and-white work above it, while the church is in a hybrid neo-Gothic style, with some 'Tudor' arches (illus. 61 and 62). The finest of the black-and-white houses was Barnes Court – a super-sized cottage (illus. 64)[12] – but the most important individual building was the Viceroy's Lodge, a creation of great splendour, commissioned by the Earl of Dufferin and built between 1881 and 1888. It was designed by Henry Irwin, who was born in Ireland, but spent most of his working life in India designing for the Raj (illus. 63).[13] The lodge's principal models were Smythson's works, especially the towering central space of Wollaton

61 Town hall, Shimla, Himachal Pradesh, India. Himalayan Tudor for British expatriates.

62 Colonel John Theophilus Boileau, Christ Church, Shimla, Himachal Pradesh, 1857. Transplanted Tudor-Gothic.

Hall. The lodge sprawls more than Smythson's works, and its towers are therefore proportionally less towering, so that despite it size the general composition is less imposing than it might have been in the hands of Smythson himself. Lord Curzon, a later viceroy, feeling that corrective measures were needed, had one of the towers heightened in order to improve the appearance.[14] It was a great palace, suited to the governor of this country, which was vastly larger and more populous than Britain itself (approximately 200 million in India, while the population of Britain was rapidly increasing from 13 million), and the splendour was adjusted to the wealth of the territory rather than to the viceroy's position as a servant of the empress in London.[15]

The main circulation axis of Shimla Mall follows the shape of the ridge, producing a relaxed layout that contrasts with the formal geometry of New Delhi.[16] Shimla seems to be the product of good planning and incremental growth, and makes a benign townscape that

63 Raj Bhaven (Governor's House) Barnes Court, Shimla, Himachal Pradesh, 1849, photographed in 1882. A palatial cottage.

64 Henry Irwin, Viceroy's Lodge, Shimla, Himachal Pradesh, 1888. More glass than wall, but with shady verandahs.

feels familiar to European visitors. Even the climate at this altitude feels European. The same power was exercised here as in Calcutta and then New Delhi, but the buildings did not express the power in the same way. The people who set up households here were mostly high-ranking civil servants and their hangers-on, including many servants and the people who brought food and messages. Others who had the means and wanted to belong in this elite group also moved here if they could, but by the end of the 1880s it was decided to discourage native Indians from buying property at Shimla. The foreign secretary wrote to the chief secretaries of all the British-administered states:

> The Viceroy has, therefore, decided that Native chiefs should in future be discouraged from owning houses in Simla... His Excellency does not wish to compel or press Chiefs who already own houses here to get rid of them. The object is to check the growth of the practice in future. At the same time, if there are any chiefs who wish to part with their houses in Simla, it is desirable that they should avail themselves of any suitable opportunities which may offer for so doing.[17]

The result was that Shimla's Britishness was ensured, and the summer idyll of tranquil domesticity could continue unchallenged by intrusions from local manners, even the splendid and refined manners of Indian princes. 'Everything is so English and unpicturesque here,' said one visitor, an artist, 'that except the people one meets are those who rule and make history – a fact one can hardly realize – one would think oneself at Margate.'[18] The speaker was Valentine Prinsep, whose use of the word 'picturesque' is idiosyncratic, since the Himalayan views would definitely be picturesque by others' standards. He, however, was travelling in search of orientalist subject matter, and plainly Shimla was a disappointment for him.

The evident permanence of the masonry buildings makes it clear that they are rooted to the spot, but everything else about them is deracinated, and now the colonial agents have themselves long gone, so the buildings do not make sense in their original way. The settlement must always have had something of the quality of a hallucination, even more so in the past when its exclusivity would have made the break with the locality even more complete, and before the buildings' decay began to express nature's reasserted claim. The buildings have not all been maintained to the highest standards, and sheets of corrugated iron valuably protect some of the structures in a manner that diminishes the Tudoresque effect. Since Independence (1947) the buildings have been reclaimed for the indigenous population, the Lodge (which is well maintained) becoming at first a summer palace for the President of India, but then from 1965 a base for research (the Indian Institute of Advanced Study).[19] The settlement continues to flourish, now as a popular tourist destination, so perhaps on the functional level it is now more than ever like Margate.

The use of Tudoresque styles in these buildings reproduced exactly the relation between the manor house and its dependent cottages, except that here the 'cottages' were often substantial houses with many servants. The viceroy was almost a monarch, and his palace was correspondingly grand, even though it was called a 'lodge' and within the settlement had the role of the manor house. A house like Barnes Court was substantial enough to have been a manor in an English village, but here it is a cottage, and that is what the building style expresses. The whole settlement, with its cultivation of British manners and exclusion of Indian influence, was a refuge from the daily challenges of life in urban India. It was a place of recuperation for the colonial administrators, where they could act out for one another their polite British identities, before returning to the heat and dust of the city to exert their authority in classical buildings. It was an oasis of safety from cultural challenge or contamination of the city, and from the jungle's natural dangers. It was a place where, against the odds, one could feel at home.

Tudoresque prestige

The indigenous population of the area now known as the Cameron Highlands subsisted on the produce of the rainforest. They, the Oran Asli, built flimsy timber constructions on stilts, which allowed penetration of air, as one would expect in a humid tropical climate. As at Shimla, the British colonials liked this area because its high altitude made it cooler and more comfortable than Kuala Lumpur, the big city that is about 100 miles to the south. Kuala Lumpur itself has a prominent and assertive Tudoresque building from the colonial era in the Royal Selangor Club, which presides over the city-centre cricket ground (illus. 65). Next to it there is the Anglican cathedral – which is the size of a parish church, in the Early English Gothic style, with a black-and-white gabled porch. A side chapel has the date of construction (1894) emblazoned on it. The clubhouse dates from 1910, and was designed by Brigadier General Arthur Benison Hubback, who is also known as the architect of Kuala Lumpur's old railway station, which translated the Gothic pinnacles of the London terminus of St Pancras into an orientalist, Indian-style fantasy. There are other orientalizing buildings around the cricket ground, which is an important public site in a densely built city – the place where Malaysia's independence was formally enacted in a ceremony in 1963 – but the clubhouse in its choice of architectural style identified itself as a place for British recuperation.

In the Cameron Highlands areas of the forest were cleared and businesses were started: tea plantations, and farms producing honey, roses and strawberries. Alongside them from the 1930s the area established itself as a hill-station resort, sustained by visitors from Kuala Lumpur. The older Tudoresque buildings here were built in a way that made British visitors feel at home. The oldest, most famous and most visited of them is The Old Smokehouse, which was built in the 1930s for the owner of a tea plantation and now runs as a hotel (illus. 66). Even here the black lines of the timberwork are treated as a decorative effect rather than making any serious effort to suggest a structural

65 Royal Selangor Club, Merdeka Square, Kuala Lumpur, Malaysia, 1884 with later renovation. City-centre recreation for the colonial elite.

frame. There are no timbers near the ends of the building, where they would be structurally important, but then they are vigorously present in other places and dominate the building's appearance. Its garden is an important part of the scene, which very successfully evokes an English cottage garden, but uses species that would be exotic in England. Another hotel, The Lakehouse, was built a few miles away in 1972, by a retired colonel, Stanley Foster, whose wife was Malaysian (illus. 67). It took its stylistic cues from The Old Smokehouse, but avoided the problems associated with timber construction in jungle conditions – rot and infestation – by making the building's structure in reinforced concrete. Foster ran the hotel with a policy that excluded dogs, children and Asians (all that changed when he died in 1984), so there was a clear intention to make by private decree an

66 The Old Smokehouse, Tanah Rata, Cameron Highlands, Malaysia, 1939. Home from home for expatriates.

67 Colonel Stanley Foster, The Lakehouse, Ringlet, Cameron Highlands, 1972. Continuing colonial traditions after independence.

atmosphere that was as British as possible, in this far-flung corner of the (by then) former empire.

These examples show exactly the same strategies as were to be found in nineteenth-century Shimla, but by the end of the twentieth century things had moved on. The elite now includes some Europeans, but the Asian population is no longer excluded at any level, and in the Cameron Highlands the black-and-white buildings set the style. A recent Tudor house for an Indian prince – the local raja – has high security at its entrance gates, but its commanding position makes it conspicuous from a distance (illus. 68). So the Tudoresque is continuing here as an elite style, but instead of making direct allusion to the cottage homes of England, it is, in this particular local context, making allusion to nearby high-status buildings associated with the previous governing class. Rather than repudiating the style as a foreign intrusion, it has been requisitioned by the local population.

68 Hill-top house, Tanah Rata, Cameron Highlands, 2003. Housing the new post-colonial elite.

The house is far from being an isolated example. There are other Tudoresque dwellings, but more remarkably many hotels, some of them large, have been built in the nearby town of Tanah Rata, which has flourished as a resort in the last twenty years. Typically, they are in white-rendered concrete, and have been given an idea of a sloping roof. They are 'smartened up' by the application of black lines, which may be black-painted timber or steel, or in some cases cast raised in the concrete. This black-and-white style is dominant in the area, and a version of it is used for most buildings that have aspirations beyond mere utility (illus. 70).

Within sight of The Lakehouse there is a retail and domestic development that is clearly not evocative of old England, but yet it is a development of the imported style, and shows what was important to its designers (illus. 69). The black lines on a white ground are very evidently there for decorative effect, and are not in the least trying to suggest the lines of a timber structural frame. Although these buildings are certainly Malaysian, they are not the work of the indigenous population. The Oran Asli's traditional way of life survives to some extent, selling jungle fruit and herbal remedies by the side of the road, showing tourists round traditional villages and demonstrating how to use a blowpipe, and no doubt in other less conspicuous ways. But the concrete buildings for the resort cater to the tastes of an urban elite, coming from outside the area – from Kuala Lumpur, Singapore and further afield. It is their tastes that are being reflected in the buildings here. The indigenous architecture could have been adapted, no doubt, to accommodate modern standards of comfort, but it has not been. The black-and-white style has been established in the area for as long as it has been a resort, and it also has social cachet. It has become the traditional architecture for comfortable buildings in the region.

Associations with the past

The black and white colouring is distinctive and in South-East Asia its use has migrated from its Tudoresque origins into other architectural

69 Retail and domestic development, Ringlet, Cameron Highlands. Tudor detail adopted by indigenous architects.

70 Equatorial Hotel, Kea Farm, Brinchang, Cameron Highlands. Tudoresque as the normative style for continuing development.

styles, so it is possible to find buildings that have a 'Tudoresque mood' about them, even though they are not identifiably in a style that derives from any kind of Tudor, except in their black and whiteness. This tendency finds its clearest expression in the bamboo blinds that shade the verandas of the Singaporean black-and-white houses, making their appearance prominently and with remarkable consistency (illus. 71). The black and white stripes here have no purpose in expressing structure or defining the framing of an opening: they are absolutely in the realm of applied decoration, but they evoke the black and white stripes of English Tudoresque gables. They are culturally distinct, because they tend to be grouped in enclaves, which their original occupants found reassuring, and which the colonial authorities found convenient. Also the colouring does not have such positive associations for the people who do not have the ideas of architectural Englishness in their background: for the now-dominant Chinese population in Singapore, for example, the colours seem funereal; and they are a world away from the colour sense on display in Singapore's 'Little India', where vibrant pinks and purples, oranges and greens clash exuberantly, applied to the decorative mouldings and cornices of colonial buildings that anticipated more restrained coloration.

The Singaporean black-and-white house can be seen as a fusion of a remarkable range of influences. They can absorb stylistic details from a wide range of Western styles, including classical, Tudoresque and Art Deco.[20] Most importantly, though, they are developments of the bungalow, with their expansive verandas, here used with the Malaysian tradition of building on stilts, so the bungalows in Singapore and on the Malay Peninsula are usually two-storey buildings. The black-and-white colouring looked traditional to British eyes, and had the effect of confirming cultural and racial difference in the enclaves, set apart, where the houses are normally to be found. In Singapore these houses are well maintained and their gardens are well established, so they look like very comfortably settled abodes established in clearings of a luxuriant forest. The black and white colours contrast strongly with the dominant greenery and the dwellings do not look vulnerable to

71 Black-and-white house, Singapore. Tropical Tudoresque.

the decay that would so evidently afflict a house built in untreated timber in these conditions. The illusion can be maintained with the continued application of paint and renewal of timbers. The houses present an image of resistance to the decay that was supposed to overtake the European body in tropical climes, just as they protected those bodies from contagion, by setting them apart from the local population and from one another, and from the climate by learning their spatial arrangements from local architectures.

The explicitly Tudoresque buildings here include colonial-era survivals, such as the bar at the Tanglin Club, which exactly reproduces the appearance of a British pub, and the more prominently exposed Tudor Court shopping gallery – a row of shop-houses – which were styled with a view to making British expatriates feel comforted (illus. 72). Tanglin Place, however, which is adjacent to Tudor Court, is a more recent building that has a different agenda. The scale is very

72 Tudor Court, Tanglin Road, Singapore. Colonial-era Tudor.

different, but an attempt has been made to inflect the building's style in a Tudoresque direction (illus. 73). It is profoundly different in many ways, and the chunky diagonals are sculptural in origin, not in the least an expression of the building's structure. Indeed, the whole building is less a response to its own internal conditions than it is to the building next door, which is treated as a historic relic, to be preserved with respect, while at the same time being diminished and overpowered by its changing surroundings.

There is another development on Singapore, inconspicuous and residential: Chuville, on the Pasir Panjang Road (illus. 74). Its black-and-white panels are decorative, but take their diagonal lines from the roof construction, which is permitted to develop with projections and gables that vary the form. The general appearance is evocative of the Tudoresque, but the houses are much more inventive than their outside makes clear. Internally, the rooms are grouped around an

A Global Brand: Beyond the Tropics and Back Again

73 Tanglin Place, Tanglin Road, Singapore. Post-colonial contextualism.

imposing and airy space that extends right up through the building's three storeys, which helps to keep the living rooms cool, so this is a clearly modern tropical house design, which did not find it necessary to repudiate Tudoresque overtones in the form, but could embrace them as something that enhanced the appearance, linking it with the architecture of the colonial elite. There is no conflict here between modernity and Tudorism. Neither here nor at Tanglin Place would we think that the buildings are trying to look older than they are, but they express continuity with a part of the island's longest-established building culture.

Tudoresque escape

Tudor-style architecture also has a significant presence in Shanghai, where the colonial experience was significantly different from that of Shimla or the Cameron Highlands. The city was not a resort but an important place for colonial business. It began as a fishing town on the Yangtze River where it meets the sea on China's east coast, but during the nineteenth century it grew to become a centre of industry and commerce, connecting China with the wider world. During the first Opium War British forces held Shanghai from 1839 until 1842, when the Treaty of Nanjing opened five 'treaty' ports to British residents and trading, and made British subjects exempt from local law. In addition to the British colonial presence, in 1849 the French and in 1854 the Americans were granted land in Shanghai.

In 1854 the British, French and American interests formed the Shanghai Municipal Council, which Chinese citizens were not permitted to join until 1928. By the 1930s Shanghai was firmly enmeshed in the networks of the modern world, and the would-be cosmopolitan elite Europeanized their style.[21] The city changed with the advent of the People's Republic of China in 1949, but there has been a long tradition of cosmopolitan culture in the city, which is reflected in the fact

74 Chuville, Pasir Panjang Road, Singapore. Modern tropical space, in black-and-white style.

that the British, American and French buildings built by the Shanghai Municipal Council have been allowed to remain. The clearest examples of the surviving buildings are in the Bund, in the centre of Shanghai, and variously Neoclassical, Palladian, Art Nouveau and Art Deco buildings dominate the riverfront. In addition to these formal colonial-era public buildings, there are also numerous domestic buildings and spaces that demonstrate a strong Tudoresque presence within the city. Houses in the domestic spaces of the Julu Road and Stanford Gardens (near the French Quarter) have a strong Tudoresque quality and are now home to poor and middle-class Chinese people, as well as expatriates (illus. 75).

After 1949 these buildings were not reproduced, and the repudiation of colonial-style buildings has continued in the era of rapid growth of a new industrial capitalist China from the 1990s. Central Shanghai is now dominated by modernist and post-modernist buildings, most characteristically high-rise apartment blocks, which cater for most of Shanghai's population of 20 million. In the suburban areas, however, there are alternatives, such as Songjiang New City, which is approximately 20 miles from the centre. Within it there are nine 'towns', one of which is a one-kilometre-square space called Thames Town – a site that contains a variety of neo-English architectures including Tudor, Georgian and Victorian-style buildings with the Tudoresque as the dominant signifier of the authentic English or British town (illus. 76). The density of the central area's development makes it evocative of central Chester, but most of the houses have a suburban Tudoresque character highly reminiscent of Western suburbs that might be found in the United States, the United Kingdom, Canada or Australia. In this context, although the Tudoresque buildings connote 'Englishness', they also signify much wider themes within contemporary Chinese society.

With the changes in the economy, these new houses are also viewed by the Chinese professional middle class as investments to preserve and develop personal capital. As in other housing markets across the world, these new buildings are important assets and they

75 Julu Road and Stanford Gardens, Shanghai, China. Cosmopolitan buildings from the era of the Shanghai Municipal Council.

76 Songjiang Development Corporation, Thames Town, Shanghai. Twenty-first century commercial development (see illus. 5).

are often – it seems most often – bought as investments rather than as dwellings.[22] Here the newness of the buildings is at such a premium that it is felt that the act of living in them will devalue them. In this regard these houses can be compared to toys that might be regarded as 'antique' one day in the future, and are therefore never removed from their boxes for fear of devaluation.

But for the people who do live there, these buildings are also part of a new movement in Chinese professional and middle-class culture towards having a space of escape or retreat from a frenetic urban life. This does not mean that the new Tudor buildings are valued as ideal dwellings; rather, the evidence points to them being seen as 'second homes' to be used for holidays or at weekends. On an ordinary weekday the town is completely deserted. The intense 'old-English' references – not only in the black-and-white architecture, but also in the public art: statues of Shakespeare, Florence Nightingale, Sherlock Holmes and Harry Potter – allow the few residents and many visitors to enter into a 'fun' world or hyper-real 'holiday space'; to be abroad at home. Thames Town can be seen as a miniature England, a microcosm that one may enter to escape the pressures of modern Shanghai urban and corporate life. It is unimportant whether or not the experience of this place matches exactly the experience of visiting a place in England. It is a place that enables escapism: it sanctions the activation of a different range of ideas and ways of behaving from those that are required in the workplace and the city of everyday life.

Thames Town is seen as a cultural sieve that has caught the exotic highpoints of English cultural and architectural life. So, rather than going on holiday to England, the town allows its residents to experience the imagined best of England, and because the visit does enable people to distance themselves from their workaday habits, it really does have the effect of a holiday, without the discomforts of long-haul travel. Actual foreign travel is relatively rare among the Chinese, and it seems to be reasonable there to bring the world's highlights to China. There is a striking parallel in the United States, where only a minority of people have passports, and where the real old London Bridge is to be found at Lake Havasu City, and parts of Venice are evoked in Las Vegas. The practice is far from unknown in Europe, but as foreign countries are so much closer at hand, the habit is less developed. We have an imitation of the Eiffel Tower in Blackpool, but the most pervasive use of this method of design was in the habit of eighteenth-century Grand Tourists of commissioning Roman and Italianate buildings when they returned. The Palladian country house has been repeated so many times in the English countryside that we think of it as the very type of the English country house, but it was a very deliberately evocative import – reminding the house's owner of his youthful travels.[23]

This exotic, 'holidayesque' interpretation of Thames Town is further supported by the numerous Chinese tourists who visit the place. Some come here to marry, and have their wedding photos taken next to the town's most impressive English-style buildings. The happy couples will also wear traditional Western wedding clothes, with brides clothed in white gowns and grooms adopting a traditionally English Edwardian morning suit with top hat and tails.

Tudoresque multiplicity

It will have become clear by now why this book has not been set up with a continuous story to guide the reader through it. There is nothing built into the idea of a Tudor building that would link it in any way with all the uses to which it has been put, in later ages and in far-flung places. All the examples can be traced back to Tudor England, usually at several removes, but despite some strong similarities between some of the buildings' external appearances, it is impossible to predict what they will mean when they are taken up by a new culture. The 'new' cultures here are all more or less remote from the Tudors, but as we saw at the outset 'the Tudors' were an eighteenth-century construction. The most stable meaning that is associated with the buildings is that they represent 'old England', and that is not a meaning they could have had in the actual Tudor century.

The sixteenth century saw fundamental change in society, and looking back we see a move from the medieval to the early modern period, which included building production in many distinct styles. In masonry there were Gothic buildings and fortresses, manor houses and showy mansions with huge windows. There were timber-framed buildings, which could include palaces and manor houses, and also more modest cottages. These buildings are all available in the imaginations of later designers, to be evoked if they so choose. Historical accuracy is usually beside the point. Horace Walpole was an antiquarian scholar, who thought of the Tudors as belonging in his evocation of the Gothic at Strawberry Hill, with its 'Holbein Chamber' displaying copies of Holbein portrait drawings of members of the Tudor court. He bought some intricately carved Indian furniture in ebony, in the belief that it had come from Hampton Court and was from the reign of Henry VIII.[24] In order to understand Walpole's vision, we need to be able to accept this detail as a legitimate part of it, and to see that for him it had some of the same charge as Cardinal Wolsey's broad-brimmed hat, which was hanging on the wall alongside.[25]

Antiquarian scholars like Walpole were turning their attention to British archaeology, and progress was being made in illuminating the various shifts in taste and architectural development through the preceding centuries. At a popular level the national character was personified in Britannia, especially after James Thomson's and Thomas Arne's masque *Alfred*, of 1740, introduced 'Rule Britannia!' to the world.[26] Britannia was a personification of the nation: defiant and with a right to rule not only the island, but also 'the waves' around it. In the masque it is the Anglo-Saxon king, Alfred the Great, defending the island against predatory Vikings, but in the nineteenth century the song was popularly sung as an anthem of imperial destiny. The other national character was John Bull, a no-nonsense everyman figure, who regularly appeared in eighteenth-century political cartoons, such as James Gillray's (though he originated as a literary figure invented by Dr John Arbuthnot in 1712) – a stocky, well-fed character, with conventional views and disinclined to be persuaded out of them.[27] It is this sense of national character that was elaborated by Edmund Burke, as unrepresented in the grasshopper-chirrupings of the press.[28]

The story of Tudoresque architecture that is to be found in the mainstream twentieth-century architectural history books, if it is mentioned at all, is that the good architecture of the nineteenth-century Arts and Crafts movement went on to influence modernism in Germany, while in Britain the mass market of the 1920s and '30s built increasingly degraded versions of Arts and Crafts buildings. Other views are possible, and the history is much longer than is generally appreciated. When Anthony Bertram said that 'economic depression and the fear of war are the chief promoters of the Tudoresque',[29] he cast the Tudoresque as a psychological illness that would heal when economic depression and the fear of war were things of the past. He might have had a point. But his suggestion that Tudoresque and Tudoristic architecture is *more* bogus now than it was at some time in the past is wide of the mark.

If Tudoresque buildings give reassurance to the inhabitants of Middle England when they are faced with uncertainty, peril or foreigners, then these are the cultural conditions of the time in which the Tudoresque architecture is being produced, and it is a real and authentic response to the cultural conditions. It may be that the future is wonderful and welcoming and should be embraced, but for many people that is not the way it looks. If the John Bull citizen has anxieties about the future, when there is so much to feel uncertain about, then it is not too surprising that the Tudoresque continues to be with us. Rather than vilify the style, it is better to try to see what it means; and what it means is that its hugely increased use through the twentieth century is an indication that the 'ordinary' voices of unremarkable citizens were having their say.

Industrialization brought prosperity for some, but produced appalling conditions in the cities for many.[30] The spread of the suburbs and the take-up of suburban housing by the lower-middle class made for a vulgarization of architectural style, by the standards of elite architectural taste, but on the other hand it also represents (at the same time and through the same buildings) a great improvement in the living conditions of a huge number of people. The important point to make is not that the architectural quality of mass housing was lower than it had previously been for a small elite group, but that for the masses it was better than it had ever before been.

After this important point about social change there is a point about style and taste: many of these people ended up in cottage-like Tudoresque houses. Why was that? What did the Tudoresque mean for them? The answer is that it meant security, homeliness and tradition. It was old-fashioned, which was a well-established sign of good character, and it future-proofed the house by ensuring that it would not go out of fashion. It was an architecture of common sense, the sedimented wisdom of the ages, rather than of experimental thought. That made it the antithesis of modernism, where architects were enjoined to think from first principles. 'A good design', said Anthony Bertram, 'must always be original.'[31]

It is by no means certain that he was correct. Even Le Corbusier, whom Bertram admired, praised certain *objets-types* – the wine bottle, the violin, the briar-pipe – which had achieved definitive form over the course of generations. If a new wine bottle is much like an old wine bottle then the new bottle may not be a new design, but it would still be a good bottle. If it is an altogether new design then it might be original, but it is unlikely to be as good. Le Corbusier proposed a new type of house, raised on stilts above the ground, with a free plan, long horizontal windows and a flat roof that could be used as outdoor space.[32] The first such design would be original, but not those that came after, and Le Corbusier was arguing for it as an *objet-type*. All houses would be like that in the future. It had its logic, and it made sense. Some architects could see the appeal, but the common-sense citizens of Middle England never did.

Their reaction is represented in Evelyn Waugh's novel of 1928, *Decline and Fall*, in which a flighty creature of fashion (Margot Beste-Chetwynde) demolishes the finest Tudor house in England in order to replace it with 'something clean and square'.[33] It has just been completed when it enters the story, and 20 pages on we learn that it is demolished some years later.[34] The architect is an unsympathetic character, who would prefer to be designing for machines than for people. He is German, from Hamburg, has spent time in Moscow and at the Bauhaus at Dessau, and is himself so machine-like that he does not sleep.[35] The house itself is unforgiving and alienating. There is an aluminium lift, balustrade and window blinds – aluminium being a very new material in the 1920s – and much glass: a green glass floor, a colonnade of black glass columns – and a vulcanite table. There is a luminous ceiling, a room with a tank of octopuses prominent in it, and a floor that is a kaleidoscope, set in motion by an electrical switch.[36] This is architecture for fashion victims. It is cultivatedly surreal and programmatically disorienting, but most significantly it is presented as foreign. Not only that, but as coming from a country with which Britain had recently been at war; and building it involved demolishing an emblematically British house. Waugh's fictional foreign architect is presented as annihilating the British past. The architect Sir Reginald Blomfield spoke for Middle England when he said:

> Since the war, Modernism, or '*Modernismus*', as it should be called on the German precedent, has invaded this country like an epidemic, and though there are signs of reaction, its attack is insidious and far-reaching, with the wholly fallacious prospect of a new heaven and earth which it dangles before the younger generation.[37]

Blomfield presents Continental modernist architecture's arrival as an attack – an invasion, a disease – there is no need to read between the lines: that is what he says. And he goes on:

> The most formidable claim of our young lions in architecture is that they are starting a new manner of their own, and they keep on assuring each other and the public that this is so, in order, I take it, to prevent any misgivings in

themselves. They consider that the past has no meaning for them, and that all they have to do is look to the present.[38]

That was then

Things have certainly moved on since Blomfield was writing. The version of modernism that became popular during the 1950s and '60s is now available as second-hand furniture on eBay (search for 'retro'). Old-fashioned houses, many of them Tudoresque, are still being built. They are more technically advanced than ever before, better insulated, with more sophisticated systems for controlling heating and lighting, more cables buried in the plasterwork and more radio waves making wireless connections with household appliances. Nevertheless, it seems that we remain comforted by the sight of an old-fashioned house and are made slightly anxious by dwellings that seem futuristic. We can enjoy looking round them, marvelling at the technical gadgetry, but when it comes to borrowing the money to pay for one, our tastes (collectively, as a nation) are cautious. If a genuinely old house is available, then that is ideal: it can be refurbished and equipped with the latest technology without disturbing the appearance. When old houses are in short supply, then the house-builders put up new ones, but make them look old-fashioned, so that we will be happy with them.

Why would that be? One role of the house is as an off-stage space, where we can recuperate. When we are there we do not want to have to try too hard. A dwelling that suggests the future suggests uncertainty and effort. A Tudoresque dwelling suggests stability and self-reliance. It is the *objet-type* of British domesticity. We know where we are with it. It is unpretentious, trustworthy and enduring. It is the architecture of Middle England. We might doubt that Middle England is still with us, but the Tudoresque suburbs are its breeding ground.

Despite newspaper sales being in general decline, the *Daily Mail*, aimed at a lower-middle-class readership, still sells about two million copies daily in the UK.[39] The Ideal Home Show, which the *Daily Mail* started in 1908, is still running. *Ideal Home* magazine is not what it was, and had a major re-launch in 1996 to stop its slide in sales, but it is still aimed at the 'middle market' and has a readership of about one million.[40] *This England* ('Britain's loveliest magazine') sells about 150,000 copies quarterly, and claims a readership of two million. Many of these readers are British expatriates, hungry for its supply of information about and photographs of ultra-traditional English fare – daffodils, village cricket, country churches, royalty and so on.[41] *Country Life* is available in the suburban supermarkets, for sale to people who think they have aristocratic tastes, and has an estimated readership in the region of 215,000.

The *Architectural Review*, which promotes modernism mainly to architects, is by contrast catering to a minority. It sells about 20,000 copies each month, going out to 190 countries round the world. Copies of the magazine are often kept for reference so the readership would be significantly higher than that figure, but it is an international readership.[42] *Elle Decoration*, the most popular architectural journal with a broadly modernist outlook, sells about 60,000 copies a month in the UK, two million across Europe, including about 190,000 in France (which has a population similar to the UK's).[43]

The British no longer think of modernity as Continental. After 1945 it probably came to seem to be more American and inevitable, and could more comfortably be imported as the style of an ally, even if it had been taken to the USA by German émigrés.[44] Professionals who have had a design education tend to think of modernism as 'normal', sometimes as the only way to design with conviction in the modern age. However, although in Europe the USA looks as if it embodies modernity, that is not actually the way that the mainstream population of the USA sees itself. Martha Stewart's website, which is trained on the mainstream with the accuracy of a heat-seeking missile, includes pictures of four of her homes, which are all more or less 'contemporary traditional'.[45] Meanwhile, the people of Middle England deal with modernity in the home much as Edmund Burke said they would, by quietly ignoring it, in the conviction that sooner or later it will leave them alone.

It is different in the workplace. An individual has many identities, and the workplace identity derives from the job that is to be done, so it is future-oriented, looking towards what must be achieved. Therefore an idea of efficiency and progress seems to be accepted as part of the workplace, and modernity is welcomed into the designs for offices and factories. Perhaps when we are at work, we can embrace modernity, but when we are at home we want to be allowed to revert to a more traditional sense of who we are. This would account for the sense of identity projected in the British pavilions at international expositions and world fairs.

The British internationally tend to be seen as home-loving, as Muthesius said,[46] and despite the acclaim that met the Crystal Palace when it was built for the first such exhibition in 1851, the British pavilion at overseas events tended to have a traditional domestic and Tudor character. That changed in the 1930s, and the pavilions now aim squarely at demonstrating Britain's creativity, the promotion of which is of interest to British businesses. The arresting spectacle of Thomas Heatherwick's pavilion for Shanghai in 2010, for example, was plainly designed to make the inhabitants of that city see that there is more to Britain than is portrayed in Thames Town, but equally we can be sure that it will have little impact on the UK's domestic architecture.

This divergence, however, is fully recuperated within the Tudoresque tradition. Cragside, for example, is not only in Tudor style, it was also the home of an inventor and the seat of creativity. The equivalent modern popular image is of Wallace and Gromit, and their unemphatically Tudoresque house, 62 West Wallaby Street, Wigan. Wallace's inventions owe more to Heath Robinson than Armstrong, but there is no doubting his creativity, and he is a decent representation of the British understanding of the spirit of the lower-middle-class Tudoresque.[47] He is also recognizably part of a tradition of self-reliance that stretches back to the Elizabethan charter and beyond. It is this aspect of creative independence, each householder feeling that in their own household they are not answerable for their tastes to anyone else, least of all to cosmopolitan elites, that the depiction of traditional quaint old England misses completely. The Tudoresque suburbs may look from the outside like a place of conformity, but the inhabitants are more likely to think of themselves as eccentric individualists, no longer actually supported by their three acres and a cow, but psychologically as independent. This is the environment from which springs Britain's eccentric creativity: from people making up their own minds about what to make with the tools in the shed in the garden, where to go in the caravan, what to play in the garage band. It is a world where there are model railway layouts, cathedrals made of matchsticks, ships in bottles, home-made fitted cupboards and old cars endlessly being rebuilt. Maybe it is a world that is passing, as computer games and celebrity gossip take over the world, but even if it is fading, its buildings will remain for some time yet. They might become meaningless without the activity that they once made possible, but it is more likely that they will be invested with new meaning as the new world makes sense of them in its own way.

A thousand Tudorisms

The three-acres-and-a-cow Tudorism of the suburbs is the most important for understanding Britain. It had its last explicit airing under the sponsorship of Chesterton and Belloc in the 1920s and '30s, but it might yet make a return as a model of sustainability. But it is far from being the only type around, even in Britain. There is the manorial Tudor, as at Wightwick and Hammerford; Romantic Tudor, as at Cragside; the simple-life Tudor that treats the suburban home as a *cottage orné* at Upper Binsford; and the naturalized-émigré Tudor at Ascott. The Tudoresque building fits into a particular assemblage and produces a different result each time: an independence machine, a social prestige machine, an English identity machine.[48] Each one is a machine for living in, and for living through, and each can be calibrated to produce a range of effects that houses on Le Corbusier's model have yet to achieve, as well as decent comfortable living conditions and self-effacing tranquillity. There are many actual variant ways in which the Tudoresque has been put to use, and no theoretical upper limit. Each way needs its own *milieu* in which to work – it is not something that the building can do in isolation – but given a set of conditions it can be surprisingly effective. The colonial administrators at Shimla, for example, who had ample means at their disposal, set in place the buildings that produced a set of environments and social interactions like Margate's. It was the Tudoresque buildings that actualized the Margate-becoming of the Himalayan slopes when they were brought into *agencement* with the administrators and their social formation. When it happened there, so far from home, it was a comfort, but if they had visited Margate itself – a coastal resort in Kent – it is unlikely that they would have felt the same, at least not so intensely. When T. S. Eliot went there he turned it into an existential wasteland:

> On Margate sands.
> I can connect
> Nothing with nothing.[49]

At Shimla the Margate machine is no longer working in quite the same way, since its visitors are not acculturated in the old expatriate way, but the Indian visitors find something like the 'holiday' *milieu* that is found by the Chinese visitors to Thames Town. The various cues given by the place prompt a personal reorientation, suggest a certain mood and bring to mind a range of possibilities that would be out of reach on a normal work day. Again the feeling of 'being at home' that was assisted by the Tudoresque buildings here or in Malaysia, when they were built by expatriate British settlers, is not quite what is produced when similar buildings are constructed by natives. For example, when Shui Hiung Chin built himself a Tudoresque house in Kota Kinabalu, Sabah, in 1994, he did so because his education had taken him to England. He spent important formative years there, and he wanted to bring a little piece of England back with him (illus. 77).[50] He was building in a foreign style, which his neighbours might see as exotic, but for him it was not to produce the 'holiday' effect,

77 Shui Hiung Chin, House in Kota Kinabalu, Sabah, Malaysia, 1994. Cosmopolitan Tudoresque.

but to remind him of Chester, for which he developed a fondness when he was studying medicine in Liverpool. So the building is not bringing his home to a far-away place, nor transporting him to an exotic realm without having to travel, but reminding him of a favourite place where he was learning to become the person he is. There is a close parallel with the classical buildings built for people who had been on the Grand Tour. It is cosmopolitan Tudor. Dr Chin's was the first indigenous rather than colonial production of Tudoresque in Kota Kinabalu, but now (thanks to his example) they are everywhere.[51] This tendency of an original idea to reproduce tells us something about the spread of fashion, and is different again.

An architecture of resistance

Dr Chin's son, Ross Chinn, has studied architecture in England and has learnt that his father's house is 'a symbol for bad architecture', but understandably finds that view problematic, since it is, more importantly, a personal symbol of 'what he wanted to achieve in his life, so the house only needs to satisfy one critic, and that is my father himself'.[52] This is the voice of Tudoresque autonomy, not feeling answerable to the critical establishment, only to one's own judgement. It lacks the conventional modernist architect's aversion to applied decoration, but finds an alternative kind of authenticity even in the stone cladding that is applied near the front door. The stones came from a nearby riverbed, not as a matter of principle for the doctor, but because artificial products were then unavailable.[53] When the building has this level of personal investment in it, who is going to listen to the critic who says that this is 'bogus' Tudor? Certainly not the person who wants to build it. And it is what a surprising number of people choose to build, when they have a choice.

The magazine *Homebuilding and Renovation*, which styles itself 'Britain's best-selling self-build magazine', gives practical advice and sets in train many hours of daydreaming, and there is much Tudoresque work illustrated on its pages. One of the best-organized self-build schemes was a group of houses in Honor Oak, south London, which was constructed making use of a radically simplified building method, devised by Walter Segal.[54] The houses were built with timber frames that supported the insulated wall panels. The joint between the panels was covered over with a timber strip. There is a very clear constructional rigour at work here, which finds expression undemonstratively at the building's surface. One of the original builder-residents noticed that if these cover strips were painted in a contrasting colour (black) and a few diagonal boards were added, then the house took on a Tudoresque appearance. For a few years that is how the house stood, but its Tudorisms have since been suppressed (illus. 78).

The Tudoresque can come to symbolize common-sense resistance to a spirit-crushing modernity. For example, in *Fahrenheit 451*, François

Truffaut's film of Ray Bradbury's novel, the book-reading Clarisse (one of the two roles in the film that is played by Julie Christie) lives in a small simple Tudoresque house (illus. 79). The drama is set in a future where the reading of books is prohibited, because it does not bring happiness. The official culture is hedonistic and consumerist, with tranquillizing drugs and enormous televisions. The narrative follows the protagonist, a 'fireman', whose job it is to burn books, as he comes to realize books' value, through meeting Clarisse. Her character is therefore pivotal in the story, and it is established by seeing her in connection with her house. It is small, so she is identified as marginal to society, and it is old-fashioned: a site of resistance to the official culture, which is represented by modernist dwellings, including blocks of flats at Roehampton, which were very well known to and much admired by architects.

Similarly, the dystopian future imagined in *A Clockwork Orange* (1971), Stanley Kubrick's film of Anthony Burgess's novel, the scenes of cruel ultra-violence are enacted for the most part in award-winning modernist buildings. The one point in the film where unofficial violence is turned against the protagonist, Alex, is after he has undergone

78 Walter Segal and the house-owner, Self-build house in Segal Close, Honor Oak, Lewisham, London, 1977–82. Accidentally almost Tudoresque.

79 A book-lover's house, in François Truffaut's *Fahrenheit 451*, 1966. A site of resistance to modernity.

aversion therapy. The state authorities have 'cured' him of his violent tendencies, partly by making him unable to listen to Beethoven without feeling pain. (It's a long story . . . .) When he is recognized by a former victim, now disabled because of Alex's attack, his revenge takes the form of playing recordings of Beethoven to him, which makes Alex in his torment leap from the window of the Tudor manor house in which, it turns out, he was being held.

The Tudoresque in these examples is presented as the site of resistance to modernity, as places where individuality can take a stand against conformity to state-enforced norms. When we look at the small would-be cottages in the suburbs from the outside, we might feel dismay at the conformity and mediocrity on display, but seen from within this environment is a product of autonomy and individualism that, for profound and deeply ingrained cultural reasons, finds expression in the same way each and every time.

This could be seen as a failing of artistry, but the houses would not be judged in that way if these were mass expressions of conformity to a modernist or a classical ideal. There is harmony here, and consistency – even rigour. These unassuming little houses address commonly felt needs. Those needs could certainly be met in more artfully accomplished and sophisticated ways, but actually *this* is the means that the mass culture has found to meet them.

Perhaps, like Virginia Woolf, one would choose death rather than live in Richmond, but given the limited means that most of us have at our disposal, we should celebrate the fact that so many of us can feel individualistic and self-possessed by availing ourselves of accommodation that is not showy or attention-seeking, but puts us in touch with the memory of the four Elizabethan acres that at some primitive level of the unconscious every inhabitant of Middle England knows to be their birthright.

References

Preface

1 See, for example: J. M. Richards, *The Castles on the Ground: Anatomy of Suburbia* (London, 1946); Alan Jackson, *Semi-Detached London: Suburban Development, Life and Transport, 1900–39* (London, 1973); John Betjeman, *Metro-land* (London, 1977); Arthur Edwards, *The Design of Suburbia* (London, 1981); Paul Oliver, Ian Davis and Ian Bentley, *Dunroamin: The Suburban Semi and its Enemies* (London, 1981); Elain Harwood and Andrew Saint, *London Suburbs* (London, 1999); Museum of Domestic Design and Architecture, *Little Palaces* (London, 2003); Gavin Stamp, 'Neo-Tudor and its Enemies', *Architectural History*, XLIX (2006), pp. 1–33.
2 Anthony Bertram, *Design* (Harmondsworth, 1938; reprinted 1943), p. 51.
3 Nikolaus Pevsner, *Pioneers of the Modern Movement* (London, 1936), p. 38.
4 At www.retrotogo.com, accessed 12 January 2011.

Chapter One

1 *The Private Lives of Elizabeth and Essex*, directed by Michael Curtiz (Warner Brothers, 1939); W. C. Sellar and R. J. Yeatman, *1066 and All That: A Memorable History of England, Comprising All the Parts You Can Remember, including 103 Good Things, 5 Bad Kings and 2 Genuine Dates* (London, 1930); see also Terry Deary and Neil Tonge, *The Terrible Tudors* (London, 1993), which is more accurate, and re-tells major myths, while pointing out that they are myths. By contrast, the humour in *1066 and All That* depends on the reader having prior knowledge of the historical events, in order to recognize the howling inaccuracies.
2 Fernand Braudel, *La Méditerranée et le monde méditerranéen à l'époque de Philippe II*, 3 vols (Paris, 1949); as *The Mediterranean and the Mediterranean World in the Age of Philip II*, trans. Sian Reynolds, 2 vols (London, 1972).
3 David Starkey, *The Reign of Henry VIII: Personalities and Politics* (London, 1985).
4 Exodus, chapter 5.
5 John Steel and Michael Wright, *The English House: 1,000 Years of Domestic Architecture* (London, 2007); Maurice Howard, *The Building of Elizabethan and*

6.   Henry Fielding, *Tom Jones* (London, 1749), book 1, chapter 4.
7.   Ibid., book 1, chapter 4.
8.   Bede, *Ecclesiastical History of the English People* (AD 731); Geoffrey of Monmouth, *The History of the Kings of Britain* (1136); William Camden, *Britannia* (1586).
9.   Linda Van Norden, 'The Elizabethan College of Antiquaries', unpublished Ph.D thesis (University of California at Los Angeles, 1946), cited in Daniel Woolf, *The Social Circulation of the Past* (Oxford, 2003), p. 162.
10. See Dana Arnold and Stephen Bending, *Tracing Architecture: The Aesthetics of Antiquarianism* (Oxford, 2003); Stephen Bending, 'Everyman is Naturally an Antiquarian: Francis Gross and Polite Antiquities', in ibid. pp. 100–110; Woolf, *The Social Circulation of the Past*; and Rosemary Sweet, *Antiquaries: The Discovery of the Past in Eighteenth-century Britain* (London, 2004).
11. Horace Walpole, letter to Horace Mann, 14 April 1743, in *The Yale Edition of Horace Walpole's Correspondence*, ed. W. S. Lewis, 48 vols (New Haven, 1937–83), vol. XVIII, p. 211.
12. James Stuart and Nicholas Revett, *The Antiquities of Athens*, 4 vols (London, 1762–1816); Richard Payne Knight, *A Discourse on the Worship of Priapus, and its Connexion with the Mystic Theology of the Antients* (London, 1786).
13. Bending, 'Everyman Is Naturally an Antiquarian', p. 101.
14. Argyro Loukaki, *Living Ruins, Value Conflicts* (Aldershot, 2008); Lynne Withey, *Grand Tours and Cooks Tours* (London, 1997); Bending, 'Everyman is Naturally an Antiquarian', p. 100.
15. Tim Richardson, *The Arcadian Friends: Inventing the English Landscape Garden* (London, 2007), p. 354; Clive Aslet and Alan Powers, *The National Trust Book of the English House* (Harmondsworth, 1985), pp. 125–6.
16. David M. Wilson, *The British Museum: A History* (London, 2002).
17. George Lipscombe, *Journey into South Wales in the Year 1799* (London, 1802), pp. xv–xviii.
18. William Gilpin, *Observations on the Mountains and Lakes of Cumberland and Westmoreland*, 2 vols (London, 1786), vol. II, p. 188; Gilpin, *Observations on the River Wye, and Several Parts of South Wales etc., Relative Chiefly to Picturesque Beauty: Made in the Year 1770* (London, 1782), pp. 32–3.
19. Gerald Newman, *The Rise of English Nationalism: A Cultural History, 1740–1830* (London, 1987), p. 57.
20. Victor Kiernan, 'Nationalist Movements and Social Classes', in *Nationalist Movements*, ed. Anthony D. Smith (New York, 1976), p. 112, cited by Newman, *Rise of English Nationalism*, p. 53.
21. Kiernan, 'Nationalist Movements and Social Classes', p. 112, cited by Newman, *Rise of English Nationalism*, p. 53.

22 Newman, *Rise of English Nationalism*, p. 57.
23 *Gentleman's Magazine*, XXXVI (1766), p. 592, cited by Newman, *Rise of English Nationalism*, p. 37.
24 Michael Snodin, *Horace Walpole's Strawberry Hill* (New Haven and London, 2009); Martin Battestin and Ruthe Battestin, *Henry Fielding: A Life* (London, 1989).
25 Dafydd Moore, *Ossian and Ossianism*, 4 vols (London, 2004); Andrew Ballantyne, 'Two Nations, Twice: National Identity in "The Wild Irish Girl" and "Sybil"', in *Cultural Identities and the Aesthetics of Britishness*, ed. Dana Arnold (Manchester, 2004), pp. 87–98.
26 The painting is by Girodet (Anne-Louis Girodet-Trioson, one of Jacques-Louis David's pupils), *L'Apothéose des héros français morts pour la Patrie pendant la guerre de la Liberté, conduits par la Victoire viennent habiter l'Elysée aérienne où les ombres d'Ossian et de ses valeureux guerriers s'empressent de leur donner dans ce séjour d'immortalité et de gloire la fête de la Paix et de l'Amitié* (1801).
27 Samuel Johnson, 'Preface to Shakespeare', in *The Plays of William Shakespeare in Ten Volumes* (London, 1765).
28 Stuart Piggott notes that 'of the thirty or forty books published between 1670 and 1740 concerned with British or Romano-British antiquities about half appeared around 1710–30'; see Piggott, *William Stukeley: An Eighteenth-century Antiquary* (London, 1950; revised 1985), p. 18; see also Woolf, *The Social Circulation of the Past*; and Sweet, *Antiquaries*.
29 Inigo Jones, *The Most Notable Antiquity of Great Britain, Vulgarly Called Stone-Heng, on Salisbury Plain, Restored* (London, 1655); Andrew Ballantyne, 'Misprisions of Stonehenge', in *Architecture as Experience: Radical Change in Spatial Practice*, ed. Dana Arnold and Andrew Ballantyne (London, 2004), pp. 11–35.
30 Geoffrey of Monmouth, *History of the Kings of Britain*.
31 William Stukeley, *Stonehenge: A Temple Restor'd to the British Druids* (London, 1740); Stukeley, *Avebury: A Temple of the British Druids* (London, 1743).
32 Richard Gough, *Anecdotes of British Topography* (London, 1768); John Whitaker, *The Genuine History of the Britons Asserted* (London, 1772); Sharon Turner, *History of the Anglo-Saxons* [1799–1805], 4th edn, 3 vols (London, 1823), cited in Sweet, *Antiquaries*, p. 198.
33 Harold McCarter Taylor and Joan Taylor, *Anglo-Saxon Architecture*, 3 vols (Cambridge, 1965–78).
34 Horace Walpole, *The Castle of Otranto* (London, 1764); Michael McCarthy, *The Origins of the Gothic Revival* (New Haven and London, 1987).
35 Clifford S. L. Davies, 'The Tudor Delusion', in *Times Literary Supplement* (11 June 2008), at http://entertainment.timesonline.co.uk/tol/arts_and_entertainment/the_tls/article4111910.ece. Davies suggests that we should not be referring to 'the Tudors' at all, but by now it has become a conventional label, and we might as well use it, just as we call the inhabitants of pre-1450s Constantinople 'Byzantine', which is not what they called each other. David Hume, *History of England under the House of Tudor*, 2 vols (London, 1759).

36 Jack Lynch, *The Age of Elizabeth in the Age of Johnson* (Cambridge, 2002), p. 66.
37 Henry St John, Viscount Bolingbroke, *Historical Writings*, ed. Isaak Kramnick (Chicago, 1972), p. 69, cited by Lynch, *The Age of Elizabeth*, p. 60.
38 Samuel Johnson, *The Rambler*, ed. Walter Jackson Bate and Albrecht B. Strauss, vols III and IV of the *Yale Edition of the Works of Samuel Johnson* (New Haven, 1969), vol. IV, p. 289, cited by Lynch, *The Age of Elizabeth*, p. 61.
39 Lynch, *The Age of Elizabeth*, pp. 63–4.
40 David Hume, letter to Andrew Millar [1757], in *The Letters of David Hume*, ed. J.Y.T. Greig (Oxford, 1932), vol. I, p. 49, cited by Lynch, *The Age of Elizabeth*, p. 65.
41 Lynch, *The Age of Elizabeth*, p. 74.
42 David Hume, *The History of England from the Invasion of Julius Caesar to the Revolution in 1688*, 6 vols (Indianapolis, IN, 1983), vol. III, pp. 62–3.
43 Francis Bacon, *The Great Instauration* (London, 1620).
44 Douglas Lanier, *Shakespeare and Modern Popular Culture* (Oxford, 2002); Bill Bryson, *Shakespeare: The World as a Stage* (London, 2007); and Jack Lynch, *Becoming Shakespeare: How a Dead Poet Became the World's Foremost Literary Genius* (London, 2008).
45 Shakespeare editions included: Nicholas Rowe (1709), Alexander Pope (1725), Lewis Theobald (1733), Thomas Hanmer (1744), Samuel Johnson (1765), Edmond Malone (1790), among many others. See Lanier, *Shakespeare and Modern Popular Culture*, p. 29. Charles Lamb and Mary Lamb, *Tales from Shakespeare* (London, 1807), made the plots of some of the plays accessible to children. Johanne M. Stochholm, *Garrick's Folly: The Shakespeare Jubilee of 1769 at Stratford and Drury Lane* (London, 1964).
46 A poster promoting it is archived at the British Library.
47 Aslet and Powers, *The National Trust Book of the English House*, p. 133; www.exploringsurreyspast.org.uk/GetRecord/SHHER_7371
48 Andrew Ballantyne, *Architecture, Landscape and Liberty: Richard Payne Knight and the Picturesque* (Cambridge, 1997).
49 Gavin Townsend, 'The Tudor House in America, 1890–1930', unpublished PhD thesis (University of California, Santa Barbara, 1986), p. 7.
50 Richard Payne Knight, *An Analytical Inquiry Into the Principles of Taste* (London, 1805).
51 Peter Mandler, *The Fall and Rise of the Stately Home* (New Haven and London, 1997), p. 31.
52 Deary and Tonge, *The Terrible Tudors*; John Madden, *Shakespeare in Love* (1998).
53 John Whittaker, *Ceremonial of the Coronation of His Most Sacred Majesty King George the Fourth* (London, 1823); see Timothy Mowl, *Elizabethan and Jacobean Style* (London, 1993), p. 203.
54 Sweet, *Antiquaries*, p. 339.
55 Charles Dickens, *The Old Curiosity Shop* [1841], Everyman's Library edition (New York and London, 1995), pp. 4–5.

56 Augustus Welby Northmore Pugin, *Contrasts; or, A Parallel Between the Noble Edifices of the Middle Ages and Corresponding Buildings of the Present Day; Shewing the Present Decay of Taste* (London, 1836; 2nd edn with additional plates, 1841); Pugin, *Ornaments of the Fifteenth and Sixteenth Centuries: Details of Ancient Timber Houses* (London, 1836); Pugin, *True Principles of Pointed or Christian Architecture* (London, 1841).

57 Frances Chiu, 'Faulty Towers: Reform, Radicalism and the Gothic Castle, 1760–1800', *Romanticism on the Net*, no. 44 (2006), p. 4.

58 David Watkin, 'An Eloquent Sermon in Stone', *City Journal* (Summer 1998).

59 Walter Scott, *Kenilworth* (Edinburgh, 1821).

60 Edward German and Basil Hood, *Merrie England* (1902).

Chapter Two

1 The title of this section is an allusion to Gregory Bateson, *Mind and Nature* (London, 1980).

2 James Stuart and Nicholas Revett, *The Antiquities of Athens, and Other Monuments of Greece* (London, 1762).

3 Shakespeare's birthplace reproduced as an exhibition building at Crystal Palace would be one such (see above, chapter One); and also the British pavilion, Exposition Universelle, Paris, 1900 (illus. 50), would be another.

4 Paul Oliver, 'The Galleon on the Front Door: Imagery of the House and Garden', in Paul Oliver, Ian Davis and Ian Bentley, *Dunroamin: The Suburban Semi and its Enemies* (London, 1981), pp. 155–72.

5 See Hentie Louw, 'Colour Combinations', *Architects' Journal* (4 July 1990), pp. 44–53; and subsequent response from F.W.B. Charles, 'Frame Finish', *Architects' Journal* (13 March 1991), pp. 32–5.

6 John Prizeman, *Houses of Britain: The Outside View* (London, 2003), p. 51.

7 Andrew Brown, *The Rows of Chester* (London, 1999).

8 Charles, 'Frame Finish', p. 34.

9 Nathaniel Kent, *Hints to Gentlemen of Landed Property* (London, 1775).

10 See particularly *Communications to the Board of Agriculture*, vol. 1 (London, 1797), pp. 77–117.

11 Colen Campbell, *Vitruvius Britannicus*, 3 vols (London, 1715–25). There were later volumes with the same title, compiled by different editors.

12 William Chambers, *A Treatise on Civil Architecture in which the Principles of that Art are Laid Down and Illustrated by a Great Number of Plates Accurately Designed and Elegantly Engraved by the Best Hands* (London, 1759).

13 William Chambers, *Designs of Chinese Buildings, Furniture, Dresses, Machines, and Utensils: to which is annexed a Description of their Temples, Houses, Gardens, &c* (London, 1757).

14 Nathaniel Kent, *Hints to Gentlemen of Landed Property* (London, 1775); John Wood the Younger, *A Series of Plans for Cottages or Habitations of the Labourer* (Bath,

1781); John Plaw, *Ferme Ornée; or, Rural Improvements: A Series of Domestic and Ornamental Designs* (London, 1823).
15. James Malton, *An Essay on British Cottage Architecture: Being an Attempt to Perpetuate on Principle, that Peculiar Mode of Building, which was Originally the Effect of Chance* (London, 1798).
16. Ibid., p. 4.
17. Ibid., pp. 8–11.
18. Ibid., p. 8.
19. Oliver Goldsmith, *The Deserted Village* (1770), lines 63–74.
20. Humphry Repton, *Red Book for Endsleigh*, 1814 (private collection): www.parksandgardens.ac.uk/index2.php?option=com_parksandgardens&task=site&id=1258&preview=1&Itemid=
21. Edmund Burke, *Reflections on the Revolution in France* [1790], ed. Conor Cruise O'Brien (Harmondsworth, 1982), p. 181.
22. Charles-Louis de Secondat, Baron Montesquieu, *De l'ésprit de lois* (Paris, 1748).
23. Burke, *Reflections on the Revolution in France*, p. 175.
24. John Ruskin, *The Poetry of Architecture; or, The Architecture of the Nations of Europe Considered in its Association with Natural Scenery and National Character* (London, 1837–8), pp. 156–7.
25. Sebastiano Serlio, *Tutte l'opere d'architettura et prospetiva* [1537–75]; as *Sebastiano Serlio on Architecture*, trans. Vaughan Hart and Peter Hicks, 2 vols (New Haven and London, 1996–2001). Andrea Palladio, *I quattro libri dell'architettura* [1570]; as *The Four Books of Architecture*, trans. Richard Schofield and Robert Tavernor (Cambridge, MA, 2002).
26. Andrew Ballantyne, *Architecture, Landscape and Liberty: Richard Payne Knight and the Picturesque* (Cambridge, 1997), pp. 295–9, for Wilkins; pp. 251–9, for mixed style.
27. Ibid., p. 295.
28. C. J. Richardson, *Observations on the Architecture of England During the Reigns of Queen Elizabeth and King James I* (London, 1837), p. 5. See also Henry Shaw, *Details of Elizabethan Architecture* (London, 1839).
29. Ballantyne, *Architecture, Landscape and Liberty*, pp. 242–3.
30. Thomas Rickman, *Attempt to Discriminate the Styles of Architecture in England, from the Conquest to the Reformation* (London, 1817). See above, chapter One.
31. Richardson, *Observations*, p. 7.
32. Ibid., p. 3.
33. Richardson later covered Tudoresque cottages, approvingly, in C. J. Richardson, *The Englishman's House: A Practical Guide for Selecting or Building a House* (London, 1870).
34. Richardson, *Observations*, p. 8.
35. Mark Girouard, *The Victorian Country House* (New Haven and London, 1979), p. 93.

References

36 F. Goodwin, *Domestic Architecture, Being a Second Series of Designs for Cottages, Lodges, Villas and Other Residences in the Grecian, Italian and Old English styles of architecture* (London, 1834), p. ix.
37 See above, chapter One.
38 P. F. Robinson, 'The Architecture of Old England', in Robinson, *Domestic Architecture in the Tudor Style* (London, 1837), p. 4. See also Robinson, *Designs for Lodges and Park Entrances* (London, 1833).
39 '. . . very excellent works published by Britton, Pugin and others, affording text books of the highest value to the Architects of the present day', in Robinson, *Domestic Architecture in the Tudor Style*: address, p. 1.
40 Goodwin, *Domestic Architecture*, p. xii.
41 Ibid., design no. 8, no page number.
42 Ibid., p. xii.
43 J. C. Loudon, *Encyclopaedia of Cottage, Farm, and Villa Architecture and Furniture*, 2 vols (London, 1833), vol. II, pp. 790–821.
44 Ibid., p. 792: 'The *Beau Idéal* of the English Villa'.
45 Ibid., p. 794.
46 Augustus Welby Northmore Pugin, *The True Principles of Pointed or Christian Architecture* (London, 1841), p. 62.
47 William James Audsley and George Ashdown Audsley, *Notes from Cottage Lodge and Villa Architecture* (Glasgow, 1868), p. 9.
48 Ibid., p. 2.
49 Pugin, *True Principles*, p. 61.
50 Audsley and Audsley, *Notes from Cottage Lodge and Villa Architecture*, p. 1.
51 Robert Kerr, *The Gentleman's House; or, How to Plan English Residences from the Parsonage to the Palace* (London, 1865), p. 51.
52 Ibid.
53 Jill Allibone, *George Devey, Architect, 1820–1886* (Cambridge, 1991); Jill Franklin, *The Gentleman's Country House and its Plan, 1835–1914* (London, 1981), p. 12.
54 Betteshanger, Kent, built in 1856 for Sir Walter James, later 1st Baron Northbourne, St Albans Court near Deal in Kent. The construction was finished in 1875. For more details, see Girouard, *The Victorian Country House*, p. 220.

Chapter Three

1 A. P. Thornton, *The Habit of Authority: Paternalism in British History* (Toronto, 1966); G. E. Mingay, *The Gentry: The Rise and Fall of a Ruling Class* (London and New York, 1976).
2 Roy Porter, *English Society in the Eighteenth Century* (Harmondsworth, 1982), pp. 65–6. This Joseph Banks was the uncle of the more famous Sir Joseph Banks, botanist. See Patrick O'Brian, *Joseph Banks* (London, 1987).
3 Gottfried von Bülow, 'Journey through England and Scotland by Lupold Von

Wedel in the Years 1584 and 1585', *Transactions of the Royal Historical Society*, n.s., IX (1895), pp. 223–70. Cited in J. Hurstfield and A.G.R. Smith, *Documents of Modern History: Elizabethan People, State and Society* (London, 1972), p. 16.

4 Brian Bailey, *English Manor Houses* (London, 1983), p. 132; Hurstfield and Smith, *Documents of Modern History*, p. 23.

5 Donald Lupton, 'London and the Countrey Carbonadoed' [1632], in J. D. Wilson, *Life in Shakespeare's England: A Book of Elizabethan Prose* (Cambridge, 1915), p. 225.

6 John Selden, 'Table Talk' [1654]; ed. Edward Arber in *English Reprints*, 30 vols (London, 1895), vol. VI; cited in William A. McClung, *The Country House in English Renaissance Poetry* (London, 1977), p. 33.

7 The idea of Robin Hood was crystallized by Walter Scott, in *Ivanhoe* (1819), which reached a huge popular audience. Robin's subsequent appearances all owe something to that incarnation. Benjamin Disraeli, *Sybil; or, The Two Nations* (1845).

8 Mark Girouard, *Life in the English Country House: A Social and Architectural History* (New Haven and London, 1978), p. 240. Eric Hobsbawm, *The Invention of Tradition* (Cambridge, 1983).

9 Martin Wallen, 'Lord Egremont's Dogs: The Cynosure of Turner's Petworth Landscapes', *English Literary History*, LXXIII/4 (2006), p. 14; Alun Howkins, *Reshaping Rural England: A Social History* (London, 1991).

10 Nathaniel Kent, *Hints to Gentlemen of Landed Property* (London, 1775), pp. 242–3.

11 Gerald Newman, *The Rise of English Nationalism: A Cultural History, 1740–1830* (London, 1987), pp. 11–12.

12 George Stanley Repton, Letter to John Harford, Esq., 18 August 1810, cited in Nigel Temple, *John Nash and the Village Picturesque* (Gloucester, 1979), p. 135.

13 Mavis Batey, 'The Swiss Garden, Old Warden, Bedfordshire', in *Garden History*, III/4 (Autumn 1975), pp. 40–43 (p. 40); and see John Steel and Michael Wright, *The English House: 1,000 Years of Domestic Architecture* (Woodbridge, 2007), p. 254.

14 William Cobbett, 'Winchester, Saturday 28 September 1822', in *Rural Rides*, 2 vols (London, 1830), vol. I, p. 104.

15 Adrian Tinniswood, *Life in the English Country Cottage* (London, 1995), p. 122.

16 Joseph Nash, *Architecture of the Middle Ages: Drawn from Nature and on Stone* (London, 1838); Joseph Nash, *The Mansions of England in the Olden Time*, 4 vols (London, 1839–49).

17 Nash, *Mansions*, vol. I, p. 1.

18 David Hume, cited by Richard Brown, *Domestic Architecture* (London, 1842), p. 21.

19 Benjamin Disraeli, *Coningsby* (1844); Disraeli, *Sybil* (1845); Disraeli, *Tancred* (1847); C. H. Kegel, 'Lord John Manners and the Young England Movement: Romanticism in Politics', *Western Political Quarterly*, XIV/14 (September 1961), pp. 691–7.

20 Lord John Manners, *England's Trust* (London, 1841).

21 Andrew Ballantyne, 'Two Nations, Twice: *The Wild Irish Girl* and *Sybil*', in *Cultural*

Identities and the Aesthetics of Britishness, ed. Dana Arnold (Manchester, 2004), pp. 87–98.
22 Henry Russell, 'Fine Old-English Gentleman (A Song of the Olden Time)', 11 December 1844, at www.pdmusic.org/russell.html
23 Sir George Gilbert Scott, *Remarks on Secular and Domestic Architecture, Present and Future* (London, 1857).
24 P. J. Cain and A. G. Hopkins, *British Imperialism, 1688–2000* (London, 1996), pp. 119–20.
25 Thomas Hay Sweet Escott, *England: Its People, Polity and Pursuits*, 2 vols (London, 1879), II, pp. 23–4.
26 Bailey, *English Manor Houses*, p. 237.
27 Jill Allibone, *George Devey, Architect, 1820–1886* (Cambridge, 1991), p. 25; J. Woodforde, *The Truth About Cottages* (London, 1969), p. 26; Anthony Quiney, 'A Benevolent Business', *Country Life* (29 August 1991).
28 Nigel Temple, *John Nash and the Village Picturesque* (Gloucester, 1979).
29 Ken Morley and Margaret Morley, *Wingrave: A Rothschild Village in the Vale* (Dunstable, 1999), p. 69.
30 Niall Fergusson, *The World's Banker: The History of the House of Rothschild* (London, 1998).
31 Morley and Morley, *Wingrave*, p. 66.
32 Anon., in *Bucks Advertiser and Aylesbury News* [1874]; cited in Morley and Morley, *Wingrave*, p. 73.
33 Anon., 'Wing: The Village Hall', *Leighton Buzzard Observer* (2 January 1906), p. 1.
34 Ibid., p. 1.
35 Samuel Smiles, *Self-Help* [1858]; see edition of London, 1911, p. 22.
36 Edwin Hodder, *Life of Samuel Morley* (London, 1887).
37 See Quiney, 'A Benevolent Business'.
38 William Hulme Lever, *Viscount Leverhulme by his Son* (London, 1927); Brian Lewis, *So Clean: Lord Leverhulme, Soap and Civilisation* (Manchester, 2008); Edward Hubbard and Michael Shippobottom, *A Guide to Port Sunlight Village* (Liverpool, 2006).
39 Edward Hubbard, *The Work of John Douglas* (London, 1991), p. 170.
40 Carl Chinn, *The Cadbury Story: A Short History* (Redditch, 1998); Joe Brannan and Frances Brannan, *A Postcard from Bournville* (Studley, 1992).

Chapter Four

1 Edmund Burke, *Reflections on the Revolution in France* [1790], ed. Conor Cruise O'Brien (Harmondsworth, 1982).
2 William Harrison, 'An Historicall Description of the Islande of Britayne' [1577], in *Documents of Modern History: Elizabethan People, State and Society*, ed. Joel Hurstfield and A.G.R. Smith (London, 1972), p. 50.
3 *Statutes of the Realm*, 11 vols (London, 1810–28; reprinted 1963), vol. IV, part 2, pp. 804–5 ('The Planning Act for Erecting and Maintaining Cottages, 1588–9').

4 John Guy, *The Tudors: A Very Short Introduction* (Oxford, 2000), pp. 2–3; John Guy, *Tudor England* (Oxford, 1988).
5 David M. Palliser, *The Age of Elizabeth: England under the Later Tudors, 1547–1603* (London, 1983), p. 116; Paul Slack, 'Poverty and Social Regulation in Elizabethan England', in *The Reign of Elizabeth I*, ed. Christopher Haigh (London, 1984), p. 241.
6 John Woodforde, *The Truth about Cottages* (London, 1969), p. 21.
7 John Locke, *Second Treatise of Civil Government* (London, 1690), sections 32 and 33.
8 John Archer, *Architecture and Suburbia: From English Villa to American Dream House, 1690–2000* (Minneapolis, MN, 2005), p. 26.
9 Woodforde, *The Truth about Cottages*, p. 17.
10 William Pitt (the Elder), Speech on the Excise Bill, House of Commons (March 1763).
11 Robert Beatson, 'On Cottages', in *Communications to the Board of Agriculture on Subjects Relative to the Husbandry and Internal Improvement of the Country* (London, 1796), p. 106.
12 Thomas Barker, Letter to the Board of Agriculture, 14 January 1796, in *Communications to the Board of Agriculture*, p. 80.
13 David Stemp, *Three Acres and a Cow: The Life and Works of Eli Hamshire* (London, 1995); A. W. Ashby, 'Jesse Collings', in *Oxford Dictionary of National Biography* (Oxford, 2004), vol. XII, pp. 668–9; Dennis Hardy, *Utopian England: Community Experiments, 1900–1945* (London, 2000); Arthur Lloyd, *Three Acres and a Cow: An Agricultural Lay* (London, 1885).
14 G. K. Chesterton, *What's Wrong with the World?* (London, 1910), part I, 'The Homelessness of Man', chapter 9.
15 Leo XIII, *Rerum novarum: Encyclical of Pope Leo XIII on Capital and Labour* (1891), which discussed property and subsistence; Hilaire Belloc, *The Servile State* (1912); Arthur Penty, *Post-Industrialism* (1914); G. K. Chesterton, *Utopia of Usurers* (1917); Arthur Smith, *Three Acres and Employment* (1927); G. K. Chesterton, *The Outline of Sanity* (1927); Hilaire Belloc, *An Essay on The Restoration of Property* (1936).
16 David Thistlewood, 'A. J. Penty (1875–1937) and the Legacy of Nineteenth-century English Domestic Architecture', *Journal of the Society of Architectural Historians*, XLVI (1987), pp. 327–41 (p. 331).
17 Christopher Harvie and Colin Matthew, *The Oxford Illustrated History of Britain* (Oxford, 1984), pp. 487–8.
18 George Grossmith and Weedon Grossmith, *Diary of a Nobody* (London, 1892), entries for 25–7 April (year unspecified, but the work first appeared serialized in *Punch*, 1888–9).
19 Roy Lewis and Angus Maude, *The English Middle Classes* (London, 1949), p. 66; John Stevenson, *Social Conditions in Britain between the Wars* (London, 1977), pp. 11–12.
20 Lawrence James, *The Middle Class: A History* (London, 2006), p. 449.

21 Stevenson, *Social Conditions in Britain between the Wars*, p. 15.
22 Mark Swenarton, *Homes Fit for Heroes* (London, 1981), pp. 1, 76–8.
23 Ibid., p. 79.
24 Stevenson, *Social Conditions in Britain between the Wars*, pp. 11–12.
25 Ibid., p. 17.
26 Ibid.
27 Trevor Rowley, *The English Landscape in the Twentieth Century* (Hambledon, 2006), p. 195.
28 Ibid., p. 195.
29 Ross McKibbin, *Classes and Cultures: England, 1918–1951* (Oxford, 1998), p. 77.
30 J. B. Priestley, *English Journey* (London, 1934), p. 401.
31 McKibbin, *Classes and Cultures*, p. 77.
32 Ibid., p. 73.
33 James, *The Middle Class*, p. 412.
34 Reginald Blomfield, *Modernismus* (London, 1934).
35 McKibbin, *Classes and Cultures*, pp. 75–6.
36 Ibid., pp. 75–6; Paul Oliver, Ian Davis and Ian Bentley, *Dunroamin: The Suburban Semi and its Enemies* (London, 1981).
37 See below, chapter Seven.
38 Anon., in *Ideal Home* (May 1920), p. 171.
39 M. J. Wiener, *English Culture and the Decline of the Industrial Spirit, 1850–1980* (Cambridge, 1982); David Matless, *Landscape and Englishness* (London, 1998); and McKibbin, *Classes and Cultures*.
40 McKibbin, *Classes and Cultures*, p. 76.
41 Ebenezer Howard, *To-Morrow: A Peaceful Path to Real Reform* (London, 1898), reprinted in 1902 as *Garden Cities of To-Morrow*; McKibbin, *Classes and Cultures*; Alan Jackson, *London's Metro-land* (London, 2006).
42 *Metro-land Annual Guide Book 1927* (London, 1927), p. 30.
43 Hermann Muthesius, *Das englische Haus*, 3 vols (Berlin, 1904–5; 2nd edn, 1908–11); as *The English House*, slightly abridged one-volume version of the 2nd edn, trans. Janet Seligman (New York, 1979), p. 7.
44 Muthesius, *The English House*, p. 7.
45 George Orwell, *Coming Up For Air* (London, 1939); see Harmondsworth edition of 1962, pp. 11–13. This is written in the voice of the novel's protagonist. The elisions are of characters' and fictional places' names.
46 Representation of the People Act, 1918.
47 Representation of the People (Equal Franchise) Act, 1928.
48 J. M. Richards, *The Castles on the Ground* (London, 1946; 2nd edn, 1973), p. 22.
49 Mary Douglas, *Purity and Danger* (London, 1966).
50 Deleuze and Guattari, 'Micropolitics and Segmentarity', in *Mille plateaux* (Paris, 1980); as *A Thousand Plateaus, Capitalism and Schizophrenia*, trans. Brian Massumi (London, 1987), pp. 208–31.
51 James, *The Middle Class*, p. 357; Denis Hardy and Colin Ward, *Arcadia for All: The*

   Legacy of a Makeshift Landscape (Nottingham, 1984).
52 Lord Kennett [Edward Hilton Young], 'Muddleford', in 'English Character' [1947]; in Judy Giles and Tim Middleton, *Writing Englishness: An Introductory Sourcebook* (London, 1995), p. 220; John Seymour, *The Complete Book of Self-Sufficiency* (London, 1976), p. 7.
53 Osbert Lancaster, *Pillar to Post* (London, 1938).
54 Ian Bentley, 'Arcadia Becomes Dunroamin: Suburban Growth and the Roots of Opposition', in Oliver, Davis and Bentley, *Dunroamin*, pp. 54–76 (p. 74); Alan Powers, *Oliver Hill, Architect and Lover of Life, 1887–1968* (London, 1989).
55 D. Simpson, 'Beautiful Tudor', *Architectural Review*, CLXII (July 1977), p. 36.
56 Anon., in *Ideal Home* (June 1930), pp. 476–7.
57 Simpson, 'Beautiful Tudor', p. 36.
58 Oliver, 'The Galleon on the Front Door', in Oliver, Davis and Bentley, *Dunroamin*, pp. 155–72.
59 Anon., *Ideal Home* (December 1921), p. 219.
60 W. C. Sellar and R. J. Yeatman, *1066 and All That: A Memorable History of England, Comprising All the Parts You Can Remember, including 103 Good Things, 5 Bad Kings and 2 Genuine Dates* (London, 1930).
61 See above, chapter Three.
62 Thomas Garner and Arthur Stratton, *The Domestic Architecture of England during the Tudor Period* (London, 1929).
63 Robert Wemyss Symonds, 'The "Passing Delicacie" of the English Home', *Ideal Home* (December 1952/January 1953 [double issue]), pp. 66–75.
64 George Orwell, *The Road to Wigan Pier* (London, 1937), part 2, chapter 8.
65 George Orwell, *Coming Up For Air* (London, 1939), part 4, chapter 1.
66 Le Corbusier, *Vers une architecture* (Paris, 1924); as *Towards a New Architecture*, trans. Frederick Etchells (London, 1927); as *Towards an Architecture*, trans. John Goodman (Los Angeles, 2007).

Chapter Five

1 Erving Goffman, *The Presentation of Self in Everyday Life* (Garden City, NY, 1959).
2 Ibid., p. 98.
3 Thorstein Veblen, *The Theory of the Leisure Class* (New York, 1899). John Kenneth Galbraith, 'The Higher Economic Purpose of Women', *MS Magazine* (May 1974), reprinted in *Annals of an Abiding Liberal*, ed. J. K. Galbraith (Boston, MA, 1979), pp. 36–46.
4 Andrew Ballantyne, *Deleuze and Guattari for Architects* (London, 2007), pp. 1–4; Judith Butler, *Gender Trouble* (London, 1990). Michel Foucault, *Le Souci du soi* (Paris, 1984); as *A History of Sexuality, Volume 3: The Care of the Self*, trans. Robert Hurley (New York, 1986).
5 Ignatius Phayre [William George Fitzgerald], 'Hitler's Mountain Home', *Homes and Gardens* (November 1938), pp. 193–5; and see Simon Waldman, 'At Home

with the Fuhrer', *The Guardian* (Monday, 3 November 2003), at www.guardian.co.uk/world/2003/nov/03/secondworldwar.blogging

6 Joseph Addison, in *The Spectator*, no. 15 (1711), in Joseph Addison et al., *The Spectator*, ed. G. Gregory Smith, 4 vols (Toronto, 1930), vol. I, p. 59.

7 William Shenstone, 'Unconnected Thoughts on Gardening', in *The Works in Verse and Prose, of William Shenstone, Esq.*, ed. Robert Dodsley, 2 vols (London, 1764), vol. II; see John Dixon Hunt and Peter Willis, eds, *The Genius of the Place* (London, 1975; 2nd edn, Cambridge, MA, 1988), pp. 289–97; Jill H. Casid, 'Some Queer Versions of Georgic', in *Sowing Empire: Landscape and Colonization*, ed. Casid (Minneapolis, MN, 2005), pp. 134–56.

8 Thomas Jefferson, 'Memorandums Made on a Tour to Some of the Gardens in England' [1786], in *The Genius of the Place*, ed. Hunt and Willis, p. 335.

9 Jean-Jacques Rousseau, 'Discours sur les sciences et les arts' (Dijon, 1750), trans. Roger D. Masters and Judith R. Masters as 'Discourse on the Sciences and Arts', in *The Collected Writings of Rousseau*, ed. Roger D. Masters and Christopher Kelly, 12 vols (Hanover, NH, and London, 1992), vol. II: *Discourse on the Sciences and Arts (First Discourse) and Polemics*, p. 12.

10 Jean-Jacques Rousseau, *Le Devin du village* (Paris, 1760).

11 Rousseau, 'Discours', p. 6.

12 Ibid., p. 22.

13 Marc-Antoine Laugier, *Essai sur l'architecture* (Paris, 1752), as *An Essay on Architecture*, trans. Wolfgang and Anni Herrmann (New York, 1977).

14 Johann Joachim Winckelmann, *Anmerkungen über die Geschichte der Kunst des Alterthums* (Dresden, 1767), as *History of the Art of Antiquity*, trans. Harry Francis Mallgrave (Los Angeles, 2006), p. 186.

15 Marc-Antoine Laugier, *Observations sur l'architecture* (Paris, 1765), pp. 23, 36, 119, 160, 180–85.

16 Pierre Arizzoli-Clémentel, *L'Album de Marie-Antoinette: Vues et plans du Petit Trianon à Versailles* (Paris, 2008); Antonia Fraser, *Marie Antoinette: The Journey* (London, 2001), p. 247; Ian Thompson, *The Sun King's Garden: Louis XIV, Andre Le Nôtre and the Creation of the Gardens of Versailles* (London, 2006), p. 321.

17 William Wordsworth, *The Prelude* (1805), book II, line 108.

18 William Wordsworth, 'Lines Written a Few Miles Above Tintern Abbey, on Revisiting the Banks of the Wye During a Tour, 13 July 1798', in Wordsworth and Samuel Taylor Coleridge, *Lyrical Ballads* (London, 1798), lines 102–12.

19 *Morning Post and Gazetteer*, no. 9569 (6 September 1799): at www.rc.umd.edu/editions/shelley/devil/devil.stc1799.html

20 *Communications to the Board of Agriculture on Subjects Relative to the Husbandry and Internal Improvement of the Country* (London, 1796), p. 80.

21 Thomas D. W. Dearn, *Sketches in Architecture: Consisting of Original Designs for Cottages and Rural Dwellings, Suitable to Persons of Moderate Fortune, and for Comfort and Retirement* (London, 1807), p. 5.

22 Andrew Ballantyne, 'Joseph Gandy and the Politics of Rustic Charm', in

Articulating British Classicism: New Approaches to Eighteenth-Century Architecture, ed. Barbara Arciszewska and Elizabeth McKellar (Aldershot, 2004), pp. 163–85.
23 Richard Elsam, *An Essay on Rural Architecture* (London, 1803), pp. 6–7.
24 Hunt and Willis, eds, *The Genius of the Place*.
25 Andrew Ballantyne, *Architecture, Landscape and Liberty: Richard Payne Knight and the Picturesque* (Cambridge, 1997), pp. 37–9.
26 Knight and the duke shared an admiration for the work of the painter Sir George Hayter. In 1794–5 Knight had a famous public argument with Repton.
27 John Russell, Duke of Bedford, Marquess of Tavistock: the family's titles are familiar from the names of streets and squares in the Bedford estate. See Dana Arnold, *Re-presenting the Metropolis: Architecture, Urban Experience and Social Life in London, 1800–1840* (Aldershot, 2000).
28 Stephen Daniels, 'Gothic Gallantry: Humphry Repton, Lord Byron and the Sexual Politics of Landscape Gardening', in *Bourgeois and Aristocratic Cultural Encounters in Garden Art, 1550–1850*, ed. M. Conan (Washington, DC, 2002).
29 Derek Linstrum, *Sir Jeffry Wyatville, Architect to the King* (Oxford, 1973); Peter Andrews, *The House Book* (London, 2001), p. 491; John Steel and Michael Wright, *The English House: 1,000 Years of Domestic Architecture* (London, 2007), p. 254.
30 Linstrum, *Sir Jeffry Wyatville*, p. 170.
31 Ibid., p. 172.
32 Michael Mansbridge, *John Nash* (Oxford, 1991), pp. 175–6.
33 Nikolaus Pevsner and Suzanne Lang, 'A Note on Sharawaggi', *Architectural Review*, CVI (1949); reprinted in *Studies in Art, Architecture and Design*, ed. Nikolaus Pevsner, 2 vols (New Haven, 1968), vol. I, pp. 78–107.
34 Anon., *Mirror of Literature, Amusement and Instruction* (London, 1831).
35 See Mansbridge, *John Nash*, pp. 212–13; and Steel and Wright, *The English House*, p. 254.
36 These things survive and are visible at the cottage.
37 Andrew Ballantyne and Gill Ince, 'Rural and Urban *Milieux*', in *Rural and Urban: Architecture between Two Cultures*, ed. A. Ballantyne (London, 2010), pp. 1–27.
38 James Smith, *The Cottage: An Operatic Farce in Two Acts* (London, 1796), p. 7.
39 James Malton, *An Essay on British Cottage Architecture: Being an Attempt to Perpetuate on Principle, that Peculiar Mode of Building, which was Originally the Effect of Chance* (London, 1798), p. 8.
40 Sutherland Lyall, *Dream Cottages: From 'Cottage Orné' to Stockbroker Tudor: Two Hundred Years of the Cult of the Vernacular* (London, 1988); Anne Bermingham, 'Gainsborough's Cottage Doors', in *Land, Nation and Culture, 1740–1840*, ed. Peter de Bolla, Nigel Leask and David Simpson (New York, 2005), p. 46.
41 W. F. Pocock, *Architectural Designs for Rustic Cottages, Picturesque Dwellings, Villas, etc.* (London, 1807), p. 29.
42 James Thomson, *The Seasons* (1730), 'Summer', lines 64–70.
43 John Buonarotti Papworth, *Rural Residences* (London, 1818), plate D.
44 Mark Girouard, *Life in the English Country House: A Social and Architectural History*

(New Haven, CT, 1978).
45 Jill Allibone, *George Devey, Architect, 1820–1886* (Cambridge, 1991).
46 Lee Goff, *Tudor Style* (New York, 2002), p. 20.
47 Stuart Hylton, *The Grand Experiment: The Birth of the Railway Age, 1820–45* (London, 2007); Martin Wiener, *English Culture and the Decline of the Industrial Spirit* (Cambridge, 1981), p. 66.
48 Andrew Saint, *Richard Norman Shaw* (New Haven, 1979), p. 88.
49 Alan Crawford, 'Englishness in Arts and Crafts Architecture', in *Architecture and Englishness, 1880–1914*, ed. David Crellin and Ian Dungavell (London, 2003), pp. 25–36 (p. 29).
50 Joseph Mordaunt Crook, *The Rise of the Nouveaux-Riches: Style and Status in Victorian and Edwardian Architecture* (London, 1999), p. 72.
51 Edmund Burke, *Reflections on the Revolution in France* (London, 1790); ed. Conor Cruise O'Brien (Harmondsworth, 1982). Crawford, 'Englishness in Arts and Crafts Architecture', p. 29.
52 James Nasmyth, *James Nasmyth, Engineer: An Autobiography*, ed. Samuel Smiles (London, 1883), pp. 272–3.
53 John Martin Robinson, *Ascott* (London, 2008), p. 4.
54 Michael McCarthy, *The Origins of the Gothic Revival* (New Haven and London, 1987), p. 146. The building is now owned by Damien Hirst.
55 See RCAHM Wales at www.coflein.gov.uk/en/site/29283/details/GREGYNON+HALL,+TREGYNON/
56 Peter Collins, *Concrete: The Vision of a New Architecture* (Montreal, 2004)
57 Andrew Saint, *Cragside, Northumberland* (London, 1992), p. 5.
58 Collins, *Concrete*, p. 42.
59 Anon., *The Builder*; cited by Collins, *Concrete*, p. 43.
60 Eugène Viollet-le-Duc, *Entretiens sur l'architecture*, 2 vols (Paris, 1858–72), as *Discourses on Architecture*, trans. Henry Van Brunt (Boston, MA, 1875). John Ruskin, *The Seven Lamps of Architecture* (London, 1849).
61 C.F.A. Voysey, *Individuality* (London, 1915); Arthur J. Penty, *The Restoration of the Gild System* (London, 1906).
62 Mark Girouard, *Sweetness and Light: The 'Queen Anne' Movement, 1860–1900* (Oxford, 1977).
63 Diane Haigh, *Baillie Scott: The Artistic House* (London, 1995).
64 Henry Walker, in *Ideal Home* (4 October 1919), p. 8.
65 Nikolaus Pevsner, *Pioneers*, revised as *Pioneers of Modern Design* (Harmondsworth, 1960).
66 Pevsner, *Pioneers of the Modern Movement* (London, 1936), p. 38.
67 Wendy Hitchmough, *C.F.A. Voysey* (London, 1995); Stuart Durant, *C.F.A. Voysey* (London, 1992).
68 Hitchmough, *C.F.A. Voysey*, p. 222.
69 Pevsner, *Pioneers*, pp. 32–3. Hermann Muthesius, *Das englische Haus*, 3 vols (Berlin, 1904); as *The English House*, trans. Janet Seligman and Stewart Spencer, ed.

Dennis Sharp (London, 2007).
70 P. A. Barron, *The House Desirable* (London, 1929).
71 Ibid., p. 9.
72 Ibid., p. 1.
73 Banister Fletcher, *The English Home* (London, 1910), p. 330.
74 Ibid., chapter 18, 'Modern English Homes', pp. 246–357.
75 Charles James Richardson, *The Englishman's House: From Cottage to Villa* (London, 1871); cited by F.R.S. Yorke, *The Modern House* (London, 1934), p. 13.
76 Le Corbusier, *Vers une architecture* (Paris, 1924); as *Towards a New Architecture*, trans. Frederick Etchells (London, 1927); as *Towards an Architecture*, trans. John Goodman (Los Angeles, 2007).
77 Paul Oliver, 'The Galleon on the Front Door', in Oliver, Ian Davis and Ian Bentley, *Dunroamin: The Suburban Semi and its Enemies* (London, 1981), pp. 155–72 (p. 162).
78 Duncan Simpson, 'Beautiful Tudor', *Architectural Review*, CLXII (July 1977), p. 31.
79 Osbert Lancaster, *Pillar to Post* (London, 1938), p. 76.
80 Anthony Bertram, *Design* (West Drayton, Middlesex, 1938; reprinted 1943), p. 51.
81 J. M. Richards, *The Castles on the Ground* (London, 1946; 2nd edn, 1973), p. 16.
82 Ibid., p. 63.
83 This is a term used by the sociologist Manuel Castells. See Andrew Ballantyne and Chris L. Smith, *Architecture in the Space of Flows* (London, 2011)

Chapter Six

1 Rosemary Sweet, *Antiquaries: The Discovery of the Past in Eighteenth Century Britain* (London, 2004); J. E. Sharwood-Smith, 'Latin, the Elite Tradition in Education and Dr Flann Campbell', *British Journal of Education Studies*, XX/1 (February 1972), pp. 5–11.
2 Joseph Addison, *Letter from Italy* [1701], cited in Tim Richardson, *The Arcadian Friends: Inventing the English Landscape Garden* (London, 2007), p. 123.
3 Andrew Ballantyne, *Architecture, Landscape and Liberty: Richard Payne Knight and the Picturesque* (Cambridge, 1997).
4 Ian Thompson, *The English Lakes: A History* (London, 2010).
5 William Stukeley, *Stonehenge: A Temple Restor'd to the British Druids* (London, 1740); Stukeley, *Avebury: A Temple of the British Druids* (London, 1743).
6 John Claudius Loudon, 'Second Tour from London to Manchester, Chester, Liverpool and the Lake District, May–July 1831', in *In Search of English Gardens: The Travels of John Claudius Loudon and his Wife Jane*, ed. Priscilla Boniface (Wheathampstead, 1987), p. 61; see also his third tour, of 1833, ibid., p. 102.
7 Andrew Ballantyne, 'Misprisions of Stonehenge', in *Architecture as Experience*, ed. Dana Arnold and Ballantyne (London, 2004), pp. 11–35.
8 Thomas Frederick Hunt, 'Address', in *Half a Dozen Hints, on Domestic Picturesque*

Architecture (London, 1825), unnumbered page.
9 Thomas Frederick Hunt, *Exemplars of Tudor Architecture, Adapted to Modern Habitations* (London, 1830), p. v.
10 Ibid., pp. v–vi.
11 See above, chapter Two.
12 Humphry Repton, date unknown, but possibly 1810; see Stephen Daniels, 'Gothic Gallantry: Humphry Repton, Lord Byron and the Sexual Politics of Landscape Gardening', in *Bourgeois and Aristocratic Cultural Encounters in Garden Art, 1550–1850*, ed. Martin Conan (Washington, DC, 2002), p. 324; Sutherland Lyall, *Dream Cottages: From 'Cottage Orné' to Stockbroker Tudor: Two Hundred Years of the Cult of the Vernacular* (London, 1988), p. 84.
13 Lyall, *Dream Cottages*, p. 85.
14 Hunt, *Exemplars of Tudor Architecture*.
15 P. F. Robinson, *Designs for Lodges and Park Entrances* (London, 1833), notes for design no. 6.
16 Ibid., notes for design no. 3.
17 John Claudius Loudon, *Encyclopaedia of Cottage, Farm and Villa Architecture* (London, 1833), p. 1147.
18 Sylvain Ageorges, *Sur les traces des expositions universelles: Paris, 1855–1937* (Paris, 2006), p. 63.
19 Edward Said, *Orientalism* (London, 1978).
20 At www.dkolb.org/sprawlingplaces/images/fullsize/theme.epcot001.jpg
21 Arroll Gellner and Douglas Kleister, *Storybook Style: America's Whimsical Homes of the Twenties* (New York, 2001).
22 Andrew Ballantyne, *What is Architecture?* (London, 2002).
23 Lee Goff, *Tudor Style* (New York, 2002), p. 62.
24 David Thistlewood, 'A. J. Penty (1875–1937), and the Legacy of Nineteenth-century Domestic Architecture', *Journal of the Society of Architectural Historians*, XLVII (December 1987), pp. 327–41.
25 Raymond Unwin, *Town Planning in Practice* (London, 1909), p. 172; Unwin, *Town Planning and Modern Architecture at the Hampstead Garden Suburb* (London, 1909), p. 86.
26 Susan L. Klaus, *A Modern Arcadia: Frederick Law Olmsted Jr and the Plan for Forest Hills Gardens* (Amherst, MA, 2002), p. 41.
27 Ibid., p. 9.
28 David Gebhardt and Robert Winter, *Los Angeles: An Architectural Guide* (Layton, UT, 1994), p. 125.
29 Goff, *Tudor Style*, p. 158.
30 Nikolaus Pevsner, *The Buildings of England: Berkshire* (Harmondsworth, 1966).
31 John Seiberling and Steve Love, *Stan Hywet Hall and Gardens* (Akron, OH, 2000), p. 13.
32 Ibid., p. 12.
33 Eloise L. Morgan and Bob Marshall, *Building a Suburban Village: Bronxville, New York,*

1898–1998 (Bronxville, NY, 1998).
34 Ibid., p. 15, citing the undoubtedly partisan local newspaper, the *Bronxville Review* (9 April 1915).
35 Ibid., p. 18.
36 Ibid.
37 Ibid., p. 29.
38 Pascal James Imperato, *Tudor Village: The History of a Unique Community in Queens County, New York* (New York, 2003), p. 43.
39 Ibid., p. 46.
40 The romance has worn thin. Residents now complain of infestations of mice, cockroaches, inadequate heating and brown water.
41 Andrew S. Dolkart, 'Hudson View Gardens: A Home in the City', *Sites*, 20 (May 1988), pp. 34–43.
42 Louis Napoleon Parker, *Pomander Walk* (London, 1910).
43 *Report of Landmarks Preservation Commission* (14 September 1982), designation list 159, LP-1279. Built in 1921, architects King and Campbell.
44 At www.tudorcity.com/History1.html
45 Walter Barrett, *The Old Merchants of New York City* (New York, 1863).
46 Anonymous, *Glimpses of East River Homes* (New York, 1893).

Chapter Seven

1 Sir William Stevenson Meyer et al., *Imperial Gazetteer of India*, 24 vols (Oxford, 1908–31), vol. II: *The Indian Empire, Historical*, p. 454.
2 Mark Harrison, *Climates and Constitutions: Health, Race and British Imperialism in India, 1600–1850* (New Delhi, 1999), and see review by Warwick Anderson in *Journal of Political Ecology: Case Studies in History and Society*, IX (2002). Gyan Prakash, *The Other Reason: Science and the Imagination of Modern India* (Princeton, NJ, 1999).
3 Anthony King, *The Bungalow: The Production of a Global Culture* (Oxford, 1995), p. 27.
4 Ibid., p. 38.
5 James Gray, *Life in Bombay and Neighbouring Out-Stations* (London, 1852), p. 13.
6 Ibid., p. 14.
7 Ibid., p. 15.
8 Ibid., p. 16.
9 Ibid., p. 18.
10 Jan Morris, *Stones of Empire: The Buildings of the Raj* (Oxford, 1983; 2nd edn, with new foreword by Simon Winchester, 2005), p. 202.
11 Vikram Bhatt, *Resorts of the Raj: Hill Stations of India* (Ahmedabad, India, 1997), p. 14.
12 Ibid., p. 102.
13 Ibid., pp. 96–7.
14 Ibid., p. 97.
15 Robert Woods, *The Population of Britain in the Nineteenth Century* (Cambridge, 1995).

16 The capital of India was moved from Calcutta to New Delhi in 1911, and new government buildings by Sir Edwin Lutyens were built to house it.
17 Pamela Kanwar, *Imperial Simla: The Political Culture of the Raj* (New Delhi, 2003), p. 97.
18 Valentine Prinsep (1838–1904), a British artist of the Pre-Raphaelite circle, born in India, cited by Jan Morris in Morris and Simon Winchester, *Stones of Empire*, p. 202.
19 Bhatt, *Resorts of the Raj*, p. 101.
20 Julian Davison, *Black and White: The Singapore House, 1898–1941* (Singapore, 2006).
21 Richard Gaulton, 'Political Mobilization in Shanghai, 1949–1951', in *Shanghai: Revolution and Development in an Asian Metropolis*, ed. Christopher Howe (Cambridge, 1981), pp. 35–65 (p. 40).
22 Information from meetings with developers and pubic relations representatives at the site.
23 Andrew Ballantyne, *Architecture, Landscape and Liberty: Richard Payne Knight and the Picturesque* (Cambridge, 1997).
24 Michael Snodin, *Horace Walpole's Strawberry Hill* (New Haven and London, 2009), p. 304.
25 Ibid., p. 305.
26 Thomas Arne, *Alfred: A Masque*, libretto by David Mallet and James Thomson (1740).
27 Dr John Arbuthnot, *Law Is a Bottomless Pit* (London, 1712); Angus Ross, *A Political Biography of John Arbuthnot* (London, 2010).
28 Edmund Burke, *Reflections on the Revolution in France* [1790], ed. Conor Cruise O'Brien (Harmondsworth, 1982).
29 Anthony Bertram, *Design* (West Drayton, Middlesex, 1938; reprinted 1943), p. 51.
30 Frederick Engels, *The Condition of the Working Class in England in 1844*, trans. Florence Kelley Wischnewetzky (New York, 1887).
31 Bertram, *Design*, p. 14.
32 Le Corbusier, *Vers une architecture* (Paris, 1924); as *Towards a New Architecture*, trans. Frederick Etchells (London, 1927); as *Towards an Architecture*, trans. John Goodman (Los Angeles, 2007).
33 Evelyn Waugh, *Decline and Fall* (London, 1928); page references to the Everyman edition (London, 1993), pp. 98, 100.
34 Ibid., p. 121.
35 Ibid., pp. 103, 108.
36 Ibid., pp. 105, 106, 108, 120, 121.
37 Reginald Blomfield, *Modernismus* (London, 1934), pp. v–vi.
38 Ibid., p. 9.
39 At http://en.wikipedia.org/wiki/Newspaper_circulation
40 At http://en.wikipedia.org/wiki/Ideal_Home
41 At http://en.wikipedia.org/wiki/This_England

42 At www.emap.com/brands/architectural-review
43 At www.mandmglobal.com/company-profiles/Superguide/elledeco
44 Murray Fraser and Joe Kerr, *Architecture of the Special Relationship* (London, 2007).
45 At www.marthastewart.com/
46 Hermann Muthesius, *Das englische Haus*, 3 vols (Berlin, 1904); as *The English House*, trans. Janet Seligman and Stewart Spencer, ed. Dennis Sharp (London, 2007).
47 For stills of the house, see any of the films in the Wallace and Gromit series, such as *A Grand Day Out* (1989), *The Wrong Trousers* (1993), *A Close Shave* (1995), *The Curse of the Were-Rabbit* (2005) and *A Matter of Loaf and Death* (2008).
48 Andrew Ballantyne, *Deleuze and Guattari for Architects* (London, 2007).
49 T. S. Eliot, *The Wasteland* (New York, 1922).
50 Ross Chinn, 'My Father's House: Memory and the Malay Mock Tudor', unpublished BA dissertation (University of Plymouth, 2009), p. 9.
51 Ibid., p. 24.
52 Ibid., p. 28.
53 Ibid., p. 7.
54 Jon Broome, 'The Segal Method', *Architects' Journal*, CLXXXIV/45 (November 1986), pp. 31–68; Jon Broome, 'Segal Method Revisited', *Architects' Journal*, CCII/20 (November 1995), pp. 53–5; *Architects' Journal*, CLXXXVII/ 22 (May 1988), was a special issue devoted to Segal, pp. 37–91.

Bibliography

Addison, Joseph, et al., *The Spectator*, ed. G. Gregory Smith, 4 vols (Toronto, 1930)
Ageorges, Sylvain, *Sur les traces des expositions universelles: Paris, 1855–1937* (Paris, 2006)
Allibone, Jill, *George Devey, Architect, 1820–1886* (Cambridge, 1991)
Andrews, Peter, *The House Book* (London, 2001)
Anon., *Mirror of Literature, Amusement and Instruction* (London, 1831)
Anon., *Glimpses of East River Homes* (New York, 1893)
Arbuthnot, John, *Law Is a Bottomless Pit* (London, 1712)
Archer, John, *Architecture and Suburbia: From English Villa to American Dream House, 1690–2000* (Minneapolis, MN, 2005)
Arizzoli-Clémentel, Pierre, *L'Album de Marie-Antoinette: Vues et plans du Petit Trianon à Versailles* (Paris, 2008)
Arnold, Dana, *Re-presenting the Metropolis: Architecture, Urban Experience and Social Life in London, 1800–1840* (Aldershot, 2000)
——, and Stephen Bending, *Tracing Architecture: The Aesthetics of Antiquarianism* (Oxford, 2003)
Aslet, Clive, and Alan Powers, *The National Trust Book of the English House* (Harmondsworth, 1985)
Atkinson, William, *Views of Picturesque Cottages with Plans, Selected from a Collection of Drawings Taken in Different Parts of England and Intended as Hints for the Improvement of Village Scenery* (London, 1805)
Audsley, William James, and George Ashdown Audsley, *Cottage, Lodge and Villa Architecture* (Glasgow, 1868)
Bacon, Francis, *The Great Instauration* (London, 1620)
Bailey, Brian, *English Manor Houses* (London, 1983)
Baillie Scott, M. H., *Houses and Gardens* (London, 1906)
Ballantyne, Andrew, *Architecture, Landscape and Liberty* (Cambridge, 1997)
——, *What is Architecture?* (London, 2002)
——, 'Two Nations, Twice: National Identity in "The Wild Irish Girl" and "Sybil"', in *Cultural Identities and the Aesthetics of Britishness*, ed. Dana Arnold (Manchester, 2004), pp. 87–98

—, 'Joseph Gandy and the Politics of Rustic Charm', in *Articulating British Classicism: New Approaches to Eighteenth-century Architecture*, ed. Barbara Arciszewska and Elizabeth McKellar (Aldershot, 2004), pp. 163–85

—, 'Misprisions of Stonehenge', in *Architecture as Experience: Radical Change in Spatial Practice*, ed. Dana Arnold and Andrew Ballantyne (London, 2004), pp. 11–35.

—, *Deleuze and Guattari for Architects* (London, 2007)

—, and Gill Ince, 'Rural and Urban "Milieux"', in *Rural and Urban: Architecture between Two Cultures*, ed. Andrew Ballantyne (London, 2010), pp. 1–27

—, and Andrew Law, 'Tudoresque Vernacular and the Self-Reliant Englishman', in *Built from Below: British Architecture and the Vernacular*, ed. Peter Guillery (London, 2010), pp. 123–44

—, and Chris L. Smith, *Architecture in the Space of Flows* (London, 2011)

Barrett, Walter, *The Old Merchants of New York City* (New York, 1863)

Barron, P. A. *The House Desirable: A Handbook for Those Who Wish to Acquire Homes that Charm* (London, 1929)

Bartell, Edmund, *Hints for Picturesque Improvements in Ornamented Cottages, and their Scenery: Including some Observations on the Labourer and his Cottage, in Three Essays* (London, 1804)

Bateson, Gregory, *Mind and Nature* (London, 1980)

Batey, Mavis, 'The Swiss Garden, Old Warden, Bedfordshire', *Garden History*, III/4 (Autumn 1975), pp. 40–43

Batsford, Harry, and Charles Fry, *The English Cottage* (London, 1938)

Battestin, Martin, and Ruthe Battestin, *Henry Fielding: A Life* (London, 1989)

Beattie, Susan, *A Revolution in London Housing: LCC Housing Architects and their Work, 1893–1914* (London, 1980)

Bede, *Ecclesiastical History of the English People* (AD 731)

Beeson, Edward William, *Port Sunlight: The Model Village of England* (London, 1911)

Belloc, Hilaire, *The Servile State* (London, 1912)

—, *An Essay on The Restoration of Property* (London, 1936)

Bermingham, Ann, *Sensation and Sensibility: Viewing Gainsborough's 'Cottage Door'* (New Haven, CT, and London, 2005)

Bertram, Anthony, *Design* (Harmondsworth, 1938; reprinted 1943)

Betjeman, John, *Metro-land* (London, 1977)

Bhatt, Vikram, *Resorts of the Raj: Hill Stations of India* (Ahmedabad, India, 1997)

Blomfield, Reginald, *Modernismus* (London, 1934)

Bolingbroke; see St John

Bolla, Peter de, Nigel Leask and David Simpson, *Land, Nation and Culture, 1740–1840* (New York, 2005)

Borer, Pat, and Cindy Harris, *Out of the Woods: Environmental Timber Frame Designs for Self Build* (Machynlleth, Powys, 1999)

Brannan, Joe, and Frances Brannan, *A Postcard from Bournville* (Studley, 1992)

Braudel, Fernand, *La Méditerranée et le monde méditerranéen à l'époque de Philippe II*, 3 vols (Paris, 1949); as *The Mediterranean and the Mediterranean World in the Age of Philip II*,

trans. Sian Reynolds, 2 vols (London, 1972)
Broome, Jon, 'The Segal Method', *Architects' Journal*, CLXXXIV/ 45 (November 1986), pp. 31–68
——, 'Segal Method Revisited', *Architects' Journal*, CCII/20 (November 1995), pp. 53–5
Brown, Andrew, *The Rows of Chester* (London, 1999)
Brown, Jane, *Lutyens and the Edwardians: An English Architect and his Clients* (London, 1996)
Brown, Richard, *Domestic Architecture* (London, 1842)
Bülow, Gottfried von, 'Journey through England and Scotland by Lupold von Wedel in the Years 1584 and 1585', *Transactions of the Royal Historical Society*, n.s., IX (1895), pp. 223–70
Burke, Edmund, *Reflections on the Revolution in France* [1790]; ed. Conor Cruise O'Brien (Harmondsworth, 1982)
Burn, Robert Scott, *Model Designs for Mansions, Villas, Dwelling-Houses, Cottages, Gates, and Stables . . . with Hints on Sanitary Construction, and an Essay on Dwellings for the Working Classes* (London, 1853)
Bryson, Bill, *Shakespeare: The World as a Stage* (London, 2007)
Butler, Judith, *Gender Trouble* (London, 1990)
Cain, P. J., and A. G. Hopkins, *British Imperialism, 1688–2000* (London, 1996)
Camden, William, *Britannia* (London, 1586)
Campbell, Colen, *Vitruvius Britannicus*, 3 vols (London, 1715–25)
Casid, Jill H., *Sowing Empire: Landscape and Colonization* (Minneapolis, MN, 2005)
Chambers, William, *Designs of Chinese Buildings, Furniture, Dresses, Machines, and Utensils: to which is annexed a Description of their Temples, Houses, Gardens, &c* (London, 1757)
——, *A Treatise on Civil Architecture in which the Principles of that Art are Laid Down and Illustrated by a Great Number of Plates Accurately Designed and Elegantly Engraved by the Best Hands* (London, 1759)
Charles, F.W.B., 'Frame Finish', *Architects' Journal* (13 March 1991), pp. 32–5
Chesterton, G. K., *What's Wrong with the World?* (London, 1910)
——, *Utopia of Usurers* (New York, 1917)
——, *The Outline of Sanity* (New York, 1927)
Chinn, Carl, *The Cadbury Story: A Short History* (Redditch, 1998)
Chinn, Ross, 'My Father's House: Memory and the Malay Mock Tudor', unpublished BA dissertation (University of Plymouth, 2009)
Chiu, Frances, 'Faulty Towers: Reform, Radicalism and the Gothic Castle, 1760–1800', in *Romanticism on the Net*, issue 44 (2006)
Clavel, Sylvie, and Isabelle Chalet-Bailhache, *Paris et ses expositions universelles: architectures, 1855–1937* (Paris, 2008)
Cobb, Ruth, *Village Story* (London, 1945)
Cobbett, William, 'Winchester, Saturday 28 September 1822', in *Rural Rides*, 2 vols (London, 1830)
Collins, Peter, *Concrete: The Vision of a New Architecture* (Montreal, 2004)
Crellin, David, and Ian Dungavell, *Architecture and Englishness, 1880–1914* (London, 2003)

Crook, J. Mordaunt, *The Rise of the Nouveaux-Riches: Style and Status in Victorian and Edwardian Architecture* (London, 1999)

Daniels, Stephen, *Humphry Repton: Landscape Gardening and the Geography of Georgian England* (New Haven, CT, and London, 1999)

——, 'Gothic Gallantry: Humphry Repton, Lord Byron and the Sexual Politics of Landscape Gardening', in *Bourgeois and Aristocratic Cultural Encounters in Garden Art, 1550–1850*, ed. Martin Conan (Washington, DC, 2002)

Davies, Clifford S. L., 'The Tudor Delusion', *Times Literary Supplement* (11 June 2008)

Davison, Julian, *Black and White: The Singapore House, 1898–1941* (Singapore, 2006)

Davison, T. R., *Port Sunlight: A Record of its Artistic and Pictorial Aspect* (London, 1916)

Dearn, Thomas D. W., *Sketches in Architecture: Consisting of Original Designs for Cottages and Rural Dwellings, Suitable to Persons of Moderate Fortune, and for Comfort and Retirement* (London, 1807)

Deary, Terry, and Neil Tonge, *The Terrible Tudors* (London, 1993)

Deleuze, Gilles, and Félix Guattari, *Mille plateaux* (Paris, 1980); as *A Thousand Plateaus: Capitalism and Schizophrenia*, trans. Brian Massumi (London, 1987)

Dickens, Charles, *The Old Curiosity Shop* (London, 1841)

Disraeli, Benjamin, *Sybil; or, The Two Nations* (London, 1845)

——, *Coningsby* (London, 1844)

——, *Tancred* (London, 1847)

Dolkart, Andrew S., 'Hudson View Gardens: A Home in the City', *Sites*, 20 (May 1988) pp. 34–43

——, *Guide to New York City Landmarks* (New York, 1992)

Douglas, Mary, *Purity and Danger* (London, 1966)

Durant, Stuart, *C.F.A. Voysey* (London, 1992)

Edwards, Arthur, *The Design of Suburbia: A Critical Study in Environmental History* (London, 1981)

Eliot, T. S., *The Wasteland* (New York, 1922)

Elsam, Richard, *An Essay on Rural Architecture, Being an Attempt, Also to Refute the Principles of Mr James Malton's 'Essay on British Cottage Architecture'* (London, 1803)

——, *Hints for Improving the Condition of the Peasantry, with Plans, Elevations and Descriptive Views of Characteristic Designs for Cottages* (London, 1816)

Engels, Friedrich, *Die Lage der arbeitenden Klasse in England* (Leipzig, 1845); as *The Condition of the Working Class in England in 1844*, trans. Florence Kelley Wischnewetzky (New York, 1887)

Escott, Thomas Hay Sweet, *England: Its People, Polity and Pursuits*, 2 vols (London, 1879)

Fielding, Henry, *The History of Tom Jones, a Foundling* (London, 1749)

Fitzgerald, William George; *see* Ignatius Phayre

Fletcher, Banister, *The English Home* (London, 1910)

Foucault, Michel, *Le Souci du soi* (Paris, 1984); as *A History of Sexuality, Volume 3: The Care of the Self*, trans. Robert Hurley (New York, 1986)

Franklin, Jill, *The Gentleman's Country House and its Plan, 1835–1914* (London, 1981)

Fraser, Antonia, *Marie Antoinette: The Journey* (London, 2001)

Select Bibliography

Galbraith, John Kenneth, *Annals of an Abiding Liberal* (Boston, MA, 1979)
Gandy, Joseph Michael, *Designs for Cottages, Cottage Farms, and Other Rural Buildings, Including Entrance Gates and Lodges* (London, 1805)
——, *The Rural Architect; Consisting of Various Designs for Country Buildings, Accompanied with Ground Plans, Estimates and Descriptions* (London, 1805)
Garner, Thomas, and Arthur Stratton, *The Domestic Architecture of England during the Tudor Period* (London, 1929)
Gaulton, Richard, 'Political Mobilization in Shanghai, 1949–1951', in *Shanghai: Revolution and Development in an Asian Metropolis*, ed. Christopher Howe (Cambridge, 1981)
Gebhardt, David, and Robert Winter, *Los Angeles: An Architectural Guide* (Layton, UT, 1994)
Gellner, Arroll, and Douglas Kleister, *Storybook Style: America's Whimsical Homes of the Twenties* (New York, 2001)
Geoffrey of Monmouth, *The History of the Kings of Britain* [1136], trans. and Intro. Lewis Thorpe (Harmondsworth, 1973)
Giles, Judy, and Tim Middleton, *Writing Englishness: An Introductory Sourcebook* (London, 1995)
George, Walter Lionel, *Labour and Housing at Port Sunlight* (London, 1990)
Gilpin, William, *Observations on the Mountains and Lakes of Cumberland and Westmoreland*, 2 vols (London, 1786)
——, *Observations on the River Wye, and Several Parts of South Wales etc., Relative Chiefly to Picturesque Beauty: Made in the Year 1770* (London, 1782)
Girouard, Mark, *Sweetness and Light: The 'Queen Anne' Movement, 1860–1900* (Oxford, 1977)
——, *Life in the English Country House: A Social and Architectural History* (New Haven, CT, and London, 1978)
——, *The Victorian Country House* (New Haven, CT, and London, 1979)
——, *The English Town* (London, 1990)
Goff, Lee, *Tudor Style* (New York, 2002)
Godfrey, Walter H., *Our Building Inheritance: Are We To Lose It?* (London, 1944)
Goffman, Erving, *The Presentation of Self in Everyday Life* (Garden City, NY, 1959)
Goldsmith, Oliver, *The Deserted Village* (1770)
Goodwin, Francis, *Domestic Architecture, Being a Second Series of Designs for Cottages, Lodges, Villas and Other Residences in the Grecian, Italian and Old English Styles of Architecture* (London, 1834)
Gough, Richard, *Anecdotes of British Topography* (London, 1768)
Government Papers, *Communications to the Board of Agriculture*, vol. 1 (London, 1797)
Government Papers, *Statutes of the Realm*, 11 vols (London, 1810–28; reprinted 963)
Gradidge, Roderick, *Dream Houses: The Edwardian Ideal* (London, 1980)
Gray, James, *Life in Bombay and Neighbouring Out-Stations* (London, 1852)
Grossmith, George, and Weedon Grossmith, *Diary of a Nobody* (London, 1892)
Guy, John, *Tudor England* (Oxford, 1988)
Haigh, Diane, *Baillie Scott: The Artistic House* (London, 1995)

Hardy, Dennis, *Utopian England: Community Experiments, 1900–1945* (London, 2000)
——, and Colin Ward, *Arcadia for All: The Legacy of a Makeshift Landscape* (Nottingham, 1984)
Harrison, Mark, *Climates and Constitutions: Health, Race and British Imperialism in India, 1600–1850* (New Delhi, 1999)
Harrison, William, 'An Historicall Description of the Islande of Britayne' [1577], in *Documents of Modern History: Elizabethan People, State and Society*, ed. Joel Hurstfield and A.G.R. Smith (London, 1972)
Harvey, William Alexander, *The Model Village and its Cottages: Bourneville* (London, 1906)
Harvie, Christopher, and Colin Matthew, *The Oxford Illustrated History of Britain* (Oxford, 1984)
Harwood, Elain, and Andrew Saint, *London Suburbs* (London, 1999)
Hawkes, Dean, *Modern Country Homes in England: The Arts and Crafts Architecture of Barry Parker* (Cambridge, 1986)
Hayden, Dolores, *Building Suburbia: Green Fields and Urban Growth, 1820–2000* (New York, 2003)
Henderson, Paula, *The Tudor House and Garden: Architecture and Landscape in the Sixteenth and Early Seventeenth Centuries* (New Haven, CT, and London, 2005)
Hitchmough, Wendy, *C.F.A. Voysey* (London, 1995)
Hobsbawm, Eric, *The Invention of Tradition* (Cambridge, 1983)
Hodder, Edwin, *Life of Samuel Morley* (London, 1887)
Howard, Ebenezer, *To-Morrow: A Peaceful Path to Real Reform* (London, 1898); reprinted in 1902 as *Garden Cities of To-Morrow*
Howard, Maurice, *The Building of Elizabethan and Jacobean England* (New Haven, CT, and London, 2007)
Howkins, Alun, *Reshaping Rural England: A Social History* (London, 1991)
Hubbard, Edward, *The Work of John Douglas* (London, 1991)
——, and Michael Shippobottom, *A Guide to Port Sunlight Village* (Liverpool, 2006)
Hume, David, *History of England under the House of Tudor*, 2 vols (London, 1759)
——, *The History of England from the Invasion of Julius Caesar to the Revolution in 1688*, 6 vols (Indianapolis, 1983)
——, *The Letters of David Hume*, ed. J.Y.T. Greig (Oxford, 1932)
Hunt, John Dixon, and Peter Willis, *The Genius of the Place* (London, 1975; 2nd edn, Cambridge, MA, 1988)
Hunt, Thomas Frederick, *Half A Dozen Hints, on Domestic Picturesque Architecture* (London, 1825)
——, *Designs for Parsonage Houses, Alms Houses, etc.* (London, 1827)
——, *Exemplars of Tudor Architecture, Adapted to Modern Habitations* (London, 1830)
Hurstfield, J., and A.G.R. Smith, *Documents of Modern History: Elizabethan People, State and Society* (London, 1972)
Hutton, Ronald, *The Rise and Fall of Merry England: The Ritual Year* (Oxford, 1994)
Hylton, Stuart, *The Grand Experiment: The Birth of the Railway Age, 1820–45* (London, 2007)

Imperato, Pascal James, *Tudor Village: The History of a Unique Community in Queens County, New York* (New York, 2003)

Jackson, Alan, *Semi-Detached London: Suburban Development, Life and Transport, 1900–39* (London, 1973)

——, *London's Metro-land* (Harrow, 2006)

Jackson, Allen W., *The Half-Timber House: Its Origin, Design, Modern Plan and Construction* (New York, 1912)

James, Lawrence, *The Middle Class: A History* (London, 2006)

Jarvis, J., *A Correct Detail of the Ceremonies Attending the Shakespearean Gala at Stratford-Upon-Avon 1827; Together with some Account of Garrick's Jubilee in 1769* (Stratford-upon-Avon, 1827)

Jenkins, Peter, and Waveney Jenkins, *The Planter's Bungalow: A Journey Down the Malay Peninsula* (Singapore, 2007)

Johnson, Samuel, 'Preface', to *The Plays of William Shakespeare in Ten Volumes* (London, 1765)

——, *The Rambler*, ed. Walter Jackson Bate and Albrecht B. Strauss, vols III and IV of the *Yale Edition of the Works of Samuel Johnson* (New Haven, 1969)

Jones, Inigo, *The Most Notable Antiquity of Great Britain, Vulgarly Called Stone-Heng, on Salisbury Plain, Restored* (London, 1655)

Kanwar, Pamela, *Imperial Simla: The Political Culture of the Raj* (New Delhi, 2003).

Kegel, C. H., 'Lord John Manners and the Young England Movement: Romanticism in Politics', *Western Political Quarterly*, XIV/14 (September 1961), pp. 691–7

Kent, Nathaniel, *Hints to Gentlemen of Landed Property* (London, 1775)

Kerr, Robert, *The Gentleman's House; or, How to Plan English Residences from the Parsonage to the Palace* (London, 1865)

Kiernan, Victor, 'Nationalist Movements and Social Classes', in *Nationalist Movements*, ed. Anthony D. Smith (New York, 1976)

King, Anthony, *The Bungalow: The Production of a Global Culture* (Oxford, 1995)

Klaus, Susan L., *A Modern Arcadia: Frederick Law Olmsted Jr and the Plan for Forest Hills Gardens* (Amherst, MA, 2002)

Knight, Richard Payne, *A Discourse on the Worship of Priapus, and its Connexion with the Mystic Theology of the Antients* (London, 1786)

——, *The Landscape: A Didactic Poem* (London, 1794; 2nd edn, 1795)

——, *An Analytical Inquiry into the Principles of Taste* (London, 1805)

Laing, D., *Hints for Dwellings: Consisting of Original Designs for Cottages, Farm-Houses, Villas, etc.* (London, 1800)

Lamb, Charles, and Mary Lamb, *Tales from Shakespeare* (London, 1807)

Lancaster, Osbert, *Pillar to Post: The Pocket Lamp of Architecture* (London, 1938)

Lanier, Douglas, *Shakespeare and Modern Popular Culture* (Oxford, 2002)

Laugier, Marc-Antoine, *Essai sur l'architecture* (Paris, 1752); as *An Essay on Architecture*, trans. Wolfgang and Anni Herrmann (New York, 1977)

——, *Observations sur l'architecture* (Paris, 1765)

Law, Andrew, 'English Townscape as Cultural and Symbolic Capital', in *Architectures: Modernism and After*, ed. Andrew Ballantyne (Oxford, 2004), pp. 202–26

Lawrence, Gary, and Anne Surchin, *Houses of the Hamptons, 1880–1940* (New York, 2007)

Le Corbusier, *Vers une architecture* (Paris, 1924); as *Towards a New Architecture*, trans. Frederick Etchells (London, 1927); as *Towards an Architecture*, trans. John Goodman (Los Angeles, 2007)

Leo XIII [Vincenzo Pecci], Pope, *Rerum novarum: Encyclical of Pope Leo XIII on Capital and Labour* (1891)

Lever, William Hesketh [Lord Leverhulme], *The Six-Hour Day and Other Industrial Questions* (London, 1918)

Lever, William Hulme, *Viscount Leverhulme by his Son* (London, 1927)

Lewis, Brian, *So Clean: Lord Leverhulme, Soap and Civilisation* (Manchester, 2008)

Lewis, Roy, and Angus Maude, *The English Middle Classes* (London, 1949)

Linstrum, Derek, *Sir Jeffry Wyatville, Architect to the King* (Oxford, 1973)

Lipscombe, George, *Journey into South Wales in the Year 1799* (London, 1802)

Lloyd, Arthur, *Three Acres and a Cow: An Agricultural Lay* (London, 1885)

Locke, John, *Second Treatise of Civil Government* (London, 1690)

Loudon, John Claudius, *A Treatise on Forming, Improving and Managing Country Residences* (London, 1806)

——, *Encyclopaedia of Cottage, Farm, and Villa Architecture and Furniture*, 2 vols (London, 1833)

——, 'Second Tour from London to Manchester, Chester, Liverpool and the Lake District, May–July 1831', in *In Search of English Gardens: The Travels of John Claudius Loudon and his Wife Jane*, ed. Priscilla Boniface (Wheathampstead, 1987)

Lugar, Robert, *Architectural Sketches for Cottages, Rural Dwellings and Villas* (London, 1805)

——, *The Country Gentleman's Architecture* (London, 1807)

Lukacher, Brian, *Joseph Gandy: An Architectural Visionary in Georgian England* (London, 2006)

Lupton, Donald, *London and the Countrey Carbonadoed* (London, 1632)

Lyall, Sutherland, *Dream Cottages: From Cottage Orné to Stockbroker Tudor: Two Hundred Years of the Cult of the Vernacular* (London, 1988)

Lynch, Jack, *The Age of Elizabeth in the Age of Johnson* (Cambridge, 2002)

——, *Becoming Shakespeare: How a Dead Poet Became the World's Foremost Literary Genius* (London, 2008)

McCarthy, Michael, *The Origins of the Gothic Revival* (New Haven and London, 1987)

McClung, William A., *The Country House in English Renaissance Poetry* (London, 1977)

McKean, John, *Walter Segal's Life, Work and Influence* (Basel, 1988)

McKibbin, Ross, *Classes and Cultures: England, 1918–1951* (Oxford, 1998)

Malton, James, *An Essay on British Cottage Architecture: Being an Attempt to Perpetuate on Principle, that Peculiar Mode of Building, which was Originally the Effect of Chance* (London, 1798)

Mandler, Peter, *The Fall and Rise of the Stately Home* (New Haven and London, 1997)

Manners, Lord John [Duke of Rutland], *England's Trust* (London, 1841)

Mansbridge, Michael, *John Nash* (Oxford, 1991)

Marder, Louis, *His Exits and his Entrances: The Story of Shakespeare's Reputation* (London, 1963)
Matless, David, *Landscape and Englishness* (London, 1998)
Metropolitan Railway Company, *Metroland Annual Guide Book, 1927* (London, 1927)
Meyer, Sir William Stevenson, et al., *Imperial Gazetteer of India*, 24 vols (Oxford, 1908–31)
Montesquieu, Baron [Charles-Louis de Secondat], *De l'ésprit de lois* (Paris, 1748)
Middleton, Charles, *Picturesque and Architectural Views for Cottages, Farm Houses and Country Villas* (London, 1793)
Mingay, G. E., *The Gentry: The Rise and Fall of a Ruling Class* (London, 1976)
Moore, Dafydd, *Ossian and Ossianism*, 4 vols (London, 2004)
Morgan, Eloise L., and Bob Marshall, *Building a Suburban Village: Bronxville, New York, 1898–1998* (Bronxville, 1998)
Morley, Ken, and Margaret Morley, *Wingrave: A Rothschild Village in the Vale* (Dunstable, 1999)
Morris, Jan, *Stones of Empire: The Buildings of the Raj* (Oxford, 1983; 2nd edn, with new foreword by Simon Winchester, 2005)
Morrison, William, *The Main Line: Country Houses of Philadelphia's Storied Suburb, 1870–1930* (New York, 2002)
Mowl, Timothy, *Elizabethan and Jacobean Style* (London, 1993)
Museum of Domestic Design and Architecture, *Little Palaces* (London, 2003)
Muthesius, Hermann, *Das englische Haus*, 3 vols (Berlin, 1904–5; 2nd edn, 1908–11); as *The English House*, trans. Janet Seligman (New York, 1979); as *The English House* trans. Janet Seligman and Stewart Spencer, ed. Dennis Sharp (London, 2007)
Nash, Joseph, *Architecture of the Middle Ages: Drawn from Nature and on Stone* (London, 1838)
——, *The Mansions of England in the Olden Time*, 4 vols (London, 1839–49)
Nasmyth, James, *James Nasmyth Engineer: An Autobiography*, ed. Samuel Smiles (London, 1883)
Newman, Gerald, *The Rise of English Nationalism: A Cultural History, 1740–1830* (London, 1987)
O'Brian, Patrick, *Joseph Banks* (London, 1987)
Oliver, Paul, Ian Davis and Ian Bentley, *Dunroamin: The Suburban Semi and its Enemies* (London, 1981)
Orwell, George, *The Road to Wigan Pier* (London, 1937)
——, *Coming up For Air* (London, 1939)
Andrea Palladio, *I quattro libri dell'architettura* [1570]; as *The Four Books of Architecture*, trans. Richard Schofield and Robert Tavernor (Cambridge, MA, 2002)
Palliser, David M., *The Age of Elizabeth: England Under the Later Tudors, 1547–1603* (London, 1983)
Papworth, John Buonarotti, *Rural Residences* (London, 1818)
Parker, Barry, and Raymond Unwin, *The Art of Building a Home: A Collection of Lectures and Illustrations* (London, 1901)

Parker, Louis Napoleon, *Pomander Walk* (London, 1910)
Penty, Arthur Joseph, *The Restoration of the Gild System* (London, 1906)
——, *Post-Industrialism* (London, 1914)
——, *Old Worlds for New: A Study of the Post-Industrial State* (London, 1918)
Pevsner, Nikolaus, *Pioneers of the Modern Movement* (London, 1936); revised as *Pioneers of Modern Design* (Harmondsworth, 1960)
——, *The Buildings of England*, 42 vols (Harmondsworth, 1951–74)
——, and Suzanne Lang, 'A Note on Sharawaggi', *Architectural Review*, CVI (1949); reprinted in *Studies in Art, Architecture and Design*, ed. Nikolaus Pevsner, 2 vols (New Haven, 1968), vol. I, pp. 78–107
Phayre, Ignatius [William George Fitzgerald], 'Hitler's Mountain Home', *Homes and Gardens* (November 1938), pp. 193–5
Plaw, John, *Rural Architecture; or, Designs from the Simple Cottage to the Decorative Villa* (London, 1785)
——, *Ferme Ornée; or, Rural Improvements: A Series of Domestic and Ornamental Designs* (London, 1795)
——, *Sketches for Country Houses, Villas and Rural Dwellings* (London, 1800)
Piggott, Stuart, *William Stukeley: An Eighteenth-Century Antiquary* (London, 1950; revd 1985)
Pocock, William Fuller, *Architectural Designs for Rustic Cottages, Picturesque Dwellings, Villas, etc.* (London, 1807)
Porter, Roy, *English Society in the Eighteenth Century* (Harmondsworth, 1982)
Powers, Alan, *Oliver Hill, Architect and Lover of Life, 1887–1968* (London, 1989)
Prakash, Gyan, *The Other Reason: Science and the Imagination of Modern India* (Princeton, NJ, 1999)
Priestland, Pamela, and Beryl Cobbing, *Village Life in Tudor and Stuart Times: A Study of Radcliffe-on-Trent* (Radcliffe-on-Trent, 1996)
Priestley, Harold, *The English Home* (London, 1970)
Priestley, J. B., *English Journey* (London, 1934)
Prizeman, John, *Houses of Britain: The Outside View* (London, 2003)
Pugin, Augustus Welby Northmore, *Ornaments of the Fifteenth and Sixteenth Centuries: Details of Ancient Timber Houses* (London, 1836)
——, *Contrasts; or, A Parallel Between the Noble Edifices of the Middle Ages and Corresponding Buildings of the Present Day; Shewing the Present Decay of Taste* (London, 1836; 2nd edn with additional plates, 1841)
——, *True Principles of Pointed or Christian Architecture* (London, 1841)
Quiney, Anthony, 'A Benevolent Business', *Country Life* (29 August 1991)
Repton, Humphry, *The Landscape Gardening and Landscape Architecture of the Late Humphrey Repton, Esq: Being His his Entire Works on These these Subjects*, ed. J. C. Loudon (London, 1840)
Richards, J. M. [Sir James], *An Introduction to Modern Architecture* (Harmondsworth, 1940)
——, *The Castles on the Ground: Anatomy of Suburbia* (London, 1946)

Select Bibliography

Richardson, Albert Edward, and Harold Donaldson Eberlein, *The English Inn, Past and Present* (London, 1925)

Richardson, Charles James, *Observations on the Architecture of England during the Reigns of Queen Elizabeth and King James I* (London, 1837)

——, *The Englishman's House: A Practical Guide for Selecting or Building a House* (London, 1870)

——, *The Englishman's House: From Cottage to Villa* (London, 1871)

Richardson, Tim, *The Arcadian Friends: Inventing the English Landscape Garden* (London, 2007)

Rickman, Thomas, *Attempt to Discriminate the Styles of Architecture in England, from the Conquest to the Reformation* (London, 1817)

Robinson, John Martin, *Ascott* (London, 2008)

Robinson, Peter Frederick, *Rural Architecture; or, A Series of Designs for Rural Cottages* (London, 1823)

——, *Village Architecture, being a Series of designs . . . illustrative of the Observations contained in the Essay on the Picturesque, by Sir Uvedale Price* (London, 1830)

——, *Designs for Lodges and Park Entrances* (London, 1833)

——, *Domestic Architecture in the Tudor Style* (London, 1837)

Ross, Angus, *A Political Biography of John Arbuthnot* (London, 2010)

Rousseau, Jean-Jacques, *The Collected Writings of Rousseau*, ed. Roger D. Masters and Christopher Kelly, 12 vols (Hanover, NH, and London, 1992)

Rowley, Trevor, *The English Landscape in the Twentieth Century* (Hambledon, 2006)

Ruskin, John, *The Poetry of Architecture; or, The Architecture of the Nations of Europe Considered in its association with Natural Scenery and National Character* (London, 1837–8)

——, *The Seven Lamps of Architecture* (London, 1849)

Said, Edward, *Orientalism* (London, 1978)

Saint, Andrew, *Richard Norman Shaw* (New Haven, 1976)

——, *Cragside, Northumberland* (London, 1992)

St John, Henry [Viscount Bolingbroke], *Historical Writings*, ed. Isaak Kramnick (Chicago, 1972)

Scott, Sir George Gilbert, *Remarks on Secular and Domestic Architecture, Present and Future* (London, 1857)

Scott, Sir Walter, *Ivanhoe* (Edinburgh, 1819)

——, *Kenilworth* (Edinburgh, 1821)

Schultz, R. Weir, et al., *The Arts Connected with Building: Lectures on Craftsmanship and Design*, ed. J. Raffles Davison (London, 1909)

Scruton, Roger, *England: An Elegy* (London, 2001)

Segal, Walter, *Home and Environment* (London, 1948)

——, *Housing: The Post-War Work of London County Council* (London, 1949)

Seiberling, John, and Steve Love, *Stan Hywet Hall and Gardens* (Akron, OH, 2000)

Selden, John, *Table Talk* (London, 1654)

Sellar, W. C., and R. J. Yeatman, *1066 and All That: A Memorable History of England, Comprising All the Parts You Can Remember, including 103 Good Things, 5 Bad Kings and 2 Genuine Dates* (London, 1930)

Serlio, Sebastiano, *Tutte l'opere d'architettura et prospetiva* [1537–75]; as *Sebastiano Serlio on Architecture*, trans. Vaughan Hart and Peter Hicks, 2 vols (New Haven and London, 1996–2001)

Seymour, John, *The Complete Book of Self-Sufficiency* (London, 1976)

Sharwood-Smith, J. E., 'Latin, the Elite Tradition in Education and Dr Flann Campbell', *British Journal of Education Studies*, XX/1 (February 1972), pp. 5–11

Shaw, Henry, *Details of Elizabethan Architecture* (London, 1839)

Shaw, Richard Norman, *Architectural Sketches from the Continent* (London, 1858)

——, *Sketches for Cottages and Other Buildings Designed to be Constructed in the Patent Cement Slab System of W. H. Lascelles . . . drawn by Maurice B. Adams* (London, 1878).

——, and Thomas Graham Jackson, *Architecture: A Profession or an Art? Thirteen Short Essays on the Qualifications of Architects* (London, 1892)

Shenstone, William, *The Works in Verse and Prose, of William Shenstone, Esq*, ed. Robert Dodsley, 2 vols (London, 1764)

Shuter, Jane, *The Poor in Tudor England* (London, 1995)

Simpson, Duncan, 'Beautiful Tudor', *Architectural Review*, CLXII (July 1977)

——, *C.F.A. Voysey: An Architect of Individuality* (London, 1979)

Skinner, Tina, *Hollywood Homes: Postcard Views of Early Stars' Estates* (Atglen, PA, 2005)

Slack, Paul, 'Poverty and Social Regulation in Elizabethan England', in *The Reign of Elizabeth I*, ed. Christopher Haigh (London, 1984)

Smiles, Samuel, *Self-Help* (London, 1858)

Smith, Anthony D., *Nationalist Movements* (New York, 1976)

Smith, Arthur, *Three Acres and Employment* (1927)

Smith, G., *Essay on the Construction of Cottages Suited for the Dwellings of the Labouring Classes* (Edinburgh, 1834)

Smith, Graham Paul, *Ernest George Trobridge, 1884–1942: Architect Extraordinary* (Oxford, 1982)

Smith, J. T., *Remarks on Rural Scenery, with Ttwenty Eetchings of Ccottages, from Nnature, and some Oobservations and Pprecepts Rrelative to the Ppicturesque* (London, 1797)

Smith, James, *The Cottage: An Operatic Farce in Two Acts* (London, 1796)

Smith, J. [pseud. Ædituus], *Metrical Remarks on Modern Castles and Cottages, and Architecture in General* (London, 1813)

Snodin, Michael, *Horace Walpole's Strawberry Hill* (New Haven and London, 2009)

Soane, John, *Sketches in Architecture; Containing Plans and Elevations of Cottages, Villas, and Other Useful Buildings, with Characteristic Scenery* (London, 1793)

Sonne, Christian R., and Chiu yin Hempel, *Tuxedo Park: The Historic Houses* (New York, 2007)

Stamp, Gavin, 'Neo-Tudor and its Enemies', *Architectural History*, XLIX (2006), pp. 1–33

——, and André Goulancourt, *The English House, 1860–1914* (London, 1986)

Starkey, David, *The Reign of Henry VIII: Personalities and Politics* (London, 1985)

Stemp, David, *Three Acres and a Cow: The Life and Works of Eli Hamshire* (London, 1995)

Steel, John, and Michael Wright, *The English House: 1000 Years of Domestic Architecture* (London, 2007)

Stevenson, John, *Social Conditions in Britain between the Wars* (London, 1977)
Stochholm, Johanne M., *Garrick's Folly: The Shakespeare Jubilee of 1769 at Stratford and Drury Lane* (London, 1964)
Stuart, James, and Nicholas Revett, *The Antiquities of Athens*, 4 vols (London, 1762–1816)
Stukeley, William, *Stonehenge: A Temple Restor'd to the British Druids* (London, 1740)
——, *Avebury: A Temple of the British Druids* (London, 1743)
Sweet, Rosemary, *Antiquaries: The Discovery of the Past in Eighteenth-century Britain* (London, 2004)
Swenarton, Mark, *Homes Fit for Heroes* (London, 1981)
——, *Building the New Jerusalem: Architecture, Housing and Politics, 1900–1930* (Bracknell, 2008)
Symonds, Robert Wemyss, 'The 'Passing Delicacie' of the English Home', *Ideal Home* (December 1952/January 1953 [double issue]), pp. 66–75
Taylor, Harold McCarter, and Joan Taylor, *Anglo-Saxon Architecture*, 3 vols (Cambridge, 1965–78)
Temple, Nigel, *John Nash and the Village Picturesque* (Gloucester, 1979)
Thompson, Ian, *The Sun King's Garden: Louis XIV, Andre Le Nôtre and the Creation of the Gardens of Versailles* (London, 2006)
——, *The English Lakes: A History* (London, 2010)
Thornton, A. P., *The Habit of Authority: Paternalism in British History* (Toronto, 1966)
Thistlewood, David, 'A. J. Penty (1875–1937) and the Legacy of Nineteenth-century English Domestic Architecture', *Journal of the Society of Architectural Historians*, XLVI (1987), pp. 327–41
Tinniswood, Adrian, *Life in the English Country Cottage* (London, 1995)
Townsend, Gavin, 'The Tudor House in America, 1890–1930', unpublished PhD thesis (University of California, Santa Barbara, 1986)
Trendall, E. W., *Examples for Exterior and Interior Furnishings in the Italian, Grecian and Tudor Styles of Architecture* (London, 1848)
Turner, Sharon, *History of the Anglo-Saxons, 1799–1805*, 4th edn, 3 vols (London, 1823)
Unwin, Raymond, *Town Planning in Practice* (London, 1909)
——, *Town Planning and Modern Architecture at the Hampstead Garden Suburb* (London, 1909)
Van Norden, Linda, 'The Elizabethan College of Antiquaries', unpublished PhD thesis (University of California at Los Angeles, 1946)
Veblen, Thorstein, *The Theory of the Leisure Class* (New York, 1899)
Viollet-le-Duc, Eugène, *Entretiens sur l'architecture*, 2 vols (Paris, 1858–72); as *Discourses on Architecture*, trans. Henry Van Brunt (Boston, MA, 1875)
Voysey, C.F.A., *Individuality* (London, 1915)
Wallen, Martin, 'Lord Egremont's Dogs: The Cynosure of Turner's Petworth Landscapes', *English Literary History*, LXXIII/4 (2006)
Walpole, Horace, *The Castle of Otranto* (London, 1764)
——, *The Yale Edition of Horace Walpole's Correspondence*, ed. W. S. Lewis, 48 vols (New Haven, 1937–83)
Watkin, David, *English Architecture* (London, 1979)

——, 'An Eloquent Sermon in Stone', *City Journal* (Summer 1998)
Watters, Sam, *Houses of Los Angeles*, 2 vols (New York, 2007) [vol. I: 1885–1919; vol. II: 1920–35]
Waugh, Evelyn, *Decline and Fall* (London, 1928)
Weaver, Lawrence, *The 'Country Life' Book of Cottages* (London, 1913)
Winckelmann, Johann Joachim, *Anmerkungen über die Geschichte der Kunst des Alterthums* (Dresden, 1767); as *History of the Art of Antiquity*, trans. Harry Francis Mallgrave (Los Angeles, 2006)
Whitaker, John, *The Genuine History of the Britons Asserted* (London, 1772)
Whittaker, John, *Ceremonial of the Coronation of His Most Sacred Majesty King George the Fourth* (London, 1823)
Wiener, Martin, *English Culture and the Decline of the Industrial Spirit* (Cambridge, 1981)
Wilson, David M., *The British Museum: A History* (London, 2002)
Wilson, J. D., *Life in Shakespeare's England: A Book of Elizabethan Prose* (Cambridge, 1915)
Withey, Lynne, *Grand Tours and Cooks Tours* (London, 1997)
Wood, John [the Younger], *A Series of Plans for Cottages or Habitations of the Labourer* (Bath, 1781)
Woods, Robert, *The Population of Britain in the Nineteenth Century* (Cambridge, 1995)
Woodforde, John, *The Truth about Cottages* (London, 1969)
Woolf, Daniel, *The Social Circulation of the Past* (Oxford, 2003)
Wordsworth, William, and Samuel Taylor Coleridge, *Lyrical Ballads* (London, 1798)
Worthington, T. Locke, *Remnants of Old English Architecture: Thirty-five plates of Measured and Perspective Drawings* (London, 1888)
Yorke, F. R. S., *The Modern House* (London, 1934)

Acknowledgements

We are very grateful to the AHRC, which supported the research that went into this book. Our intellectual debts are formally acknowledged in the References, but the Tudoresque is a subject about which everyone seems to have a view, and our work was also informed by many conversations, in different parts of the world. We spoke with, and listened to, colleagues, students, family, friends, the owners of some buildings and custodians of others, delegates at academic conferences and some people we met in the street. Their initial reactions to the Tudoresque could range from enthusiasm to bemusement, but they all helped by encouraging and stimulating ideas. Local guides steered us towards buildings we would not otherwise have reached. We would particularly like to thank: Emily Apter, Architectural Humanities Research Association, Dana Arnold, Raaja Bashin, Steve Basson, Martin Beattie, Barry Bergdoll, Neil Bingham, Kati Blom, Geoffrey Buck, Sandy Buck, Malcolm Bull, Zeynep Celik, Chang Jiat-Hwee, Chang Ying, Tony Champion, Lillian Chee, Ross Chinn, Nathaniel Coleman, Vivian Constantinopoulos, Martyn Dade-Robertson, Hugh Dixon, Andrew Dolkart, European Architectural History Network, English Heritage, Elvan Ergut, Crista Ermiya, Gary Exu, Carolyn Fahey, Rose Gilroy, Pru Goodwin, Adrian Green, Pyrs Gruffudd, Peter Guillery, Suna Guven, Mark Halpin, Han Ling Mei, David Haney, Vaughan Hart, Jean Hillier, Joseph Hwang, Zeynep Kezer, Joanna Klein, Peter Klein, Lakeland Trust, Lai Chee Kien, Kathy Law, Malcolm Law, Richard Law, Sue Lawson, Leigh Historical Society, Gerard Loughlin, Hentie Louw, Kim McCartney, Elizabeth McKellar, Emma Main, Neil Moat, The National Trust, Belgin Turan Ozkaya, John Pendlebury, Alan Powers, Qin Qianqian, Karen Ritchie, Chris Rowley, Alan Ramsbottom, Andrew Saint, Clare Sherriff, Society of Architectural Historians (USA), Society of Architectural Historians of Great Britain, Sue Speak, Gavin Stamp, Nancy Stieber, Tatiana String, Bill Tavernor, Ian Thompson, Anthony Vidler, Dave Webb, Bobby Wong, Wong Yunn Chii, Joris Van Wezemael and Brendan Woods.

PHOTOS: Andrew Ballantyne: pp. 51, 166, 170, 181, 185, 188, 189, 191, 193, 195, 196, 197, 199, 213, 214, 215, 217, 219, 220, 221, 222; The British Library: pp. 49, 63, 142, 157, 176, 177; Ross Chinn, p. 236; FreeFoto: p. 37; Hotel Endsleigh, Tavistock, Devon: p. 52; Courtesy of Lakeland Arts Trust: p. 159 (Nick Wood); Andrew Law: pp. 45, 72, 73, 92, 95, 98, 100, 101, 104, 110, 148, 149, 150, 152, 154, 165, 207, 208, 209, 224, 238; The National Library of Scotland: pp. 118, 124; National Monuments Record: pp. 58, 93; The National Trust: pp. 19, 81; John Piper Estate: p. 169; Rex Features: p. 180 (Roger-Viollet); Robinson Library, Newcastle University: p. 86; Thornton Manor Hotel, Wirral, Cheshire: pp. 102–3.

Index

Addison, Joseph
   Letter from Italy 172
   The Spectator 133–4, 140
Aldersyde, York (Penty) *25*, 110
allotments 122–3
Anglo-Saxon architecture 29
antiquity, interest in 23–8
   see also classical styles
Arcadian landscape 21, 25, 36, 173
Architectural Review (magazine) 232
aristocratic culture, 18th century 26–7
Armstrong, Lord, Cragside (Shaw) *34*, 153–5, 233
Arts and Crafts Movement 157–9, 160–61, 228
Ascot House, Wing (Devey) *32*, 150–51
Aspley Wood cottage (Repton) *46*, 175–6
Atterbury, Grosvenor, Forest Hills Gardens, New York *52*, 185–6
Audsley, George and William 68, 69

Baillie Scott, Mackay Hugh, Blackwell, Bowness *37*, 158–9, 162
Banks, Sir Joseph 76, 77, 78–9
barge-boards, carved *46*, 176
Baring, Sir Thomas and Lady 83
Baronial, Scottish 58
Barron, P. A., *The House Desirable* 161–2

Barry, Sir Charles, New Palace of Westminster 66
Bateman, Richard 142–3
Bedford, Duke of, Endsleigh Cottage (Wyatt) *8*, 52–3, 64, 140, 141, 175
Bedfordshire, Old Warden (Robinson) 83, 91
Belloc, Hilaire 111
Berkshire
   Ockwells Manor 190
   Princess Elizabeth's Cottage, Windsor *30*, 142–4
   Windsor Castle, King's Cottage *29*, 141–2
Bertram, Anthony 10, 167, 228, 229
Bill of Rights (1689) 107
black-and-white work
   history of 44–6
   launch of (19th century) 147
   popularity of (early 20th century) 125–6, 159–60
   see also individual buildings
Blackwell, Bowness (Baillie Scott) *37*, 158–9
Blaise Hamlet, Bristol (Nash) *7*, 51–2, 82–3
Blomfield, Sir Reginald 230–31
Blue Stockings Society, harvest dinners 79
Brighton Pavilion 70, 142

276

Bristol, Blaise Hamlet (Nash) 7, 51–2, 82–3
British character
  assessment 53–6
  Merry England 39–40, 68–9, 87, 126–7
  personification 227–8
  self-sufficiency 105–11, 121–3, 151, 155
  see also lower middle classes; middle classes
Bronxville, New York 55, 192
Brown, Richard, *Domestic Architecture* 86–7
Bucks
  Ascott House, Wing (Devey) 32, 150–51
  Mentmore Towers (Paxton) 16, 91, 92, 93
  Wing village (Devey) 17, 94–6
  Wingrave, (Huckvale) 15, 91–2
budget housing 160, 164–6, 193–4
bungalows
  Indian origins 117, 204–6
  Singapore 71, 218–19
Burke, Edmund 53–5, 148, 228, 232

Cadbury, George, Northfield Manor, Birmingham (Harvey) 24, 99, 104, 149
Cambridge, Selwyn College 180
Camden, William, *Britannia* 23
Campbell, Colen, *Vitruvius Britannicus* 47–8
Castle Village, New York (Pelham) 198
Chambers, William, *Civil Architecture* 48
Chaplin, Charlie, studio and homes, California (Meyer and Holler) 54, 188, 189
Cheshire
  Little Moreton Hall 151
  Port Sunlight 22, 99, 101, 185
  St Michael's Row, Chester

(Lockwood) 5, 45
  Thornton Manor, Port Sunlight 23, 99, 102–3
Chesterton, G. K. 110–11
Chicago World's Fair 49, 178, 179
chimney stacks 82
China
  British pavilion, Beijing (Heatherwick) 182, 233
  Julu Road and Stanford Gardens 75, 223, 224
  Shanghai cosmopolitan culture 221–3
  Thames Town, Shanghai 76, 223–5, 226, 233
  travel, rarity of foreign 225
Chinn, Ross 237
Chrysler Building, New York 200
class struggle 115–19
classical styles
  and allusion 172–3
  and antiquity interest 23–8
  architectural detail 35–8
  and British Empire and sense of self-importance 173
  and Gothic 59
  and Grand Tour 171–2
  Greek 24, 58, 61, 136, 171–3
  Neoclassicism 43–4, 47–8, 58
  Roman 23–4, 28–9, 47–8, 57, 59, 152
A Clockwork Orange (film) 238–9
college building 178–81
commuters 147–8
concrete
  cement slab construction 155–7
  panels, Gregynog Hall, Newtown 33, 151, 152–3
  panels, Paris Exposition Universelle (1900) 50, 178, 180
consumer culture 115
Corcoran, Paddy 201
Cornwall, Tregothnan (Wilkins) 9, 57, 58

277

cottage orné (second home) 50, 129, 138, 139–40, 143, 145–6
cottages
    British Cottage Architecture (Malton) 6, 48–51, 79, 138–9, 145, 163, 174
    Cottage, Farm and Villa Architecture (Loudon) 65–6, 177–8
    cottage law (Elizabethan) 105–6, 109–10, 130
    country house styled as 8, 52–3
    design improvement 6, 7, 47, 48–52, 82–3
    Designs for Cottages (Gandy) 38, 160, 163
    Germany, Black Forest cottage style 183–4
    and informal domestic style 64–5
    and paternalism *see* paternalism
    Rustic Cottages (Pococke) 145–6
    Sketches for Cottages (Shaw) 36, 155–7
    super-scale 146–51
    traditional building methods 46
    Victorian Tudoresque villages 90–96
    see also individual buildings
Country Life (magazine) 123, 124, 232
craftmanship, increasing importance of 157–70
Cragside, Northumberland (Shaw) 34, 153–5, 233
Cumbria, Blackwell, Bowness (Baillie Scott) 37, 158–9

Dalmeny, West Lothian (Wilkins) 58, 92
Davies, Marion 188
Dearn, Thomas, *Sketches in Architecture* 139
Derbyshire, Hardwick Hall (Smythson) 1, 19, 198
Desperate Housewives (TV show) 191–2
Devey, George 147
    Ascott House, Wing 32, 150–51

Betteshanger, Kent 12, 73–4
Hammerfield, Kent 31, 149–50
Leigh Hall and village 18–19, 97–9
Penshurst Place, Kent 11, 72–3
Rothschild Tudor cottages 17, 91–2, 94–6
Wing village 17, 94–6
Wingrave, Buckinghamshire 15, 91–2
Devon
    Endsleigh Cottage (Wyatt) 8, 52–3, 64, 140, 141, 175
    Luscombe (Nash) 58
Dickens, Charles, *The Old Curiosity Shop* 39–40
Disney, EPCOT 182
Disraeli, Benjamin 87, 88
    Sybil; or, The Two Nations 88, 90, 101
Doheny mansion, Beverly Hills (Kaufmann) 53, 187, 188
Dorset
    Kingston Maurward 151
    Milton Abbas 91
Douglas, John, Thornton Manor, Port Sunlight 23, 99, 102–3
Douglas Smith and Barley, Hanger Hill Garden Estate 40, 164, 165
Downton Castle, Herefordshire 57–8, 140
Druids 29, 173

East Cowes Castle, Isle of Wight (Nash) 58
East Midlands, Wollaton Hall, Nottingham (Smythson) 92, 207–8
economic depression, effects of 10–11, 167–8, 228
Egremont, Lord, Petworth estate fête 13, 79, 81
electricity provision 114, 153, 154–5
Elizabeth I 2, 31–2, 33, 40, 76–7
    Cottage Law 105–6, 109–10

Elizabethan design
  conflicting views on 40–41, 66–70, 71–2
  Hardwick Hall, Derbyshire (Smythson) 1, 19
  Jacobethan 18
  Leigh Hall, Kent 18–19, 97–9
  prodigy houses 1, 19
  as representation of olden days 59, 60–61, 64–5, 127, 148
  Ruskin on 55–6
  Thornton Manor, Port Sunlight 23, 99, 102–3
  Wollaton Hall, Nottingham (Smythson) 92, 207–8
Elle Decoration (magazine) 232
Elsam, Richard 139–40
Endsleigh Cottage, Devon (Wyatt) 8, 52–3, 64, 140, 141, 175
Enlightenment 134–8
Esher Place (Kent) 36
Europe, vernacular revival 183–4

Fahrenheit 451 (film) 79, 237–8, 239
Fenham, Newcastle upon Tyne 42, 164–6
Fielding, Henry 27, 28, 30
  Tom Jones 20–22, 37, 55, 91, 191
Fifth Avenue, New York 59, 196, 197
'Fine Old-English Gentleman' (song) (Russell) 88–9
Fletcher, Sir Banister 'Modern English Homes' 162
Foster, Stanley, The Lakehouse, Cameron Highlands 67, 213–15
Four Acres and a Cow (Cottage Law) 105–6, 109–10
France
  French Revolution 36–7, 46–7, 53–5, 138
  petit hameau, Versailles (Mique) 137
  le style normande 137

French, Frederick F.
  Hudson View Gardens, New York (Pelham) 58, 196, 199
  Tudor City, New York 60, 199–201

Gandy, Joseph 139, 160
  Designs for Cottages 38, 160, 163
Garden Cities 111, 118, 184–5
Garner, Thomas, *The Domestic Architecture of England* 125–6
Garrick, David 35
George, Ernest, Leigh village 97–9
George IV 39, 141–2
Georgian architecture 20–22, 70, 124
  Neo-Georgian 116–18, 123
  Palladian style 70, 71, 204, 226
German, Edward, *Merrie England* (operetta) 41
Germany, Black Forest cottage style 184
Gilpin, William, *Observations on the River Wye* 25
Goldsmith, Oliver, *The Deserted Village* 49–50
Goodwin, Francis 61–2, 64–5
Gothic architecture 18, 20–22, 30, 176–7
  conflicting views on 59, 61–2, 66–7, 69–70, 89
  Gothic Revival 36, 40, 66, 88, 125–6
  New Palace of Westminster 40
  and Renaissance, influence of 57–9
  Strawberry Hill, Twickenham 30, 38–9
  Toddington Manor, Gloucestershire 151
Grand Tour 24, 28–9, 171–2, 226, 236
Greek classical style *see under* classical styles
Greenwich (Jones) 57
Gregynog Hall, Newtown 33, 151, 152–3

Grimshaw, Nicholas, British pavilion, Seville 182
Grossmith, George and Weedon, *Diary of a Nobody* 112–13

Hammerfield, Penshurst (Devey) *31*, 149–50
Hampstead Garden Suburb (Penty) *26*, 111, 185
Hamshire, Eli 110
Hanger Hill Garden Estate, Ealing *40*, 164, 165
Hardwick Hall, Derbyshire (Smythson) *1*, 19
Harford, John, Blaise Hamlet (Nash) *7*, 51–2, 82–3
Harvey, William Alexander, Northfield Manor (Harvey) *24*, 99, 104, 149
Hearne, Thomas, *The Landscape* (illus.) *4*, 36–8
Heatherwick, Thomas, British pavilion, Beijing 182, 233
Hennebique, François 152
Henry VII 16–17, 30–32, 86–7
Henry VIII 41–2, 59, 86–8
Herefordshire, Downton Castle 57–8, 140
Hill, Oliver 124
Hitler, Adolf 133
Hollenden, Lord, Leigh Hall and village 18–19, 97–9
Holler, Gabriel, Chaplin studio, California *54*, 188, 189
home ownership 119–23
Homebuilding and Renovation (magazine) 237
homes
    designated spaces in 131–2
    and social identity 132–3
    as spaces of escape 131–45, 231
Homes and Gardens (magazine) 123, 124, 133
Honor Oak self-build housing, Lewisham *78*, 237, 238

housework 120–21
Howard, Ebenezer 118
Hubback, Arthur Benison, railway station and Royal Selangor Club, Kuala Lumpur 212
Huckvale, William, Wingrave, Buckinghamshire *15*, 91–2
Hudson View Gardens, New York (Pelham) *58*, 196, 198
Hume, David 31–2, 32–4, 86–7
Hunt, Thomas
    Domestic Picturesque Architecture 45, 174, 175
    Exemplars of Tudor Architecture 174–5, 176

Ideal Home (magazine) 27, 28, 117, 118, 123–7, 159–60, 231–2
India
    bungalow 204–6
    East India Trading Company 203
    Shimla village, Himalayas 61–4, 206–11, 235
indigenous culture, interest in 173–7
industrialists' Tudor 96–104, 147–51
inter-war years, housing initiative 113–15, 116, 125
international exhibitions 178–82, 233
Ireland, Swiss Cottage, Cahir (Nash) 144
Irwin, Henry, Viceroy's Lodge, Himalayas *64*, 207–8, 209
Isle of Wight, East Cowes Castle (Nash) 58

Jim Henson Studios, California *54*, 188
Johnson, Samuel 27–8, 31
Jones, Inigo 28–9
    Greenwich 57

Kaufmann, Gordon, Doheny mansion, Beverly Hills *53*, 187, 188

Kent
  Hammerfield, Penshurst (Devey) 31, 149–50
  Leigh Hall and village 18–19, 97–9
  Penshurst Place (Devey) 11, 72–3
Kent, Nathaniel, *Hints to Gentlemen of Landed Property* 46, 48, 79–80, 81, 109
Kent, William, Esher Place 36
Kerr, Robert 71–2
Kingsbury, London 41, 164, 165
Kingston Maurward 151
Knight, Richard Payne 59, 60–61
  Downton Castle 57–8, 140
  The Landscape 4, 36–8

land ownership, and self-sufficiency 105–11
Lascelles, W. H. 152, 155
Laugier, Marc-Antoine 136, 137
Le Corbusier 129, 159, 163, 229
  Pavillon Suisse 181
The Leasowes, Dudley 134
Leetham, Ernest, Aldersyde, York (Penty) 25, 110
Leigh Hall and village, Kent 18–19, 97–9
Leverhulme, Lord
  Port Sunlight, Cheshire 22, 99, 101, 186
  Thornton Manor, Port Sunlight 23, 99, 102–3
Levinson, David J., Tudor Village, New York 56, 193–4
Leys Wood, Sussex (Shaw) 35, 153, 155
Little Moreton Hall, Cheshire 151
Lloyd, Arthur, 'Three Acres and a Cow' (song) 110
Lloyd George, David 113–14
Locke, John 107–8, 110, 111
Lockwood, William, St Michael's Row, Chester 5, 45
London
  Greenwich (Jones) 57
  Hampstead Garden Suburb (Penty) 26, 111, 185
  Hanger Hill Garden Estate, Ealing 40, 164, 165
  Honor Oak self-build housing, Lewisham 78, 237, 238
  Strawberry Hill, Twickenham 30, 38–9, 227
Loudon, John Claudius 173
  Cottage, Farm and Villa Architecture 65–6, 177–8
Lovell Health House, Hollywood (Neutra) 187
lower middle classes 112–15
  budget housing 160, 164–8, 193–4
  and class struggle 115–19
  and home ownership 119–23
  moderation in taste and design 163–8, 228–9, 231, 233–4
  simple life, dream of 127–30, 133
  suburbia *see* suburbia
  see also British character; middle classes
Luscombe, Devon (Nash) 58
Lutyens, Edwin 162
  British pavilion, Paris Exposition Universelle 50, 178, 180

Malaysia
  Equatorial Hotel, Brinchang 70, 216, 217
  hill-top house, Tanah Rata 68, 215
  Kota Kinabalu house, Sabah 77, 235–6, 237
  The Lakehouse, Ringlet 67, 213–15
  old railway station, Kuala Lumpur (Hubback) 212
  The Old Smokehouse, Tanah Rata 66, 212–13, 214
  retail and domestic development, Ringlet 69, 216, 217
  Royal Selangor Club, Kuala Lumpur (Hubback) 65, 212, 213

281

Malton, James, *British Cottage Architecture* 6, 48–51, 79, 138–9, 145, 163, 174
Mander family, Wightwick Manor, Wolverhampton 20–21, 99, 100, 149
Manners, Lord John 87–8
Marie-Antoinette, Queen, *petit hameau*, Versailles (Mique) 137
Martin, Pierre, Collège Franco-Britannique 51, 178, 180–81
medieval architecture 18–19, 30–32, 39–40, 57–8, 59–60, 84–5
Mentmore Towers (Paxton) 16, 91, 92, 93
Merrie England (operetta) (German) 41
Merry England 39–40, 68–9, 87, 126–7
  see also British character
Metro-land 118–19, 167
Meyer, Mendel, Chaplin studio, California 54, 188
middle England
  suburbia *see* suburbia
  value system 55, 105–6, 229–30, 231
middle-classes
  Cottage Residences (Shaw) 36, 156–7
  cultural interest in old-fashioned things 39–40, 84, 123
  increased confidence of 27–8
  lower *see* lower middle classes
  mobility, increased 161–2
  see also British character
Milton Abbas, Dorset 91
Mique, Richard, *petit hameau*, Versailles 137
Mock Tudor 12, 123–7
Modern Movement 160–61, 229, 230–31, 232–3
modernity, resistance to 237–40
Morgan, Julia 189
Muthesius, Hermann 119, 161, 233

Nash, John
  Blaise Hamlet, Bristol 7, 51–2, 82–3, 144
  East Cowes Castle, Isle of Wight 58
  King's Cottage, Windsor Castle 29, 141–2
  Luscombe, Devon 58
  Swiss Cottage, Cahir, Co. Tipperary 144
Nash, Joseph, *The Mansions of England* 14, 84–6, 94, 126, 131, 159
nature, cult of 133–8
Naysmith, James, Hammerfield, Kent (Devey) 31, 149–50
Neoclassicism 43–4, 47–8, 58
  see also classical styles
Nesfield, William Eden 147, 151
Neutra, Richard, Lovell Health House, Hollywood 187
New Palace of Westminster 40, 63, 66, 88
Newton, Ernest, *Sketches for Cottages and Other Buildings* 36, 155–7
Northfield Manor, Birmingham (Harvey) 24, 99, 104, 149

Ockwells Manor, Berkshire 190
ogee arch 36
Old Warden, Bedfordshire (Robinson) 83, 91
Olmsted Jr, Frederick Law, Forest Hills Gardens, New York (Atterbury) 52, 185–6
Ongley, Lord, Old Warden, Bedfordshire (Robinson) 83, 91
Orwell, George 120, 128–9
Ossian 28
Ould, Edward, Wightwick Manor, Wolverhampton 20–21, 99, 100
Oxford, Magdalen College 180

Palladian style 70, 71, 204, 226
  see also Georgian architecture

Papworth, John Buonarotti, *Rural Residences* 146
Paris
  Collège Franco-Britannique (Martin and Vieu) *51*, 178, 180–81
  Exposition Universelle 48, 50, 178, 179, 180
  see also France
Parker and Unwin, Hampstead Garden Suburb *26*, 111, 185
paternalism 75–104
  and expected practices 75–8, 89–90, 189
  festivals of altruism 78–83
  industrialists' Tudor 96–104, 147–51
  newly rich and Old English manor house 83–7, 91
  and philanthropy 87, 91, 93, 97–9, 101–2
  and poverty 79–81, 139
  and rich and poor reconciliation 87–90
  and tenants' clothing and morals 83
  Victorian Tudoresque villages 90–96
Paterno, Charles V.
  Castle Village, New York (Pelham) 198
  Hudson View Gardens, New York (Pelham) *58*, 196, 198
Paxton, Joseph, Mentmore Towers *16*, *91*, *92*, *93*
Pelham, George F., Hudson View Gardens, New York *58*, 196, 198
Pelham II, George F., Castle Village, New York 198
Penshurst Place, Kent (Devey) *11*, 72–3
Penty, Arthur
  Aldersyde, York *25*, 110
  Hampstead Garden Suburb *26*, 111, 185

Peto, Harold, Leigh village 97–9
Petworth estate fête *13*, 79, 81
Pevsner, Nikolaus 10, 11, 190
  Pioneers of the Modern Movement 160–61
Picturesque 25, 48–9, 84–5, 141, 163, 174
  Cragside, Northumberland (Shaw) *34*, 153–5, 233
  The Landscape (poem) *4*, 36–8
  Penshurst Place, Kent (Devey) *11*, 72–3
  Tregothnan, Cornwall (Wilkins) *9*, 57, 58
Piper, John *43*, 168, 169
Pococke, William, *Designs for Rustic Cottages* 145–6
Pomander Walk, New York 198
Porphyrios Associates, college building 180
Port Sunlight, Cheshire *22*, 99, 101, 186
poverty 79–81, 106–8, 139
Priestley, J. B., *English Journey* 115
Princess Elizabeth's Cottage, Windsor *30*, 142–4
prodigy houses *1*, 19, 198
  see also Elizabethan design
Pugin, Augustus 40, 62, 66–8
  New Palace of Westminster 66

Queen Anne style 158

Reform Bill (1832) 81
Renaissance effects 57–63
Repton, George Stanley, Blaise Hamlet, Bristol *7*, 51–2, 82–3
Repton, Humphry
  Aspley Wood cottage *46*, 175–6
  Endsleigh Cottage, Devon (Wyatt) *8*, 52–3, 64, 140, 141, 175
  Landscape Gardening 46, 176
Richards, J. M. 120–21
  The Castles on the Ground *43*, 167–8, 169

Richardson, C. J. 59, 60
  The Englishman's House 39, 163, 164
Rickman, Thomas, *Styles of English Architecture* 30, 59–60
Robinson, P. F. 62
  Designs for Lodges and Park Entrances 47, 176–7
  Domestic Architecture in the Tudor Style 10, 62–3
  Old Warden, Bedfordshire 83, 91
Roman classical style *see under* classical style
Romanticism 135–8
Rothschild family
  Ascott House, Wing (Devey) 32, 150–51
  Mentmore Towers (Paxton) 16, 91, 92, 93
  Tring Park, Aylesbury 91–2, 93–4
  Wing village (Devey) 17, 94–6
  Wingrave, Buckinghamshire (Huckvale) 15, 91–2
Rousseau, Jean-Jacques 134–7
  Le Devin du village (opera) 135–6
Ruskin, John 55–6, 156, 157–8
Russell, Henry, 'Fine Old-English Gentleman' (song) 88–9
Russell Sage Foundation, New York (Atterbury) 185–6

Sassafras Estate, Long Island 189
Schneider, Charles Sumner, Stan Hywet Hall, Akron 190
Scotland, Dalmeny, West Lothian (Wilkins) 58, 92
Scott, Sir George Gilbert, *Secular and Domestic Architecture* 89
Scott, Sir Walter, *Kenilworth* 40
second homes *see* cottage orné
Segal, Walter, Honor Oak self-build housing, Lewisham 7, 238
Seiberling, Frank, Stan Hywet Hall, Akron (Schneider) 190–91

self-build housing, and accidental Tudoresque 78, 237, 238
self-sufficiency 151, 155
  and land ownership 105–11
  and suburbia 121–3, 231, 233–4
Shakespeare, William 3, 28, 31, 34–5, 37, 40, 60, 200, 225
Shaw, Richard Norman 147, 148, 151
  cement-slab construction 155–6
  Cragside, Northumberland 34, 153–5, 233
  Leys Wood, Groombridge 35, 153, 155
  Sketches for Cottages and Other Buildings 36, 155–7
Shenstone, William, The Leasowes, Dudley 134
Sherwood Terrace, New York 57, 195–6
Shimla village, Himalayas 61–4, 206–11
Shute, John, *The First and Chief Groundes of Architecture* 47
simple life, dream of 127–30, 133
  see also lower middle classes
Singapore
  bamboo blinds 71, 218–19
  bungalows 218
  Chuville 74, 220–21, 222
  Tanglin Place 73, 219–20, 221
  Tudor Court shopping gallery 72, 219, 220
Smiles, Samuel, *Self-Help* 97, 104
Smirke, Robert 24, 62
Smith, Arthur, *Three Acres and Employment* 111
Smythson, Robert 199
  Hardwick Hall 1, 19
  Wollaton Hall 92, 207–8
Society of Dilettanti 23–4, 25, 58
Somerset, Warleigh Manor (Webb) 59
Spain, British pavilion, Seville (Grimshaw) 182
Stan Hywet Hall, Akron (Schneider) 190–91

steel-framed houses 152, 178, 187
Stonehenge 28–9, 173
storybook style houses 184
Stratton, Arthur, *The Domestic Architecture of England* 125–6
Strawberry Hill, Twickenham 30, 38–9, 227
Stukeley, William 29, 173
suburbia 114–15, 116–18
    budget housing 164–7, 228–9
    and mass-market housing 161
    and self-reliance 121–3, 231, 233–4
    see also lower middle classes; middle England
Sudeley, Lord
    Gregynog Hall, Newtown *33*, 151, 152–3
    Toddington Manor 151
Surrey, Esher Place (Kent) 36
Sussex
    Brighton Pavilion 70, 142
    Leys Wood (Shaw) *35*, 153, 155
    Petworth estate fête *13*, 79, 81
Swiss Cottage, Cahir, County Tipperary (Nash) 144
Symonds, Robert 126–7

technical innovation 151–7, 178
This England (magazine) 232
Thornton Manor, Port Sunlight *23*, 99, 102–3
'Three Acres and a Cow' (song) (Lloyd) 110
transport provision 114, 115
travel, effects of foreign 171–82
    and college architecture abroad 178–81
    Grand Tour 24, 28–9, 171–2, 226, 236
    and indigenous culture, interest in 173–7
    international exhibitions 178–82, 233

and old-fashioned image of Tudoresque 182
and overseas building developments *see* individual countries
Tregothnan, Cornwall (Wilkins) *9*, 57, 58
Tring Park, Aylesbury 91–2, 93–4
Tudor, meaning of 15–18
Tudor arch 18, 57, 195, 207
Tudor City, New York *60*, 199–201
Tudor Village, New York *56*, 193–4
Tuxedo Park, New York 189
Tyndale, Sir Walter 190
Tyne and Wear, Fenham, Newcastle upon Tyne *42*, 164–6

Unwin, Raymond, Hampstead Garden Suburb *26*, 111, 185
USA
    apartments 194–9
    aspirational housing 193–4
    Black Forest cottage style 184
    Bronxville, New York *55*, 192
    Chaplin studio buildings and homes (Meyer and Holler) *54*, 188, 189
    Chrysler Building, New York 199, 200
    college building 178–80
    Doheny mansion, Beverly Hills (Kaufmann) *53*, 187, 188
    Fifth Avenue, New York *59*, 198
    Forest Hills Gardens, New York (Atterbury and Olmsted) *52*, 184–6
    Hudson View Gardens, New York (Pelham) *58*, 196, 198
    Lovell Health House, Hollywood (Neutra) 187
    modernism 232
    Pomander Walk, New York 198
    rarity of foreign travel 225–6
    revivalist styles and up-market housing 187–93

Sassafras Estate, Long Island 189
Sherwood Terrace, New York 57, 195–6
Stan Hywet Hall, Akron (Schneider) 190–91
Tudor City, New York 60, 199–201
Tudor glamour 199–201
Tudor Revival 12
Tudor uses, overview 201–2
Tudor Village, New York 56, 193–4
Tuxedo Park, New York 189

Victorian Tudoresque villages 90–96
Vieu, Maurice, Collège Franco-Britannique 51, 178, 180, 181
Viollet-le-Duc, Eugène 36, 156
Voysey, Charles Francis Annesley 160, 161, 162

Wales, Gregynog Hall, Newtown 33, 151, 152–3
Walker, Henry 159–60
Wallace and Gromit 233–4
Walpole, Horace 30
    Strawberry Hill 30, 38–9, 227
Warleigh Manor, Somerset (Webb) 59
Waugh, Evelyn, *Decline and Fall* 229–30
Webb, Neale, Warleigh Manor, Somerset 59
West Midlands
    The Leasowes, Dudley 134
    Northfield Manor, Birmingham (Harvey) 24, 99, 104, 149
Wightwick Manor, Wolverhampton 20–21, 99, 100, 149
Wilkins, William
    Dalmeny, West Lothian 58, 92
    Tregothnan, Cornwall 9, 57, 58
Windsor Castle, King's Cottage 29, 141–2
Wing village (Devey) 17, 94–6
Wingrave, Buckinghamshire (Huckvale) 15, 91–2

Winthrop, F. B. 201
Witherington, William Frederick, *Fête in Petworth Park* 13, 79, 81
Wollaton Hall, Nottingham (Smythson) 92, 207–8
Wordsworth, William 137–8, 139
workplace identity 233
Wotton, Sir Henry, *The Elements of Architecture* 47
Wright, Frank Lloyd, Hollyhock House 187
Wyatt (Wyatville), Sir Jeffry
    Endsleigh Cottage, Devon 8, 52–3, 64, 140, 141, 175
    King's Cottage, Windsor Castle 29, 141–2

Yorke, F.R.S., *The Modern House* 38, 39, 163, 164
Yorkshire, Aldersyde, York (Penty) 25, 110
Young England club 87–8